# ANIMAL WISDOM

Other titles in this series:
*Flower Wisdom*
*Tree Wisdom*

# ANIMAL WISDOM

THE DEFINITIVE GUIDEBOOK TO THE
MYTH, FOLKLORE AND MEDICINE POWER OF ANIMALS

Jessica Dawn Palmer

Element
An Imprint of HarperCollins*Publishers*
77–85 Fulham Palace Road,
Hammersmith, London W6 8JB

The website address is: www.thorsonselement.com

and *Element* are trademarks of
HarperCollins*Publishers* Limited

First published by Thorsons,
an Imprint of HarperCollins*Publishers* Limited 2001
This edition published by Element 2002

10 9 8 7



A catalogue record for this book
is available from the British Library

ISBN 0 00 710218 6

Illustrations by Andy Farmer

Printed and bound in Great Britain by
Martins the Printers Limited, Berwick upon Tweed

This book is dedicated to Wa Na Nee Che
as both spiritual advisor and friend
who told me to share my knowledge with others,
and to Dave and Kate, and Lawrence
who encouraged me in this task.
To the people of Fontmell Magna.

# CONTENTS

# INTRODUCTION

Humanity's fascination with animals dates back to pre-history. As symbols they have been interwoven into the fabric of religious belief of both the Old World and the New. Evidence of early man's preoccupation with animals is found throughout Europe, especially in the Mediterranean region, in the cave paintings of southern France and temple reliefs excavated throughout Egypt.

Indeed, during the predynastic period the first divinities were strictly animals. By the 1st Dynasty the parent animal was wedded in some way with human form, either shown as an animal with the head of a human – such as in the hieroglyph for *Ba*, or soul – or the more familiar, human body with the head of an animal or bird. Bast is a good example of this transition: the cat goddess was originally portrayed as a domesticated cat. Around 2100 BC, Bast became a woman with the head of a cat.

In the centuries before Egypt adopted Christianity the populace returned to animal worship, dropping the semi-human deity – the general citizens perhaps feeling betrayed by their god-kings after the country had been overrun by a succession of conquerors from the Nubian, Greece and Rome.

The Greek and Roman pantheons maintained the association between the gods and animals, so Athena in Greece and Diana in Rome were both linked with the owl. The Greeks, though, worshipped the human form as the ultimate perfection. The Romans continued this tradition with only slight changes. Later, all things Roman were considered superior. As a result, animals and birds had been demoted to pets or helpers. The divines could shift-shape to animal form – a benefit of which both Zeus and Jupiter took full advantage. Either way, the animal was considered in some way subservient to, or lesser than, the human. This marked a major cultural shift between the European point of view and the aboriginal American one.

The Hebrews and then the Roman Church rejected any divine association with animals. The Bible gave man dominion over the creatures of land, sky and sea. Meanwhile, the Catholic hierarchy systematically suppressed the old religions. They took over old temple sites to build their cathedrals. Those who retained the old knowledge were burned as heretics. Eventually animals were denied even a soul.

Yet our Christian fathers could not expurgate human memory of their 'primitive' worship, so the Roman church conformed to popular opinion, and the fawn became the Christian symbol of purity, the hart of nobility – to list only two examples. The qualities attributed to animals by society are so universal, so ingrained, that the noted psychologist Karl Jung characterized them as a part of man's 'collective unconscious' or cultural memory.

In Europe, the Celts with their Druid priests preserved the old faith longest, attributing magic to the animals themselves. Often animal wisdom was sought without any interference from the local deity. The Celtic view of animals most closely resembles that of the Native Americans. However, the Celts too eventually succumbed to the Christian church, and much of their knowledge has been lost or obscured by time.

Consequently the European must turn to the aboriginal Americans in order to recover Animal Wisdom. Most Native American creation stories agree with the Christian that man was last born, but they differ in their interpretation of the event. Many tribes attribute creation itself to animals – variously the raven, fox and coyote. For the aboriginal American, the two-legged animal (man), as youngest, was the child, while animals, as older and more experienced, were humanity's teachers. At the core of native belief is the fact that people not only can, but must, learn from their environment in general and from animals in particular. Man was meant to adapt to his surroundings, finding his place in the world rather than trying to bend it to his will. Humankind was not superior to, the controller – or even the possessor – of the land, but a part of it and part of a far wider family. The native family included both plants and animals. This idea is encapsulated in the Lakota phrase *Mitakuye Oyasin*, or 'All our relations'.

The human position in the hierarchy is graphically illustrated by the totem pole used by northwestern Native Americans, where man's image is found at the bottom and not the top. Man was depicted at its base because he is responsible for not only the condition of the planet, but everything on it. The Native Americans, therefore, could rightly be called the first ecologists – with some chieftains speaking as early as the 1600s about how each creature was essential and how the loss of any, even as insignificant as a beetle, could damage an entire ecosystem. White society scoffed, to our detriment. Humanity tried to vanquish mother nature and discovered itself unequal to the task, for she has ways of biting back.

We are paying the price of our manipulation, and now it would seem that the Old World view has come full circle. Interest in so-called 'primitive' religions and cultures is at an all-time high precisely because science has finally recognized what the Native American knew instinctively and our forebears also understood before society became too divorced from its environment: We are the caretakers, not the conquerors, of this world we inhabit.

## POWER ANIMALS

The phrase 'power animals' is often misused, and the concept often misunderstood. The author Joseph Epes Brown in his book *Animals of the Soul* delineated three separate ideas encompassed by the overall term of 'power animals':

1 Master Guardian, or master spirit – a spirit animal that guards all the animals of a given species.
2 Power animal – the spirit or essence of an animal or a species.

3 Guardian Spirit – personal protectors; animals who appear to an individual during a dream, meditation or vision quest.[1]

The reason for this confusion in usage between power animal (animal essence) and guardian spirit (animal protector/mentor) is twofold. First, a guardian spirit is an angelic manifestation, and for the Christian it must be human. Animals, having no souls, do not qualify.

The other reason underlying the confusion is a matter of grammar. The Native American put a modifying adjective *after* the noun, as is done in Spanish or French. Thus we have 'the ball black' instead of 'the black ball'. The original translation of the term 'power animal' was literal, but in accordance with English grammar 'power' becomes the modifier and 'animal' the thing modified. The more accurate translation would be 'animal power'. Suddenly the transition from 'power animal' to animal essence becomes comprehensible.

Therefore, what most people think of as 'power animals' are in fact *guardian spirits*. They could more appropriately be called animal mentors. Yet each idea (animal power and power animal) contains the germ of the other. For our purposes, we will use the term in its current, common usage – an individual's animal protector.

Probably the best English word to describe the relationship between a person and his or her animal mentor is *affinity* – encompassing as it does not only attraction, but a certain resemblance or similarity – for often a power animal is assigned to an individual because the person is seen to possess the qualities, traits or characteristics of that animal and so, it was believed, shared its medicine or power.

This is not, however, an entirely accurate description, as it reflects a distinctly Occidental bias, because it suggests that the person does the choosing when, in fact, the reverse is true: the animal mentor adopts the individual. It might even be said that the person acquires a trait as a result of this union with the animal spirit, rather than acquiring the animal because of the inherent trait.

The number of power animals, or guardian spirits, given to an individual varied according to tradition – with the numbers cited between four and 12. Often animals were ascribed to a point on the compass both cardinal and cadent. Practically speaking, if an animal appeared often – physically, in dreams or vision – then that animal probably had particular import for the individual, either as an essence with which the person was endowed, or as a guardian spirit. If a spirit animal's visitation occurred only once, then it would be assumed that it had a particular message for the person at that time.

## TOTEM

Similarly, the term 'totem' is often used interchangeably for power animal. Like animal essence and animal mentor, totem is often misused. The totem pole, its physical manifestation, originated in the coastal northwest of America. 'Totem' as a philosophy describes animal mentors or protectors that are sacred to and/or representative of a family grouping, a clan and a tribe. In the Plains, this inherited or clan affiliation was replaced by societies. Therefore, an animal mentor could not be handed on from generation to generation unless the animal spirits were consenting. Just because one's father had bear as a guardian did not automatically mean that the family group was under bear's protection, or that the family members were known collectively as the 'bear clan'. It is only since the onset of the US census of Native American tribes in the mid-1800s that the name of the father, usually containing as it does an animal essence, becomes the family name passed on to the next generation – making the Native American way of naming illegal.

In both the northwestern United States and elsewhere, group associations with a particular animal are universal, and the term 'totem' has been adapted to refer to an individual's or society's collective animal mentors.

Since this book is written for the European or for those with European ancestry, we will use the terms *power animal* and *totem* in their current commonly accepted usage: as animal mentor, either singular or plural.

# A FURTHER WORD ABOUT LINGUISTICS

The written translation of any unwritten language is entirely dependent on the 'ear' of the listener. Hence, the Lakota divinity *Iktomi* in one book is spelled *Unktomi* elsewhere and *Unhktomi* somewhere else again. Every attempt has been made to pick the most common spelling and use it throughout the book. Still, the reader may come across more than one spelling. This does not mean that it is an error, but a matter of source. For instance, if a direct quote uses a different spelling, even a misspelling, this has been maintained. Similarly there may be some confusion in tribal names, as some tribes have dropped the insulting names given to them in the past and reverted to their original name. Other tribes have not.

Other terms require definition in usage. For instance, the words 'appearance' or 'appear' as employed in the *Medicine and Power* sections have special meaning. Although this does not preclude the physical appearance of the animal – especially in our urbanized society, where any physical manifestation of a wild animal would be considered significant – it also entails an animal seen in a dream, meditation, or the fugue state that often overcomes us when we are tired, or any creature actively sought during a vision quest. This book presupposes that the reader is willing to entertain such possibilities. Thus, references to appearance speak of something both physical and ethereal.

In the same way, when the book refers to invoking, summoning or raising a certain animal, it means to call upon an animal's energy or wisdom. This may take the form of ritual – for those who practise such things. More likely, invoking an animal is as simple as calling its image to mind. The Native Americans have special songs and dances for the different animals. They called upon a creature to lend its strength and assistance – so wolf powers were summoned before battle. The animal then decided if it would help or not.

The easiest way to raise or summon animal energy is to have something representative of it. The Native Americans used skin, fur, tooth, claw or bone – the fruits of the hunt – which they wore or held to gain closer contact. Historically the eagle feather was of particular import, and US law only allows those individuals who are able to *prove* their status as holy men in a tribe to possess eagle feathers. Even in the United Kingdom, a person like myself must be licensed to own them or bring them into the country. Within the restrictions of time and place, a picture or a figurine fulfils much the same function and is much easier to acquire.

Whether one believes in these mystical or religious aspects, there are still lessons to be learned from our fellow creatures who have lived in this world far longer than humankind. These are the species that have adapted and survived all the global disasters and climatic changes, for those who were unable to adjust perished. To survive, humanity needs to view life from a different perspective – where animals and man are interdependent upon one another and the loss of one species, plant or animal, devalues the whole. It is time for us to choose. Will we learn the lessons of our animal friends and adapt to our environment, or become another species doomed to extinction?

*Mitakuye Oyasin*,
Jessica Dawn Palmer
(Prancing Fawn)

# AUTHOR'S NOTE

## THE STRUCTURE OF THIS BOOK

*Animal Wisdom* covers both American and European animals and traditions. The desire was to include as many species as possible, listed in a simple alphabetical format. Because of the limitations of space, some animals had to be combined. Often, the magic or 'medicine' of creatures cannot be differentiated; they are credited with the same attributes of a comparable animal found in another location, or the distinction is only a matter of degree. In areas where a species did not naturally occur, another, usually similar animal, took on or absorbed the traits of the first. So in those regions beyond wolf's range, coyote acquired some, but not all, of the wolf's supernatural powers. Thus, those creatures – bird or mammal – that were similar both in physical make-up and in tradition have been consolidated into a single entry. Therefore, the reader will find raven and crow together, as they will find bobcat and lynx. Unfortunately, this tends to muddle the alphabet a bit. It is recommended if you are looking for a specific animal that you check the Table of Contents (pages vii–ix) to see where it is listed.

This consolidating device has enabled us to include animals often ignored in other texts, such as the American raccoon and the plain old domesticated tabby. The book covers the animals of the northern hemisphere and those that are shared with the south, such as the jaguar.

Each section begins with a description of the physical, biological and social characteristics of the species, genus or family. Subsequent headings discuss the legends, rituals and rites attributed to the animal. More than one tribe will be covered. The Native American view will then be compared against the European mythology, where one finds both some surprising similarities and some interesting contrasts.

The last division under each animal listing is called *Medicine and Power*. It combines the two *Healing* and *Magical* subheadings of the previous books in this series – partly because not all animals are reputed to have healing powers. More importantly, the word Medicine as it is perceived by the Native American implies a sharing of power, a gift or ability that is bestowed upon man from the animal mentor. It incorporates the concept of healing and magic, without the Western connotation attributed to the latter, manipulation. Magic would relegate animals to the status of tools or familiars rather than the spiritual advisors envisioned by the Native tradition.

# ALLIGATOR/CROCODILE

American alligator: *Alligator mississippiensis*
Crocodile family: *Crocodylidae*

## BIOLOGICAL INFORMATION

The size of the different crocodilian species can vary from 1.3 meters (4 feet) to 7 metres (23 feet), although some have been reported as large as 10 metres. The male is normally larger than the female. Alligators and crocodiles are the only remaining descendants of the *archosauri* from the Mesozoic period. They achieved their present form about 200 million years ago.

Crocodiles' and alligators' eyes, nostrils and ears project from the top of the head. The ear flaps are often mistaken for 'eyebrow ridges'. The head points directly forward and is positioned horizontal to the ground, while their legs jut from the sides of their body. The alligator/crocodile is able to stand because it swivels its ankles under its body. Despite its lumbering gait, this animal can gallop up to 10 miles per hour on dry land.

The American alligator reaches breeding maturity between 8 and 13 years of age, at which time they have attained a length of 6 to 7 feet. However, the adult alligator may grow up to 14 feet long and weigh as much as 1,000 pounds or more during its lifespan of 30 years.

## HABITAT

Alligators/crocodiles are found on all major continents – North, Central and South America, Africa, Asia and Australia. They have adapted to semi-aqueous conditions, although it is believed that there was a completely land-based species of crocodile in New Caledonia as late as 3,000 years ago. These cold-blooded creatures live mainly in low-lying areas of the tropics. None is found above elevations of 1,000 feet.

The American alligator is the only member of the crocodile family that ranges beyond the tropical band. It is found in North America along the Gulf of Mexico – stretching from Florida to Houston, Texas, and down to Freeport, Texas. Populations are particularly dense in the Florida Everglades, and in the bayous and swamps of Louisiana and Texas. They also live in the pine forests of northern Florida, Georgia and Mississippi, and can be found as far north as the Carolinas and Arkansas.

## CHARACTERISTICS

The snout of the crocodile is narrower than that of the alligator, and the crocodile's bottom teeth project from its bottom jaw so they are clearly visible when the mouth is closed. The alligator's teeth do not. The adult alligator is greyish or black in colour, while the crocodile has a distinctly brownish tint.

Both are solitary creatures by nature. Unless conditions force them into close proximity, they maintain definite territories. Confrontations tend to be limited to slapping the water with the tail or chin and other means of posturing, although during times of extreme hunger or over-crowding they have been known to eat others of their own kind.

As a predator, alligator/crocodile has had years of evolution to perfect its technique. It is endowed with highly developed senses of hearing, sight, smell and touch. It has pressure-sensitive black dots on its chin and neck upon which it can rely when submerged in murky depths. Excellent memory coupled with a need to eat only every few weeks means that alligators/crocodiles have plenty of time to size up their prey.

It is able to flatten itself into 30 centimetres (1 foot) of water, so that it is not observed until it strikes. The beast has three forms of attack:

frontal, with a tilt of the head to seize a limb, or a sideways blow. Is it any wonder that the Egyptians saw it as representative of Set, the chaos that explodes from darkness?

The alligator and crocodile kill by drowning their victims. They spin to drag the animal into the water and keep it there, using mass and momentum to maintain the grip. They eat the same way, ripping a piece off by spinning and then swallowing it whole, for the alligator/crocodile does not have jaws capable of chewing. Once they have eaten their fill, they wedge the remains into rocks, weighting it down so it will not flow away and at the same time securing an excellent refrigeration service. In the wild, some crocodiles eat only once a year.

The female lays its eggs on dry land, burying them close to the water. The temperature at which the egg is maintained determines the gender. Warmer eggs, those that are closer to the surface, hatch as males. The female stands guard over her clutch. As she waits, she will dig out a special pond where she can take her brood as soon as they break free. She lays about 60 eggs; when the babies begin to squeak she helps them hatch and lifts each one singly to carry it to the nursery pond. They stay under her protective care for the first year of their lives.

The alligator of the Everglades digs a pool, or 'gator hole', which it maintains during summer droughts. Other animals, such as fish and turtles, find refuge in these ponds, while still others like birds find sustenance. The large reptile provides protection from other predators until the local inhabitants become part of the alligator's menu.

## LEGENDS AND TRADITIONS

GODS Sobek/Sebek, Khentykhai (Egyptian)

The two-headed dragon of the Mayan was represented by the body of a reptile, one head of a crocodile and one of a serpent. Often the lower jaw was missing, from which protruded a human face. It was a blatant symbol of death. In the Peresianus Codex, a king is seen seated on a crocodile. Later this image was replaced by the two-headed dragon, which seems to indicate that the latter evolved from the former.

Archaeological digs in the Everglades and the Florida Keys have revealed a city-state culture in existence at the time of the arrival of the Spanish. Archaeologists have surmised from the altars, which resemble the pits or pools dug by the Florida alligator, that this tribe once held the alligator in high esteem – perhaps even as primary god.

One of the Native American stories to survive comes from the Creek tribe, who originated in the pine forests of Florida and Georgia along the Gulf Coast. They tell a tale of how a lowly rabbit outwitted an alligator. This gator bragged of his valour daily and threatened to eat his furry cousin. Wily rabbit challenged the alligator to prove his courage by facing a fierce demon. Proud alligator accepted. When the annual forest fires came, rabbit told alligator that this was the demon he'd long awaited. Alligator stood his ground and was burned by the flames until he could bear it no longer. His skin shrivelled and he slid his body into the water to quench the fire. There he stayed. Thus, the lesson of alligator for the children of the Creek was not to boast too much nor too loud.

Some of the first Old World myths are associated with Egypt. There, crocodile was a symbol of chaos. The hieroglyph formed the root of such words as lust, aggression, wrath or rage. It represented viciousness and destructive power.

Because it faced east each morning to greet the rising sun, the crocodile was associated with solar power. One legend said it was the tears of the crocodile that caused the annual flood. In its association with elemental water and earth, crocodile came to represent fecundity and power, and this was reflected in the hieroglyph where the crocodile curls its tail protectively around its body. This hieroglyph meant 'to gather'. Therefore, the crocodile was worshipped in many cities, the most important god being Sobek, or Sebek, guardian of the city of Krokodilopolis.

In an ancient tale of Egypt called 'Nebka and the Crocodile', a page made love to the King's wife. The court magician revealed their affair to the king by crafting a wax crocodile who then drowned the hapless page. The wife was burned and her ashes scattered upon the waters. The story illustrates several crocodilian traits, including prescience and judgement.

This concept was reinforced in the composite monster, Amem-mit, who was one-third hippo, one-third crocodile and one-third horse. In the afterlife, one's heart was weighed against the feather of truth. If the heart was found wanting, it was fed to Amem-mit.

The Medieval European view was similar to the Mayan where the reptilian crocodile was equated with dragon and serpent. Indirectly crocodile came to represent knowledge. In alchemy, crocodile symbolized inversion from which came rebirth. It was often associated with Ourboros, variously pictured as a serpent or a legged 'dragon' which bears a startling resemblance to a croc. Thus, alligator/crocodile became associated with the cyclical nature of the universe.

One oft-repeated tale relayed in bestiaries from the Middle Ages is that the crocodile weeps over its victims. Hence the expression: crocodile tears, or false tears. Interestingly enough, one later British publication (*Introduction to Heraldry*) attributes this myth to the Indians – although it does not specify whether this refers to Native Americans or the peoples of the Indian subcontinent.

## MEDICINE AND POWER

| | |
|---|---|
| DIRECTIONS | East, South |
| ELEMENTS | Water, Earth, Sun |
| TRAITS | Fury, ferocity, highly attuned senses, stealth |
| ASSOCIATIONS | Chaos, guardianship, protection, motherhood, secret knowledge |

The Egyptian crocodile would drag itself out on the bank to warm its blood under the rising sun each day, so it was linked with the east. However, the association for the aboriginal North Americans was south.

As a symbol, alligator and crocodile spoke of primal knowledge and primal power, that which originated when the earth was young. It held the secrets of the ancients before the time of man. In a way, alligator personifies all that terrifies; therefore, chaos.

For millennia it has patrolled the rivers, streams, ponds, lakes, swamps, marshes and bayous of the world. Thus, crocodile/alligator is also a guardian. It protects, and it protects fiercely. Crocodile tends its territory jealously. The alligator splits its time between water and land. A cold-blooded creature, it pulls itself out onto the bank to soak up the rays of the sun. Hence the varied associations. The connection with water and earth coupled with the generative power of the sun makes crocodile the first mother. The female watches over her young, and the same jaws that can catch and hold a water buffalo until it drowns become gentle enough to carry hatchlings from land to water without injury.

To call upon alligator is to call up protection of a most active nature, for it is a guardianship of destructive strength. Similarly, alligator/crocodile teaches the wisdom of the ancients. It is primeval. It possesses the knowledge of instinct, of a life moved by tides and eddies, and by the pull of the moon.

To view the world through alligator eyes is to see secrets. For the crocodile swims unobserved, awaiting its unwary victim. Was it not the waxen image of a crocodile that allowed the cuckolded husband to witness his wife's adultery? In that scenario the creature also provides justice.

To the alchemist, crocodile/alligator is inversion – the reversal of order as the young born on land retreat back to the swamps. And as inversion leads back to the beginning, alligator represents rebirth and renewal. Thus, it can impart strength for new beginnings.

Meanwhile, if someone needs to get back in touch with the instinctive, feeling side of nature – the subconscious or that which lies hidden – then alligator medicine is the one to try.

In many places, alligator is attributed to masculinity, rather than femininity. Alligator or crocodile dried and ground into a fine powder is used to invoke virility in some parts of Africa. Its skin can impart some of its warrior characteristics to the wearer.

Alligator medicine people are loners and extremely territorial. They tend to repel others, for people shy away from them. They may appear a bit slow-moving and stodgy unless motivated, for example, by someone invading their space. However, those with alligator medicine are not to be underestimated. They wait patiently, unnoticed by others until it is time to strike, which they do efficiently. Women with this medicine are good mothers and defend their children with ferocity.

# ANT

*Hymenoptra formicoidae*

## BIOLOGICAL INFORMATION

Ants have two-segmented bodies separated by a narrow waist. The head is topped by antennae which they use for feeling and communication. They appear to have three sections. All insects have six legs. Ants can range in size from a few millimetres to over 20 cm (8 inches). There are many different species. The fire ant of the southwestern US has a powerful, stinging bite. The soldier ant of South America can strip a carcass in a few minutes. The most common ant in Britain is the sugar ant. They range in colour from black or ruddy brown to bright red or white.

### HABITAT

Ants live in a variety of locations. They make nests in the ground, in hollow logs, in trees, even in the walls of large multi-storey buildings. They adapt to most environments, from the wet marshlands to dry deserts, from the tropics to the temperate regions of the north. Generally they cannot survive cold temperatures, staying in a state of suspended animation through the winter months.

### CHARACTERISTICS

Ants have complex instincts and social systems. Most, but not all, ants live in communities organized into a strict hierarchy of specialized workers, soldier protectors and a breeding queen where the needs of the individual are sublimated to that of the group. The queen and the male drones are winged, while the workers are not.

Like bees, ants communicate the location of food through a series of movements or dances which the others feel with their sensitive antennae. The soldier ant is completely blind, but can with thousands of others form a trail of destruction led by the scent of the ant preceding it. They plan their attack by regions, moving to strip a new area of forest each day until they have finished their circle of devastation, at which time they move en masse to the next bivouac. Thus, they never go over the same place twice.

Some ants, though, live and hunt singly. One breed of desert ant digs a pit and then lays in wait for its prey.[1]

## LEGENDS AND TRADITIONS

GODDESS Ceres (Roman)
GOD Wang-ta-hsein (Chinese)

Ant taught the price of jealousy in a Native American (Pierce Nez tribe) story about a battle of wills between the chief of the ant tribe and the chief of the yellow-jackets (wasp). Ant raided yellow-jackets's favourite rock as the latter was eating his lunch, and the two of them began to quarrel. Coyote arrived and asked them why they were fighting. Ant complained that he wanted to eat on the rock, but yellow jacket contended that the rock was his since he always ate there. Coyote remonstrated them both: 'Are there not enough rocks for everybody?' For their foolishness and envy, coyote gave them a harsh lesson: he turned the two to stone as a monument to false pride.

In Europe, the first story to spring to mind is Aesop's fable of *The Ant and the Grasshopper*. This tale, with its comic undertones, illustrates the traits for which ant is famous – its diligence and patience. Industrious ant toiled and prepared for the winter while erratic, spendthrift grasshopper laughed as he played his music and frittered the summer away. When winter came, grasshopper begged to enter the nest. The moral of the story was obvious. Ant's forethought, planning and community spirit are not only applauded but rewarded. Poor, procrastinating grasshopper – a symbol of selfishness, impulsiveness and imprudence – is forced to grovel before the creature whose ways he previously reviled.

In the temples of ancient Rome, the priestess of the corn-goddess, Ceres, observed the activity of ants in order to predict the future. Ants have often been used as a weather indicator. Any unusual or excessive activity warned of a change. Ants moving their eggs from one nest to another is a definite omen of storms.

In the medieval *Formica*, it was said that the ability of the ant to distinguish between wholesome and unwholesome foods by the odours they emit was paralleled by the Christian's power to tell between good and evil, orthodoxy and heresy.[2]

## MEDICINE AND POWER

| | |
|---|---|
| DIRECTION | East |
| ELEMENT | Earth |
| TRAITS | Patience, perseverance, industry, forethought |
| ASSOCIATIONS | Community, organization, vibration and communications, devotion to duty |

Although not what one could call a proper 'spell', at one time it was believed that if someone stepped on an ant it called forth the rains. The presence of ants is also indicative of good luck. Ants founding a nest next to a home ensured security, for it was believed ants would not build next to a shaky structure.

Ant eggs mixed with honey was supposed to nullify love magic. Although this particular spell doesn't say what to do with the mixture, one presumes it was fed to the victim or recipient of the unwelcome love magic.

Ant medicine of the Native Americans is based on careful observation of the creatures. Ants organize themselves into a social structure where each individual contributes to the good of the whole. So each person has a specific function within the tribe, and his or her desires become secondary to that of the family and the overall community. Ant truly represents the positive results of teamwork.

Ants are engineers, like beavers. Ant medicine reminds one to look ahead and plan for the future. Ant speaks of loyalty, duty and sacrifice. The appearance of ant suggests the individual step back and find his or her place within the whole. It indicates a time of preparation before making further moves. Its presence hints that the situation is one where both patience and strategy are required.

Ant also imparts these abilities when someone enlists its aid. If there is a point under contention, then the issue needs to be viewed from the angle of the greater good. It suggests that the spirit of co-operation and co-ordination should be paramount.

People who have ant as a power animal are meticulous. They scrutinize everything. They make good employees and good administrators in any kind of job that requires organizational skills. They may appear to be nit-pickers, getting lost among the detail work and forgetting the overall picture. The latter, however, is not true; ant people never forget the community – be it family, business or tribe – but these individuals accept that the best way they can contribute to the greater whole is by doing their own jobs to the best of their ability. Ant medicine imparts constancy, a strong sense of responsibility and forbearance.

# ANTELOPE (PRONGHORN)

Family name: *Antelopinae*
Pronghorn: *Antilocapra americana*

## BIOLOGICAL INFORMATION

Height at shoulder: 88 to 103 cm (33 – 41 inches); length: 125 to 145 cm (50 – 58 inches); weight: 40 to 63 kg (90 – 140 lb). The female is smaller – about half the size – 39 to 43 cm (15 – 16 inches) at the shoulder and weighing 34 kg (75 lb). The horns of the male are 30 to 50 cm (12 – 20 inches) long. They end in a split. The does' are 10 to 17 cm (4 – 5 inches) and generally not pronged.

The coat is reddish with a white underbelly. Facial markings include white stripes along the throat and a black stripe running from the outside corner of the eyes to the black nose. Each animal has a white patch on the back which only becomes exposed when it is alarmed.

The Latin family name for the pronghorn means antelope-goat. Often the name 'antelope' was given to any animal that did not fall into the other general categories of sheep, goat or oxen. Yet the American pronghorn is none of the above, not goat, sheep, oxen or true antelope. The pronghorn is the only remaining remnant of a family that dates back 200 million years. Neither goats nor antelope shed their horns and they are not branched. Like the deer, the pronghorn sheds its horns each year, and the males' are notably branched.

## HABITAT

In the 1700s the pronghorn antelope lived all across the Great Plains of America, covering a total area of 2,000 square miles that stretched from the Saskatchewan River in Canada to the Gulf of Mexico and the Rio Grande in the south. At one time it was estimated that antelopes were more numerous than buffalo. Evidence of antelope 'pounds', ending in pits and antelope hides, date to prehistory and suggest that the pronghorn were the primary food source of the nomadic peoples of the plains.

Shy creatures, the pronghorn antelope retreated from the advance of white man to some of the most remote and least inhabited regions in America. Their range is restricted to an area from the Rockies in the east to the Sierra Nevada mountains of California in the west, what is commonly known as the Great Basin region. Antelope never appear in the Plain that once was its home.

## CHARACTERISTICS

All antelopes have extraordinary eyesight. The large protruding eyes are able to sweep in a wide arc and can detect movement four miles away. Pronghorn antelope are ever-vigilant. They communicate danger to others in the herd by exposing the white patch on their rump. If alarmed, the animals flee. The buck takes rear guard, fighting off any predators with its sharp hooves.

The species is one of the fastest long-distance runners. From a standing start, pronghorn have been clocked at speeds in excess of 70 miles per hour within 20 bounds. They can maintain this speed for about four minutes. Speeds of 45 miles per hour are the norm, while speeds of around 30 mph are just a healthy trot for the pronghorn. This pace can been sustained for half an hour.

Pronghorn graze on numerous plants, including grasses and cacti. In winter they browse on sage. They can dig through light snow, but deeper snow usually forces them uphill to the exposed mountainsides to feed.

Antelope band in scattered herds, usually segregated by gender. Does and their fawns gather in groups of a dozen or so. Old males form bachelor herds of similar size. They are migratory within the limitations of terrain and human incursion. During the time they were numerous, their migratory habits over the Great Plains might have resembled those found in Africa. Even now the pronghorn have summer and winter ranges.

In the autumn the mature males will try to create a harem of 20 does. During the breeding season from September to October, males defend their territory by staring down their adversaries. They fight only if necessary. Implantation occurs one month after copulation. Gestation takes seven months, with the young born in May or June. The fawns' coats have no spots. A female's first conception usually results in one offspring, while subsequent births bring twins.

## LEGENDS AND TRADITIONS

The Cheyenne tribe would often paint their ponies with the horns of the pronghorn to confer swiftness and survival to their steed. They had a special medicine man, or holy man, who was believed to be able to call antelope to him. They could catch the creatures in large numbers by this method, driving them into large pounds.

Similarly, the western Apache tribe survived mainly on deer and antelope. Antelope bones were treated with respect, for to mishandle them would risk the anger of the spirit animal. The bones were kept for a specific length of time. The period varied between the tribes, but it could be up to a year. Then with much ceremony they were buried, burned or thrown into a river and the spirit of the dead antelope beseeched. This would be done to ensure that the next antelope hunt would be a good one. So the early Native American tribes were sustained by antelope just as the same tribes, mounted on horseback, later depended on buffalo.

The book entitled *Medicine Cards* by Jamie Sams and David Carson describes how antelope brought the medicine of survival to man. In the story they relay, when life was new upon the planet and ice travelled across the land, antelope came upon starving humanity and offered its life as sacrifice. First, though, it taught them how to hunt and trap, and in the end antelope gave man its meat to feed on and its fur to wear.

The Lakota tribe viewed all animals with branched horns or antlers with distrust. This included both deer and pronghorn. The Sioux people believed such horns reflected the split or forked tongue of deceit.

Antelopes were not native to Europe. However, they were found in Africa and, since the time of the Greeks and Romans, were known to Europeans. The bestiaries of the Middle Ages mirrored the opinion of the Lakota, and antelope became a symbol of intemperance, perhaps because of the animal's association with the land of the Saracen.

## MEDICINE AND POWER

| | |
|---|---|
| DIRECTION | West |
| ELEMENT | Wind |
| TRAITS | Speed, vision, watchfulness, guile |
| ASSOCIATIONS | Original sacrifice, first gift, correct action |

In the Native American scheme of things, the pronghorn was divine in and of itself. It was one of the first teachers. As precursors to man, all animals were mentors, and antelope as one of the most accessible to the pedestrian tribes was among the first to be shamanized.

A sash made of antelope hooves endowed upon its wearer the speed of the pronghorn and the ability to escape the wounds and arrows of one's enemy. Among its many gifts are swiftness and endurance, for pronghorn not only had the ability of rapid acceleration, but continued velocity.

Antelope medicine imparts vision (as a far-seeing animal) and preparedness. Therefore, it is associated with foresight. The pronghorn is ever alert to danger and aware of its surroundings. It relies on other strategies besides running, including staring down the enemy. Battle came only as a last resort. Antelope is the power of quick and, more importantly, appropriate action. The decisiveness to get things done. It gives an internal knowing of the right response to a given situation. So the first lesson of antelope is the ability to survive when times are harsh.

Antelope medicine is good to call upon when life becomes confused, particularly if the source of confusion is an outside threat, for it provides attentiveness and watchfulness; the pronghorn is rarely taken unawares. Antelope gives insight, as a mentor of correct response and the first shaman. Call upon antelope when initiating a new project, starting a new job or approaching a new phase of life. In Western mythology, antelope would be equated with the ram – hence, Aries.

The antelope person is the kind of individual who gets things done. This is someone who provides good advice. If one's natural talents are allowed to develop, the antelope individual makes a good leader. However, as a herd animal antelope also likes to be part of the crowd. This person is uncomfortable with being alone and will, when left in solitude for too long, be driven out to find the company of his own kind.

# ARMADILLO

*Dasypus novemcintus*

## BIOLOGICAL INFORMATION

The armadillo is a member of the sloth family. It is between 615 to 800 mm (approximately 24 – 31 inches) long. Scaly plates cover its head, body and tail. A series of nine (sometimes fewer) armoured bands protect the middle. The underside is soft. Hair is sparse, and brown, tan or yellow in colour.

### HABITAT

The only plated animal on the North American continent, the armadillo prefers creek beds and sandy soil in which it can burrow. It does not hibernate, so cannot withstand freezing weather. At one time its range was limited to Florida in the southeastern corner of the United States. In the last century it has greatly increased its territory, possibly due to global warming. The armadillo has spread both west and north, into the Carolinas, Georgia, Louisiana, Texas and Oklahoma. It can be found (though only rarely) as far north as Kansas.

### CHARACTERISTICS

The armadillo prefers areas with loose, sandy soil where it can burrow. The entrance holes to its den are about 15 cm to 20 cm (6 – 8 inches) across and roughly oblong in shape. An insect-eater, the armadillo spends most of its day digging and foraging in the dirt. It eats ants, worms and spiders. It also feeds on crayfish, amphibians and small reptiles, although it can supplement its diet with berries and fruit.

Armadillos mate in the autumn. Implantation is delayed 14 weeks. One egg splits into four, and the mother gives birth to identical 'quadruplets' in March, after a gestation period of approximately 150 days. The young are born with their eyes open. They are well-formed, perfect miniatures of the parents, except for the skin, which takes a while to harden.

Armadillos are surprisingly fast creatures, able to achieve speeds of 25 mph in short sprints. They swim by inflating their intestines to provide buoyancy; if they prefer, armadillos can walk along the bottom of riverbeds. Their primary defence mechanism is to curl up in a little ball to protect their internal organs, which may be the reason why they are the object of so many traffic fatalities that the Texas state mammal is often referred to as a 'Texas speed bump' (roughly equivalent to the British ' sleeping policeman').

## LEGENDS AND TRADITIONS

The Aztecs' name for armadillo was 'rabbit-turtle' – reflecting its two most noticeable traits, the armoured exterior and its ability to move quickly when startled. The English name is derived from the Spanish for 'little armoured one'.

Because the armadillo is a fairly recent arrival in the western US, few Native American traditions are associated with it, and those legends that may have come to us from the tribes where the armadillos were most abundant have been lost, for those cultures were among the first to be destroyed.

## MEDICINE AND POWER

| | |
|---|---|
| DIRECTION | South |
| ELEMENT | Earth |
| TRAITS | Armour, self-containment, ability to dig |
| ASSOCIATIONS | Boundaries and protection |

Even though stories of old are sparse, the armadillo's renown continues to grow in the US, where it is looked upon with laughing affection and with a grudging respect. The meaning may sound like mere pop psychology, but when it comes to establishing boundaries, if the shield fits ...

The armadillo wears its protection on its back, like knights of old. When under attack it will curl up, leaving an impenetrable barrier to the world. Therefore, armadillo medicine speaks of safety and security. It exemplifies the ability to draw the line against outside invasion. Armadillo teaches us how to set up appropriate limitations, especially when dealing with others.

Its appearance (in dreams, ritual or literally, as explained in the Introduction) can mean that one's boundaries have been breached or are about to be. Armadillo acts as a warning that the time to set limits is at hand. Likewise, it can signal a time of retreat within the safety of one's shell.

To invoke its medicine is to create healthy barriers between oneself and others. It lends the individual its thick skin, particularly when under verbal attack. Like antelope, armadillo also has the wit to know when flight is required.

Armadillo, as a burrower, can also herald the need to dig below the surface of things. In dealings with other people it may mean that not everything is open and above board. It gives people the strength to unearth plots or expose any underhanded dealings.

The armadillo individual is a private person. He or she is guarded. Like any member of the sloth family, the armadillo may appear comical and lethargic, but once threatened the armadillo person will act immediately and appropriately – either putting up their armour as a defence or revealing the great speed with which they can move when pressed.

The armadillo prefers to stay in the background. This person will freeze under the spotlight. With their ability to dig deep, the armadillo individual can unearth secrets and would make a good private investigator.

# BADGER

European: *Meles meles*
American: *Taxidea taxus*

## BIOLOGICAL INFORMATION

The American badger has bowed legs and a grizzled coat from grey to brown, with fur of varying lengths. It has a white stripe from shoulder to snout, black patches on each cheek and small ears. The face is pointed and the snout upturned. The tail is short, bushy and yellowish in colour, while the feet are dark. Length: 52 to 87 cm (20 – 34 inches); weight 3.6 – 11.4 kg (approximately 8 to 25 lb).

The English or European badger is slightly smaller, around 85 cm (30 inches) long. The head sports a broad central white bar and white cheeks. Indeed, the English badger looks like a slightly cuter, photo-negative version of the American.

### HABITAT

The plains, moorland, farmland and open woods are home to the badger. At one time the American badger was seen all over the United States and Canada, but now its range is limited to the Great Lakes region and areas west of the Mississippi River. Along this strip it can be found as far north as Saskatchewan and down into Mexico.

The American badger lives in burrows with an oval entrance (20 – 30 cm, 8 – 12 inches) to admit its rotund form. The opening is usually surrounded by loose dirt, bone, fur and other rubbish that has been cleaned from the nest. Often a badger will enlarge the dens of prairie dogs to accommodate its needs. The American badger is solitary, joining with another of its species only to mate.

Meanwhile its European cousin lives in multiple sets. Each set will have several entrances that lead to a dry central chamber. The badger of England is a much more social animal. It lives with an extended family. The young are eventually driven off when they come of mating age. Unlike the American badger who sticks to the flat lands, the European/Asian badger will occasionally live high up in the mountains.

## CHARACTERISTICS

The badger is a carnivore. It feeds on small mammals, rodents, insects and small reptiles. One of the favoured meats of the American badger is rattlesnake. It is evidently immune to the venom. The American badger often competes with coyote for prey. One of coyote's tricks is to wait until the badger has dug out a nest and then steal the badger's home. Of course, badger is also tricky. It often invades the den of its quarry and lingers until the occupant returns.

Not nocturnal by nature, badger has become so to avoid contact with man. In more remote areas it still gets out and forages during the day. The badger is not as ferocious as the old tales would have us believe. The badger would rather retreat to a place of safety, if one exists, than fight. They are so averse to confrontation they will dig a den, throwing dirt into the face of the attacker, and a badger can easily outpace a man with a shovel.

However, once cornered this clumsy runner would rather turn and fight, especially when there is no place to hide. Then, it makes a formidable adversary. Its claws can be up to 5 cm (2 inches) long, and it uses both tooth and nail to its best advantage.

Although primarily terrestrial, badger can swim and will often be seen lying in the shallows of a stream on a hot day.

During the winter, badger becomes torpid but it does not hibernate. It mates in late summer. Like the armadillo, implantation is delayed. Litters number between two and five, which are born in March or April, blind but well-furred. The young remain with the parents during the summer months, dispersing in autumn.

The mating season in Europe occurs in June and July. After a delay of seven to eight months, implantation occurs. The young are born between February and April. They grow slowly, opening their eyes 28 – 35 days after birth.

## LEGENDS AND TRADITIONS

According to Oglala (Lakota) belief, badger is an earth animal because it lives in a den and digs in the earth. Badger represents fighting qualities which a warrior would do well to emulate. It attacks when necessary, with powerful aggression, using teeth and claws that can rend hard earth. So, badger symbolizes the willingness to fight for what we want.

Badger has been linked with medicinal roots, and in some ceremonies the medicine man or woman would use a badger's claw or paw (or something representative of them, such as a rattle decorated with badger fur) to dig the disease from the affected part. The curative power of badger is similar to that of bear. Both taught man what roots and herbs were good to eat. The shaman of bear medicine also used a rattle or claw to dig at disease. Badger, as smaller than bear, was more often associated with children, and its medicine was often woman's medicine, while bear was so male that in some tribes there was an interdict against women touching or treating the skins.

In his book *Lakota Belief and Ritual*, James Walker described a rite used to predict the future where a person who killed a badger extracted everything from the body cavity, leaving only the blood. If the blood had a smooth, mirror-like surface, the person could view his reflection. If he saw himself and his head was white, then he will live a long time and become a grandfather. If the image reflected looked unwell, then the person will soon die. If, however, a red head was seen, the person will kill an enemy.

In the *History and Topography of Ireland* by Giraldus Cambrensis, written in the 1190s, badger was referred to as an unclean animal that bites and frequents rocky, mountainous places. This book further states that, digging with its feet, badger makes holes as places of refuge and defence. Ironically, given what comes before, the author of this book draws the conclusion that badgers are born to service by nature. In later times, keeping a badger's tooth in one's pocket was supposed to make a gambler unbeatable.

Throughout history badger has been on the receiving end of atrocious behaviour. The verb 'to badger' is derived from the European custom of badger-baiting and means 'to persecute' or 'to annoy'. Likewise, badger has been subjected to periods of persecution and extermination in post-Columbian America and in Europe. The farmers of the western United States regularly destroy badger nests, out of fear that the holes will trip up cattle. They forget the service badgers provide in rodent control. Recently, badgers have become infected with the tuberculosis virus in Great Britain, which can then be transferred to man via infected cows' milk. Perhaps one of the best measures of renewed hope for badger is the more measured response that this outbreak has received when compared to previous ones.

## MEDICINE AND POWER

| | |
|---|---|
| DIRECTION | North |
| ELEMENT | Earth |
| TRAITS | Courage, strength, perseverance |
| ASSOCIATIONS | Aggression, keeper of stories |

The badger is called upon to impart persistence, determination and endurance. It will dig for hours to unearth its next repast. Similarly, once it has gained access to another animal's den, badger will wait for hours for their prey to return.

Badger also gives mental energy and fighting spirit. Once badger has bitten into something it won't let go. It would die rather than give up, so badger teaches us how to stick to a project and see it through to its completion.

As a digger, badger medicine refers to the use of medicinal roots. It is considered one of the strongest medicines because of the badger's reputed tenacity. Its medicine can be called upon when others fail. Badger gives deep healing of infections. Few people own the badger fur, paws or claws – fewer still would want to – required to invoke its medicine; however, ceremonies can be performed with a rattle upon which a badger's footprint or claws have been drawn. Often this substitution is made by the Native American medicine man or woman of the current day.

Calling upon badger is supposed to allow the healing to penetrate deeper into the system. Many of the motions used by Raike healers, such as plucking out an area of blockage, are similar to those used by badger medicine people of old.

Badger's energies include not only healing but prophecy. Badger medicine could be called upon when scrying with water, crystal or glass.

A more European perspective of badger – for the Eurasian animal is a social animal – is that of storyteller. Thus, badger was the keeper of history in the form of legend and lore. Badger knows both past and future while maintaining a firm grasp on the present. This means that badger, despite its so-called aggressive nature, is a powerful mentor, a giver of strength and wisdom.

The badger person is the boss everyone fears. Chances are the rough exterior hides a lack of self-confidence, timidity and doubt. This person may be gruff, but the badger individual gets the job done. This person is unwilling to quit. The individual with badger medicine has innate healing abilities and may be interested in alternative therapy. Like armadillo, badger digs deep; therefore, it is difficult to keep secrets around a badger.

# BAT

Family: *Chirotera*

## BIOLOGICAL INFORMATION

In the US, Canada and Mexico there are 39 species of bat, all of them nocturnal. Europe has seven different kinds of bat, also nocturnal, but not all bats are night-feeders. Flying foxes and fruit bats move about during the daylight hours. Because there are so many – varying in size from smaller than a tea cup to those with a wing span of over 30 cm (1 foot) in length – it is impossible to give a specific size.

However, all bats share certain characteristics. They have hands with a thumb and four digits. The digits are elongated and then covered with a furry membrane to create a wing. The thumb remains as a kind of claw. Most have an interfemoral membrane between the legs.

### HABITAT

In North America the various species range from Mexico up into northern Canada. It seems that bats have adapted themselves to all but arctic conditions. Thus, bats are found throughout South America, Asia, Australia and Europe – in woodland, deserts, marshes, open fields and farmland.

Most bats nest in colonies, either in trees or in caves, hanging upside down. Woodland bats tend to be more solitary creatures. Usually when bats are in a more exposed environment they seek the protection of groups, caves or both.

### CHARACTERISTICS

In the US, as in Europe, the bat is a creature of the night. It uses a form of sonar, bouncing sound waves off surfaces to determine distances. Flying bats, for their part, emit between 30 and 60 squeaks per minute at speeds between 30,000 and 100,000 cycles per second. Their eyesight is poor, but not all bats are blind. Some bats are sighted and are strictly daytime flyers.

In the more temperate climates of the northern and southern hemispheres, the bat is mainly an insectivore. However, elsewhere bats eat pollen or fruit. Some have even developed a specialized relationship with a certain type of tree, proving that bats are capable of exploiting almost any environment.

Bats hibernate, but if the temperature drops below freezing they may freeze to death. They awaken quickly to danger.

Gestation periods vary. Most northern bats mate in the autumn, storing the sperm over winter for fertilization in the spring. Mother bats give birth while hanging upside down. They have one or two babies annually. The babies are born feet-first. After birth they climb to a suckling position and cling to their mother's fur to nurse. Bats can live up to 20 years.

Few generalizations can be made, though. The length of gestation depends on the species. The time of breeding depends upon the location, even within a species. The young suckle upside down and cling to their mothers until they are ready to fly, but the length of time before they reach this stage of development also varies.

## LEGENDS AND TRADITIONS

GODS Camazotz (Mayan), Wiohepeyata (Lakota)

A book from Mayan America, the *Popul Vol*, described the initiation process of the Priests of the Mayan bat god. The second book in the series referred to seven tests. The last test took place in the 'house of bats', where mammoth winged creatures flew at the proposed initiates. The god Camazotz had the head and wings of a bat and a human body. This god carried a large sword with which he tested the human soul. When Camazotz ran into unwary travellers at night, he decapitated them. The bat god was shared by the Nahua people. Some say the Mayans imported this deity from that more northern culture. Bat, with its lunar associations, became incorporated into the Mayan calendar as one of the symbols for the month. Specifically, the leaf-nosed bat represented Zotz (perhaps a shortened version of Camazotz, and certainly linked to the god) – comparable to the month of October, a time when summer's life turns to winter's death.

The Lakota associated the bat and hawk with Yata (Wiohepeyata), the west. Bat helped soldiers, counsellors, scouts, spies and the marshals who policed the tribes. Thus, the bat imparted the ability to move unseen and silent in the dark.

In China, bat was a symbol of happiness. In Western alchemy the bat has similar associations to dragon, with the wings having special demonic significance. They are often feared; some people believe bats live on blood. Only one species of bat, appropriately named vampire, does that. It is found in Mexico, but is more of a danger to livestock than to man.

Biblical references equate Satan with the nocturnal bat. In medieval times, bat was considered the devil's messenger, imp or demon. Bat's link with witchcraft under the Christian church is direct. As flying animals and creatures of the night, bats were thought to be excellent familiars. According to superstition, if a bat flies close to an individual then someone is trying to bewitch him or her.

The mixed emotions with which the bat was held in English tradition is illustrated in the *Introduction to Heraldry*, published in 1802 during the age of rationalism. Bat is listed under the name 'rere mouse', where the author confesses that the creature 'is of such a resemblance to both bird and beast, that it may be doubted of which kind it is ...'

Probably most curious is the belief that if a person keeps the right eye of a bat in his pocket, he will be rendered invisible. (Certainly the bat in question would have some difficulty seeing this individual.) Meanwhile a bat hitting any building is supposed to foretell rain (and a severe headache for the bat.).

## MEDICINE AND POWER

| | |
|---|---|
| DIRECTION | West |
| ELEMENT | Air |
| TRAITS | Flight, sensitive hearing, pollination |
| ASSOCIATIONS | Death and rebirth, initiation, transition, shamanistic rites |

The medicine of bat varies depending upon location. To the tribes of the American northwest, they were symbols of diligence. In the Great Plains regions it was believed that they imparted wisdom. Bats were associated with vision and dreams – the essence of shamanistic power. Elsewhere in the US it was thought that the appearance of a bat foretold a successful hunt and a period of prosperity.

Generally, though, the accepted view is the one that comes from the southwestern US and Mexico, that bat represents death and rebirth. Because they disappeared underground in noisy hordes at day's dawning and erupted each evening from beneath the earth, they were associated with resurrection.

This belief evolved into a shamanistic death as a result of a trial where fear dies and is replaced with magical power. Almost all the cultures of aboriginal America had some form of vision quest. In the southwest and meso-America, the person dug his own grave and then lay in it for a specified period of time, accepting his own mortality and conquering his dread. The vision quest consisted of some sort of ordeal that pushed the individual's physical and emotional strength to the limits of endurance. During the Lakota rite of Hanblechya, the individual was isolated for four days and took neither food nor drink. A four-cornered circle would be cleared, defining the boundaries of confinement. Four small wands marked the major directions, and a larger spirit pole marked the centre. The person, who was 'crying to the Great Spirit for a vision', would walk the four corners signified by the sticks, always returning to the middle pole after exploring each direction. This was a reminder that wisdom comes from the centre.

Bat as death refers to letting go of the old. It is transition. When bat appears, change is either imminent or long overdue. It portends spiritual rebirth. Hanging upside down, it implies inversion – therefore a time of trials. The appearance of bat suggests that the ordeal may be a necessary part of the transition. During the day, bats gather in large aggregate groupings in caves or trees. Thus, they also speak of colony and community.

The bat person likes to be in the company of others. These people can 'see' in the dark. Thus, they are able to observe the blackness that lies within the human soul. Bat people also have acute hearing. They can hear what people don't say and view what others would prefer to keep hidden. The individual who possesses bat medicine is a seer and a natural shaman.

# BEAR

American Black Bear: *Ursus Americanus*
European Brown (American Grizzly): *Ursus arctos*
Polar Bear: *Thalarctos maritimus*

## BIOLOGICAL INFORMATION

The bear is the largest terrestrial carnivore in Europe and the Americas.

The male black bear is 90 to 105 cm (3 – 3½ ft) at the shoulder. It is 137 to 188 cm (4½ – 6½ ft) long and weighs 92 to 267 kg (205 – 595 lb). The black bear of North America actually comes in a variety of colours: black to cinnamon, a bluish grey near Yukatat Bay, Alaska, and a white in British Columbia.

The European brown and the American grizzly are longer, hence larger – with the American grizzly measuring 152 to 183 cm (6 – 7 ft) while the European brown varies from 150 to 250 cm (5 – 8 ft). Both average about 300 kg (660 lb).

What Americans refer to as the grizzly belongs to the species *Ursus arctos*. Some biologists recognize as many as 74 kinds of American Grizzly under the heading of *Ursus horribilis*. Similarly, some believe the Alaskan Kodiak to be a larger version of the grizzly. For simplicity's sake, grizzly is equated here with the European brown bear.

The polar bear measures 198 to 203 cm (6½ – 7½ ft) in length. Its height at the shoulders ranges from 98 to 122 cm (3 – 4 ft). Its weight is between 270 and 495 kg (600 to 1100 lb). The polar bear is distinguished by its white to yellowish white coat. It has a blueish sheen to the eyes, unlike the white 'black' bear of British Columbia, and a entirely different tooth structure, with some 47 teeth. Some authors put polar bear into the genus *Ursus*; others have given it an entirely different classification. The polar bear is largest of all bears, even larger than the grizzly.

## HABITAT

The black bear is still found throughout the Rocky Mountains, in the Sierra Nevadas in California, parts of the eastern Appalachians, New England, Alaska and in most of Canada. Small populations are located in the states of Minnesota, Wisconsin and Michigan. In eastern America, black bear sticks to forests and swamps. In the west and north, they live in woodlands and mountains under elevations of 2,100 m (7,000 ft).

In the Americas the brown bear remains in the high mountains of the west – the Rockies and the Sierra Nevadas and in the tundra regions of the north. In Europe the bear is concentrated in old forests and mountain ravines. The brown bear is still found in the Pyrenees, Apennines, Alps, Carpathians and Balkans. The Carpathian bear is the largest. The brown bear's range extends into the mountainous regions of Asia.

Meanwhile, the polar bear sticks to the harshest environments – the ice floes, the rocky shoreland and remote islands of the Arctic. Therefore it can be found in Alaska, northern Canada, the islands of Scandinavia and Russia.

## CHARACTERISTICS

Bears are omnivores. They eat, fruit, nuts and honey along with prey. Bears are also scavengers and will break into a human habitation if they are sufficiently hungry. They are unlikely to attack humans, preferring to run. Such occurrences are rare in the US, since most bears have learned to fear man. The last reported incident in the continental United States happened in a park where there was a large transient human population and bears had not only lost their fear of man, but had learned that they are a good source of food.

The black bear mates in June or early July. The female has one litter of one to five cubs (usually twins and triplets) born in January and February while she is hibernating. Sows reach breeding maturity in their third year. Primarily nocturnal, the black bear is specific to the American continent. They have a home range of some 15 miles (24 km) and can run at speeds up to 30 miles per hour (48 kph) for short distances.

The brown bear should not be confused with the black bear. First and foremost, the American brown bear (Kodiak/grizzly) is larger than the black. The two have different habitats and different temperaments. Generally speaking, the grizzly is considered more unpredictable and the more ferocious of the two breeds. It has a far larger range, some 50 miles (80 km). The grizzly tends to use the same track over and over again, stepping into the same footprints in order to confuse trackers.

All bears live solitary lives, except when the female has cubs. They are most active at night. However, they may be seen foraging about during the daytime. Grizzly/brown bear eats berries, nuts, fruit and honey. It is also the largest terrestrial predator in Europe. The grizzly is able to reach speeds of between 35 and 40 miles (56 and 64 km) per hour.

Brown bears mate in April or May. The female holds the ovum before implantation. The full gestation period lasts eight to nine months, timed so the cubs – usually one or two – are born during the winter's sleep.

Not all bears (black or brown) hibernate. Those that live in more southern latitudes will awaken during the winter months.

The polar bear is the most dangerous of all bears. Living where food is sparse, particularly in the summer months, the polar bear gravitates towards human settlements in order to eat. Kept in such close proximity to humans, the polar bear thinks nothing of attacking people, while the black and brown bear usually avoid confrontation unless cornered.

The polar bear's hairs are hollow, transparent tubes – that is why the bears are white. Each hair acts like a solar heater, transmitting the weak sunlight directly to the skin. This is far different from the white bear of the *americanus* variety who has the standard fur and whose white colour is a matter of pigment, not structure.

# LEGENDS AND TRADITIONS

| | |
|---|---|
| GODDESSES | Calisto (Greek), Diana (Roman), Artio (Celtic) |
| GOD | Rhpisunt (tribe unknown), Hu Nonp, Tob Tob (Lakota) |

One way to measure the esteem in which an animal was held is by viewing the reverence given to their remains. Bear was so important to most tribes that permission had to be sought in order to hunt it; special ceremonies were held and the dead body was handled with respect. This point is illustrated in one Native American legend of uncertain origin. Once the bear was killed, feathers were placed behind its ears and ochre painted on its back. The body could not be dragged after the skin was removed. Rather, the meat was stripped from the bones and carried away piece by piece.

The Montagnu – Naskapi and the Cree of the subarctic region around Newfoundland – considered bear one of the most important animals. When one was killed, its skull was kept and carefully cleaned. Afterwards it was adorned with red stripes or dots, returned to the forest and placed in a tree to soothe its spirit. A bow was not powerful enough a weapon to kill a bear, so it was hunted with clubs and the hunters found it particularly susceptible when it stood up on two legs like a man.

Rituals of appeasement were common wherever bear was hunted, from Russia across Europe and the Americas. Native Americans prepared by fasting. The day the hunt began they made sacrifices to the spirit of the bear. When the bear was killed, the hunter lit a pipe and blew into the bowl, asking the bear not to be angry. In British Columbia the carcass of the bear was brought in and seated upright, a headdress placed on his head and offerings made to the corpse.

The bear claw necklace was a sign of prestige among the eastern Fox and Sauk tribes of the Missouri/Illinois region. The bear claw necklace was reserved for the chief of the Kansa, from whom the name of the state of Kansas was derived. Another emblem of rank was the bear and otter cape. The neighbouring woodland Sioux preserved the bear claw necklace for those who had earned it, either in warfare or the hunt, and so the young Ohiyesa (the author Charles Eastman) was advised in 1864 when he asked to wear his grandfather's bear claw necklace.

The Skidi (wolf) Pawnee people migrated north from Mexico. They carried the traditions of Central and Southern American tribes with them. They worshipped the stars. They associated bear with the northeast.

The Mandan tribe honoured grizzly in its Buffalo dance. Two men would dress as grizzlies, who acted as guardians of the dancers and the magic they invoked. If any tried to enter the circle to interrupt the ritual, they would be chased away. The purpose of the dance was to ensure the return of the herds. Thus, the grizzlies were associated with protection, plenty and the supernatural.

The woodland Dakotas' hereditary enemies were the Ojibwa (Chippewa). Before each attack, the Santee (woodland Dakota) war party would stop. The medicine man would call upon the rival spirits, those Ojibwa who had been killed in previous raids, to subdue them. It was believed that these spirits would fight to defend their people. The smoke of the pipe called the dead warrior who arrived in the form of a bear. The shaman sang to them and then vanquished them with his rattle. Once pacified, the Santee braves were assured that the battle could begin and they would only have to fight the living and not the dead. So bear was equated with death and war.

The eminence of an animal is also indicated by the number of stories attached to it. The lore of old often came as lessons for young and old alike – morality plays – thus, they tell us which traits the Native Americans admired and which they scorned. Animals were chosen because they could illustrate these traits; therefore, one can view their strengths and weaknesses from a uniquely Native American perspective.

For example, in one legend bear falls in love with puma's wife. She ran off with him. When later they discussed her husband, bear boasted that he was big and could easily defeat puma. But when his rival bursts onto the scene, bear was not ready. In his haste bear put his moccasins on the wrong feet, tripped and fell to his death. This story warned the listener against overconfidence and lack of preparedness. Bear invested his future in size and strength rather than wit and wisdom. This tale also acknowledged bear's clumsiness and vulnerability on two legs.

In the legends, bear doesn't just marry other animals, it marries humans. Able to walk on two legs, bear is one of the most human of all animals, so bear appears in several stories married to a man, or more often a woman. Its 'humanity' and generosity are revealed in one Pueblo tale. After a young mother dies, her grieving husband paid little attention to his son. The child is allowed to run wild. Eventually, the boy met up with some bear cubs and was adopted by the mother bear. When the holy man asked the father where his son was, the father didn't know. They searched for the boy and found him playing with the bears in a cave.

The father tried to call his son from the bear, but the child refused to leave. In his anger, the father armed himself for battle, but the shaman stopped him. The holy man pointed to his necklace of bear claws. 'These are my people and this is my medicine. You can't win this boy with violence, but with love.' Then the father offered honey to the bears. It was accepted gladly. He pulled his son aside and begged him to return. The boy, who by now had grown into a young man, replied: 'I will, but you must treat me and my family' – he indicated the bears – 'with friendship.' Thus, the father learned love and compassion from the bears. The young man turned out to be the best wrestler in the village, so the boy had gained bear's gift of strength.

The Lakota celebrated black bear in the form of Tob Tob (or 'four-by-four'). This was the spirit bear who ruled over all other bears. It was one of the wisest of all creatures. According to the old ways, mankind learned what was good to eat and what was not from bear, so bear was the keeper of herb lore, and the primary medicine animal. The bear was so important that it could only be hunted after certain ceremonies were performed.

It was Mato (black bear) who presided over love and hate. Mato imparted bravery, and those who had bear medicine could treat wounds. Bear was the patron of mischief and fun. When bear appeared in a vision to someone, that person became a shaman, for Mato instructed holy men in magic's secrets. The Hunka (adoption) ceremony was brought to the Sioux by a vision of Hu Nonp, the bear God.

Yet for the Sioux, bear was thought to be anathema to woman. A woman was neither allowed to handle bear skins nor to tan them, lest she sprout hair, turn into a bear herself or take on the warlike attributes of the animal and become irritable.

While Mato (black bear) had one association for the Lakota/Dakota, grizzly was something else again and acquired different attributes. For the Santee (woodland Dakota people), the 'cinnamon' or brown bear was considered the most lazy and stupid of all the bears. Meanwhile the grizzly was held in awe by most of the Plains' tribes. It was recognized as a symbol of strength and courage. Grizzly bear medicine was much sought after by warriors. Bear cults existed for those few men who had dreamed of them.

Another legend of the woodland Sioux stated that the 'chief' of the bears was made of flint, which meant another of bear's gifts was weaponry – the arrowhead, spearhead and stone knife.

When one is called to make medicine by an animal mentor, then it is unwise to try and evade the calling. Usually a ceremony was held when someone with bear medicine turned 13, or became a man. This consisted of the recipient of the medicine dressing as a bear and being 'hunted' by the male members of the tribe, who donned all the regalia of war. The successful applicant avoided capture; if, however, someone fell, this was an omen of death.

Similarities in such transformations are revealed by clan ceremonies of the Niska tribes from coastal Canada. The bear moiety was one of the most important. When a member was initiated, he was ritually killed with a thrown knife. Then he was reborn as the particular bear. The Six Nations of the Iroquois who inhabited the eastern half of the US also honour bear in their clan associations, the clans being named after the principal game of the region.

The Ojibwa, like all Native American tribes, created special medicine bundles before hunting bear, which when placed upon the bear's paw prints compressed time and space, so the hunter would find his intended prey quickly.

The classical or Old World image of bears has many similarities and a few differences. Both Viking and Celt warriors wore the fur of the bear to invoke its strength. Meanwhile bear, as companion to the goddess Diana, had feminine and lunar associations for the Greeks and Romans.

Artio of Muri was a Celtic goddess worshipped only in a small area around Berne. She was invoked to ensure a good harvest and prosperity.

The evil Egyptian god Set kept his abode in the constellation the Great Bear. The Lakota call it the hearth of the black bear.

In alchemy the bear represented *nigredo*, prime matter. Therefore it was linked with blackness, chaos and the void. For the early Christian the bear meant instinct, base matter and the cruel, dangerous side of the unconscious. This negative image evolved until Clark's *Heraldry* described the bear as fierce, naturally slothful, heavy and lumpish. The author of this 1810 book believed that the brown bear was vegetarian and the black a carnivore whose prey were killed by the bear's sucking of its blood.

Like the Niska of British Columbia, the Basque hunter killed during a bear hunt supposedly came back as a bear. The Gilyak of Siberia also believed that if a person fell to a bear, his soul migrated into its body. This group from eastern Siberia raise and then sacrifice one bear a year. Before it is killed the bear is taken into each home; its presence is supposed to confer a blessing on the occupants.

Probably the most curious traditions were held by backwoods colonial Americans. It was believed that bears only bred once every seven years. Riding the back of a bear was alleged to be a cure for whooping cough – assuming, of course, one survived the procedure.

## MEDICINE AND POWER

| | |
|---|---|
| DIRECTIONS | Northeast (Pawnee), North |
| ELEMENT | Earth |
| TRAITS | Strength, physical health and prosperity |
| ASSOCIATIONS | Wisdom, healing, the moon, first matter, the unconscious |

We can see that bears had profound influence throughout history for both Europeans and aboriginal Americans. It was warrior spirit; it was prosperity and harvest. Male yet female. An animal of the day attributed to the night. It gave strength and protection, gentleness and love. Bear is moon; it is earth. Temperamental bear presided over love and hate. It was courage and bravery. It conferred physical strength, but not endurance.

Therefore it is easy to understand that bear power can be used for good or for ill. The bear represents a spirit both unruly and wild, human and divine. The masculine power of bear was viewed with ambivalence. In this mode, bear embodies underground earth forces such as volcanoes, which it was hoped could be tamed by promises and faith, but rarely were.

Because of bear's ability to walk upright its soul was thought to be special. So, bear knew all things, wisdom and medicines. The presence of the bear at a ceremony ensures its successful completion. Vicariously, it implies success in the project for which the dance was held. In Native American rites the bear is brought to earth as a spirit. This spirit is danced to and sung for in order to gain bear's support for an enterprise. Sacred tobacco is placed on the skull of the bear as an offering. Tree-climbing black bear became a symbol of plant life.

Grizzly, unlike black bear, is not an arboreal animal. It can climb, but generally does not. It prefers to stay on the ground. Thus, grizzly medicine is used for connecting with the secret rhythms of the earth. It is invoked when incubating ideas, plans and dreams and bringing them to fruition. To call upon grizzly bear medicine enables one to tap into the creative powers of one's unconscious. Likewise it imparts energy by attuning people to the cycle of hibernation and emergence.

Grizzly/brown bear is used for cultivating strength, groundedness and power. Bears also teach the ability to retreat into the power of introspection. Bear is the sacred dreamer, the seeker of truth. Bear teaches balance, activity with rest.

Grizzly, like black bear, imparts strength. Unlike the latter, grizzly/brown is more erratic. It is much more likely to attack. Therefore it has more associations with war than the black bear and fewer links with introspection. It reveals machismo, but not wisdom. Thus the story of the boastful bear.

The brown bear is a creature of the moon. As prime matter, it speaks of returning to the primitive, and it imbues people with a strong instinct for survival. If working with the unconscious, invoke grizzly or brown bear for protection. It can also act as a guide in the murky world of the subconscious. Through Set it has links with the underworld and, vicariously, the occult.

When brown bear appears, a fight may be in the offing. It suggests a situation that's calling for brawn, might and muscle rather than intellect. It may indicate that something which the individual has hidden from himself and others is about to surface. This is not an animal for contemplation, but for action. If a battle has ensued, call upon grizzly. If it is time to meditate, raise black bear.

The grizzly individual can seem a bit crude. When provoked, he or she will become dangerous, even cruel. This person has a temper. Yet grizzly is a good protector. The 'grizzly' woman will be a reliable mother who would defend her cubs unto death; the grizzly man is a warrior. Bear people may appear fat and slow, but these people should not be underestimated; they will go to extreme lengths to win.

Black bear people are dreamers, although they have a practical side. They tend to be introspective and withdrawn. Bear people are independent, preferring to stand on their own two feet rather than ask for help. Black bear people are generally good-natured unless threatened.

# BEAVER

American beaver: *Castor canadensis*
European beaver: *Castor fibre*

## BIOLOGICAL INFORMATION

Length: 63 to 76 cm (25 – 30 inches); tail: 23 to 25 cm (9 – 10 inches); weight: 13.5 27 kg (30 to 60 lb). The beaver is a rich brown colour with a paddle-shaped, scaly tail. It has large chestnut-tinted front teeth.

### HABITAT

Rivers and streams in woodlands and forested areas. The beaver lives throughout the North American continent from Texas to Alaska, Florida to California. In Europe, the beavers' habitat is limited to the Elbe in Germany, the Rhone region of France, Poland, the Scandinavian peninsula and Lithuania, Estonia and Russia.

### CHARACTERISTICS

The beaver constructs large dome-shaped dens of sticks and logs, with underwater entrances. These, and the dams they build to create the appropriate environment for their homes, are considered engineering marvels. However, on rare occasions beavers may burrow into the bank if the current is particularly strong.

The beaver eats aquatic plants, roots and tubers and the bark of certain trees. Alder, aspen, maple, willow, birch and poplar are favoured.

Beavers are excellent swimmers and can stay underwater for 10 to 14 minutes.

Beavers live in family groups with parents, yearlings and kits. The family works co-operatively to maintain the dam and home. Thus, construction remains an ongoing process. The flat tail is used to raise the alarm in case of danger, and the beaver family will defend their territory against any rival clans.

The European beaver and American beaver are similar in size and habits, except for the breeding season. The European beaver gives birth to two to four young in the beginning of August, while the American beaver produces her litter between April and July. At the age of two the young are driven away to establish new colonies elsewhere.

## LEGENDS AND TRADITIONS

GOD Capo

For the Native Americans of the far north and east, beaver held powerful healing power. When the white man came bringing with him plague, pestilence and disease, the native peoples thought that the Beaver God had deserted them and sought revenge by helping the white man hunt the beaver to near extinction.

The initiation to the Midiwiwan Society of the northeastern Chippewa consisted of having a medicine bundle shaped like a snake hurled at the candidate, who subsequently swooned. The medicine men carried the bundles, which were made of beaver, otter, white martin or weasel. The intent was to cure the initiate of all disease, for the Chippewa were health conscious and wise in herb lore and plant medicine. The society and the rite were adapted by some of the adjacent tribes, particularly those allied with the Chippewa such as the Fox, the Sauk, Menominee, Winnebago, Potowatomi and Kickapoo.

The former medicine bundles were made by individuals. However, many tribes created special bundles for the village. Those that were held in the highest esteem were the medicine pipe bundles, the caretaker of which was called the 'medicine-pipe man'. The Blackfeet had a huge one made of beaver fur, and called the Beaver and Pipe bundle. The pipe was considered a gift of thunder; the clap of the beaver's tail emulated this sound.

The Native Americans of Alaska and western Canada took special care of beaver bones. Dogs were not allowed to gnaw on them. The hunters would keep them in a sacred place for a year and then bury them, after which the native peoples offered tobacco and prayers, as they did before each hunt.

Beaver is best known for its industry and its building skills. According to legend, beaver and ant share some common characteristics – for example their ability to plan ahead and to organize. Clark's *Heraldry* claims that beavers '... collect a magazine of winter provisions and appoint an overseer in the society, who gives a certain number of strokes with his tail, as a signal'.[1]

In the narrative *Bestiary of Physiologus*, castor (beaver) appeals to the audience for chastity – along with 'autolops, tutur, labides igniferi'.[2,3]

Beaver was a symbol of the renunciation of the flesh. Beaver was hunted for his testicles, which were supposed to have medicinal uses for fertility. To evade capture, it was believed that beaver would bite his own testes off and throw them in the face of the hunter.

## MEDICINE AND POWER

| | |
|---|---|
| DIRECTION | East |
| ELEMENTS | Water, Earth |
| TRAITS | Community, industry, flexibility and creativity |
| ASSOCIATIONS | Fidelity, comfort, home, family, construction and ingenuity |

For the Oglala, beaver was Taku Wakan (sacred). It represented work, provision and domestic faithfulness. Beaver medicine illustrated how to build, shape and create. It was associated with creature comforts. Beaver's elements were earth and water. It imparted a strong sense of family and home. Thus, beaver medicine was female medicine.

Beaver is the 'doer' of the animal kingdom – builder, architect and construction engineer. Beavers transform their environment in order to provide for their own security and comfort. Beaver teaches humanity man how to shape the future for convenience.

To invoke beaver is to bring ideas into concrete reality. Beaver is the planner and the problem-solver. It assists clear thinking. Beaver medicine should be sought at the beginning of any new project or endeavour. It provides support in re-creating the design of one's life. Its lesson is that structure, hence discipline, is a necessary part of creativity.

Beaver medicine people are diligent workers. They labour better as a team, however. Give the individual with beaver totem a project and they will get stuck in until it is finished. Beaver medicine imparts organizational skill. However, work is only part of their life; for when the day's chores are done, family and fun take precedence. Part of socializing is play. Therefore, the beaver person is a balanced individual who toils or romps when and where appropriate.

# BEE

Honey Bee: *Apis melifera*

## BIOLOGICAL INFORMATION

Length: 500 to 750 mm (1/4 – 3/4 inch). Although once fertilized, the queen becomes bloated and may measure more than an inch.

The bee descended from protohymeneoptera and carnivorous wasps. A family known as *Prosopidae* – with characteristics of both bee and wasp – still exists today. These tiny bees have a wasp mouth.

The evolution of the bee is directly linked to that of the flower. Bees did not exist before flowers appeared, while the wasp did. Bees are winged, with six legs and a segmented body. Usually the body and legs are covered with fine hairs. They collect pollen in special sacs on their legs, while a residual coats their bodies. The former is used to feed the offspring while the latter fertilizes other flowers, so bees and flowering plants are interdependent upon one another for their continued survival.

### HABITAT

Bees cover the globe, found as far north as the tundra regions down to the tip of Africa and South America. They prefer to create their nests inside dark, ill-ventilated places – such as walls or hollow trees. They will make their home inside attics or lofts, sheds or in rocky crevices out of doors. A few live underground.

### CHARACTERISTICS

The bee has evolved a highly structured society, with a resident queen or breeding female, thousands of workers (androgynous immature females) and a few select drones. The latter contribute nothing to the hive. The males' sole purpose is to fertilize the queen. Each hive consists of the parents, including the fecundated female and fertilizing males, and two generations of offspring.

A strong colony can have as many as 60,000 workers and a few hundred drones. The life expectancy of the average drone is four to five weeks, while the worker can live up to six weeks. Everything in the hive revolves around the maintenance of the queen and her offspring. Thus, the queen will usually survive the winter and can often be found alone and drowsy in the spring as she moves about to start a new hive.

When another queen is born, they will stalk each other through the hive to battle for supremacy. Eventually, the bees within the hive will swarm. Taking a certain percentage of workers and drones, the loser queen will fly off to start a new hive.

## LEGENDS AND TRADITIONS

GODDESSES Neith (Egyptian), Mellonia (Roman), Austeja (Lithuanian)
GODS Amun (Amen), Min (Egyptian)

'War upon the Bee' was a game played by Dakota boys. The children would attack a hive with sticks and clubs. The bees would fight back while the boys would stand their ground. This was supposed to prepare the children for war, teaching them courage to confront fear (the sting of the bee) and silence and stoicism in the face of the resulting pain. Any boy who cried out was sent away to sit with the women, and he wore that shame until he'd successfully completed the challenge. Even then the memory would often last a lifetime, as Charles A. Eastman's reminiscences in *Indian Boyhood* illustrate.

The lore of the Old World concerning bees is rich and varied. For the Egyptians, the bee embodied solar energy. It was the bringer of the sweetness of life. Bee meant rebirth and it was associated with many deities, including Neith, Amun and Min. Similarly, the bee had royal significance. It was the symbol for lower Egypt. Coupled with sedge, the bee was the emblem for the united kingdoms of Egypt.

In Greece, the bee represented work and obedience. According to Delphic custom, the second temple at the sacred spot of Delphi was erected by bees. In Orphic teaching, the bee symbolized the human soul because it was believed that souls swarmed to the divine as bees do to water. Lithuania and Rome each had goddesses associated with the bee, Austeja and Mellonia respectively. Later Christians picked up the tradition, as did the Moslems. In Judges XIV: 8, the bee was lauded for its industry, creativity and wealth.

Again a quote from Clark's *Heraldry* provides a unique perspective: 'Bees are the most wonderful and profitable insects yet known; they have three properties of the best kind of subjects; they keep close to their king; are very industrious for the livelihood, expelling all idle drones.'[1]

## MEDICINE AND POWER

| | |
|---|---|
| DIRECTION | East |
| ELEMENTS | Air, Sun (Egypt) |
| TRAITS | Industry, community, teamwork |
| ASSOCIATIONS | Creativity, prosperity, profit, structure, hierarchy |

Except in Clark's *Heraldry*, which reflects the male-oriented view current during the time of William IV, bee medicine is female medicine. It implies fertility and growth, home and property. Bees, like ants, work in the spirit of co-operation rather than competition. All endeavour is invested in future generations. Hence, bee represents motherhood. Neith was said to be the mother of the sun (Amun), while Min (a male god) was primarily associated with fertility and creativity. He was usually depicted with a fully erect penis.

To invoke bee is to call upon new life. Especially in group activities, bee brings not only creativity, but harmony. If there are problems to be solved, the bee brings the light of the sun to illuminate the situation. At the same time, bee provides the organizational skills required to implement the solution.

All but the queen die at the end of the season. Yet from this one source the hive begins anew. Therefore, bee holds the gift of rebirth from a single source or idea. Its appearance in spring promises a better tomorrow, and its produce provided the only sweetener the Europeans knew until the discovery of the New World. Thus, call upon bee to bring the sweetness back to life.

Bees share the ability of ant to communicate through dance and vibration. When they have found a new source of pollen, they return to the hive. Certain steps, wiggles and turns act as directional indicators that guide the other hive members to the pollen. Thus, bee imparts the ability to communicate with others, especially in a group situation or for the common weal. And they are pathfinders to new sources of supply.

Bee people, like beaver people, are industrious. They are good workers and should exhibit competent engineering skills. Bee medicine confers the ability communicate. Bee people are creative and able to find new answers for old questions. However, the individual with a bee totem is intense, and when interrupted from their given task, or frightened, they can lash out with stinging remarks.

# BOAR

American peccary: *Dicotyles tajacau*
European wild boar: *Sus scrofa*

## BIOLOGICAL INFORMATION

The European wild boar stands 91 cm (3 foot) at the shoulder. It measures 132 to 182 cm (4½ – 6 feet) in length. The average weight of the male is 75 to 20 kg (165 – 440 lb), while the female weighs between 35 and 150 kg (77 – 330 lb). The Old World boar is black or dark brown. It has guard hairs on its back which may be grizzled or white-tipped, and it develops a dense undercoat during winter. The tusks can be up to 20 cm (9 inches) long. The tusks of the European boar are elongated canines that curl up and out over the cheek.

The American peccary is also known as the Asian javalina. Its height measures 50 to 55 cm at the shoulder (20 – 22 inches); the length ranges from 87 to 102 cm (34 – 40 inches). The New World wild pig is much smaller than the European. It has a top weight of 29.5 kg (65 lb) compared to the 200 kg (440 lb) recorded for the boar. The American is grizzled grey or black. It has four toes on its front feet and three on the back, while the boar has four on both front and back. The upper tusks of the American peccary curve down instead of up as on the boar.

### HABITAT

The European boar lives in forested swamps and marshes or rocky areas. The wild boar is limited to continental Europe. Those in the south and west are smaller than those found in the east, with the Carthaginian boar reputed to be the largest.

In America, wild boar are found where they were introduced in the southeastern corner of the US, including Georgia, Alabama, Florida and parts of the Carolinas and Tennessee. It can live in restricted locations in New Hampshire, Vermont and California.

The American wild pig prefers brushy deserts, rocky canyons and wastelands. It resides mainly in southeastern Arizona, southwest New Mexico and parts of Texas.

### CHARACTERISTICS

While different in size and habitat, the American and European wild boar share many traits. Both travel in herds. In the US, the herds of the wild boar number up to 50, as against the numbers of the American peccary herds (6 to 30 per herd). However, the rich lands of the south-east are better able to support large bands than the scrub of the south-west. Males band separately or live alone until mating season. The diet varies, each eating what is available in their respective locales. The American peccary eats the fruit of the prickly pear and mesquite, while their eastern cousins concentrate more on nuts and acorns. Both are especially active at dusk and dawn, and both forage. Each breed swims and can run at high speeds, with the American peccary recorded at 40 kph (25 mph).

## LEGENDS AND TRADITIONS

| | |
|---|---|
| GODDESSES | Ceridwin (Celtic), Henwen (British), Artemis (Greek), Austeja (Lithuanian), Freya (Norse), Bajravrahi (Hindu) |
| GODS | Set (Egyptian), Freyr (Norse) |

The peccary featured in Mayan art, by which time it had been domesticated. The pig provided a source of nourishment and sustenance. It was considered sacred, which is reflected in the treatment of the bones. Skulls of peccaries located in archaeological digs were carved with human figures, along with that of the jaguar.

As a species limited to the small corner of the US, there are few Native American legends that include wild pig. As prey animal to large cats, the peccary and the feline were considered linked. The wild pig was attributed with speed, self-sacrifice and alarm, for once attacked a pig's squeal warns its mates of danger.

The boar attained greater renown in the Old World. The black hog of Egyptian mythology was the god, Set, who disguised himself as a boar in order to shoot a bolt of fire straight into the eye of Horus. As a result, the pig was cursed by Ra and its meat deemed unclean. This attitude towards pork, as unfit for human consumption, was adopted by the Jews and later the Moslems. In Syria and Palestine, the boar was considered an abomination.

Wild boar was held to have trampled to death both the Phrygean deity Attis and the Greek Adonis, whose stories show many parallels. It inflicted punishment upon Adonis and Attis for the incest of their birth, so boar delivered justice.

Most of the symbolism about boar comes from the Celts. They connected the boar with battle and leadership. It gave strength and courage. To dream of boar, or to have a vision of one, indicated the warrior or war. Its appearance to Isolt foretold the impending demise of Tristan.

Boar bristles were valued, and considered filled with innate power. In one Celtic legend, Fion steps on a boar bristle and dies, after breaking a *gaeas* (vow, or in this case prohibition) against hunting boars. In the end the bristle had more power than man, and indirectly the boar dispensed justice.

The Carnyx (battle horn) of Scotland and Wales bore the figure of the boar's head. Their helmets and shields were often adorned by its image. The Vikings also venerated boar's warlike qualities. It was invoked by Nordic warriors to give them the fortitude and determination to win.

On a more pacific level, boar was a symbol of wealth and fruitfulness. It was sacred to Freya and Freyr, the Norse god and goddess of fertility. Its skin was endowed with healing properties by the Celts. When placed upon an injury, it caused all wounds to disappear. Later the domestic pig became a symbol of fecundity, and their bodies are often found in Welsh and Celtic graves – having been placed there as food and to ensure the safe passage of the soul in the afterlife.

In Celtic mythology, Ceridwin, goddess of inspiration, was represented by boar. The crone goddess often transformed herself into a sow to address her people. Therefore the Druids were referred to as piglets, and the goddess the snow white sow.

In post-Christian Europe, just as the deer was associated with the good, the boar symbolized evil. As an animal of pagan worship, it came to be seen as the antithesis of Christian virtue. The tusks were often equated with horns, and in early medieval times the animal was likened to the devil – perhaps originating from Psalm 80, which presents the boar as Satan's agent. In the 14th century, Bastars de Buillons compared Christians with lions, the Saracens with boars. For the alchemist, boar represented the process of mortification.

Gaston Phoebes, who wrote *Livre du chase* in the 13th century, considered boar the most dangerous animal in the world. It was capable of killing man, horse, leopard or lion with one blow. Boar was often the object of the epic hero's hunt. It was hunted in the same way as the deer, but it reacted quite differently. It had greater endurance and fewer wiles. It was credited with bravery and pride; cornering a boar was described as a challenge of single combat.

The repulsive mouth made the boar the symbol of the slanderer or gossip. The opinion seems to have softened during Victorian times, when boar was viewed as a champion. Its weapons were its strong and sharp tusks. The boar walked fearless in the forest. It seldom attacked unprovoked and dreaded no one.

## MEDICINE AND POWER

| | |
|---|---|
| DIRECTIONS | North, South |
| ELEMENT | Earth |
| TRAITS | Strength, bravery, pride, wealth |
| ASSOCIATIONS | Fertility, power, justice, gossip, the hunt, evil |

Despite all the bad press, when viewing boar in the context of the divinities it represents, the boar loses a lot of this negative imagery. Two directions are given for boar. North because of its Scandinavian and Celtic associations; south for the American peccary.

To call upon boar is to invoke its strength, its endurance. It imparts the courage to turn and face one's fears head-on. Boar instills the individual with pride, which suggests its energies could be summoned if the issue is one of self-confidence or self-esteem. During confrontation, boar, like bull, confers stubborn determination. Boar would rather die than quit.

At first glance, one might think the appearance of boar could indicate battle, war or confrontation, and it may. However, this would emphasize only one aspect of boar to the exclusion of all others. Boar and pigs were also a measure of wealth for the Celts. They carried great healing. Therefore, the interpretation of boar's arrival in a vision or dream is subjective. It does not automatically indicate conflict. It, like many other animals, must be viewed contextually. Is the scene a quiet one of gentle foraging and domestic bliss? Or is it of the chase and the hunt?

Let it not be forgotten that boar is a great recycler as it roots among the leaf mould to find food that other animals have left behind. Because of this, boar confers the ability to make something out of nothing. Its appearance can mean the individual is about to enter a period of growth, wealth and prosperity. If controversy is already apparent in a person's life, then boar's arrival suggests that the contest will be settled equitably.

Boar people can dig under the surface to find treasure among refuse. They can be inspired by little and able to make the most of any situation. Boar medicine people can be a bit noisy and seem clumsy. Yet they are extremely loyal to their friends. At their worst – particularly when cornered – they can become bellicose and belligerent. This is not a person one cares to confront over trivial matters, for when the boar individual fights, they fight for keeps.

# BUFFALO (BISON)

American Buffalo: *Bison bison*
European Wisent: *Bison bonasus*

## BIOLOGICAL INFORMATION

The buffalo stands between 180 and 200 cm (6½ – 7 feet) at the shoulder. It weighs in excess of 900 kg (about 2,000 lb). The bison has dark brown fur with a shaggy mane and beard. The long bony tail has a tuft of fur at the end which is raised when agitated. The head and shoulders are broad and massive with a well-defined hump. The legs are short compared to the body. However, buffalo can run at speeds of up to 56 kph (35 mph) for short bursts. It has great acceleration. In fact, the American bison will beat the horse in short races.

The bison is the largest terrestrial mammal in both Europe and America, and it has suffered a similar fate in both continents. The last herd in Poland numbered 1,898 animals in 1857. By the end of the First World War, there were only 68 left. The last cow (female) was shot in 1922. By the time a society was formed to save the European Wisent, only 30 animals were left and these lived in captivity.

The example of the American decimation of the Plains herds is notorious, a strategy devised to subdue the tribes by starvation. Even after the bison retreated from the woodlands of the east to the Great Plains, it was estimated that the herds numbered about 60 million. By 1900 there were fewer than 1,000 American buffalo left in the wild, and a crusade to rescue the herds began from which the herds have grown to their current population of 30,000.

## HABITAT

Woodlands, marshes and plains.

In Europe, the bison is an animal of the forested regions, such as the Bowalies Forest in Poland, although at one time they were found throughout Germany and Eastern Europe.

In the US, too, bison were not restricted to the Plains' states at first. At one time, buffalo's range stretched nearly from coast to coast. In 1612 they were observed by the Potomac near present-day Washington DC. In 1722, Colonel William Byrd found a herd in the South Carolina region. By 1850, the buffalo were unknown east of the 95 meridian (the Kansas—Missouri border) and confined to areas west of the Mississippi and east of the Sierra Nevada mountains.

## CHARACTERISTICS

There are two types of what Americans call buffalo, or more accurately bison. The woodland buffalo is smaller than the Plains bison and has longer fur along the fetlocks. All buffalo have poor eyesight, although their sense of hearing and smell is acute. They, like many herd beasts, have a series of snorts and alarms that are used to communicate with others. They raise their tails when frightened or angry.

The American bison live in herds of females and their young, although young males will often hang around the periphery of the herd. More often, though, when bulls reach sexual maturity they leave to create separate all-male herds or to live singly until the next seasonal rut. The female of the species will only leave the herd for two reasons: to give birth or to die. Buffalo create wallows in the dirt for their beds.

Bison are active in early morning and late afternoon. At the time when the Plains were open, the American herds performed annual migrations of 320 km (200 miles) or more. The Canadian buffalo still covers a

240-km (150-mile) territory. In July the bulls join the cows and fight for harems of 70 cows. After a 270-day gestation period, a single calf is born to each fertilized female around May, although twins are not unknown. Most are weaned by late summer; some may nurse for up to seven months.

## LEGENDS AND TRADITIONS

GOD Tatanka (Dakota/Lakota)

The first inhabitants to cross the ice bridge into Canada were the Clovis people, fine stone-workers and creators of the Clovis spearhead. The group migrated to South America around 12,000 years ago. Within two millennia they had hunted the woolly mammoth to extinction. This left the bison as the largest herd animal in the Americas for the next 10,000 years.

Evidence of the worship of buffalo dates to 3000 BC. The mound-builders of Wisconsin often moulded the image of the buffalo into the earth. Called effigy mounds, they cover a large triangle in the southeastern corner of Wisconsin. The snake mound of Ohio though is probably the most famous.

Signs still exist in Colorado of the mass drives where the native peoples stampeded bison over a cliff. This was an annual affair done collectively by several tribes. It took place in autumn to ensure there was enough food for the winter, similar to the British tradition where excess livestock was killed around Michaelmas.

During the other seasons, the early Plains tribes usually followed the herd, culling the weak and the sick. The annual stampede was necessary for a pedestrian people who depended on the spear and therefore required close proximity to the prey. After the bow and arrow appeared on the Plains around AD 500, the danger presented by hunting the buffalo was limited and the tribes soon learned exactly where to hit the animal in order to achieve a kill.

The Arikara, Cheyenne and Sioux peoples did not always consider the buffalo a benefactor. Each tell stories of a time when buffalo (the Dakota/Lakota included deer) ate man. In the Cheyenne version of the story, a great race was run and won by magpie, who then decreed that buffalo could no longer feed upon man. Rebellious buffalo calves took human flesh one last time and it stuck in their throats. To this day, the Cheyenne will not eat the fleshy bit under the throat; it would be considered an act of cannibalism.

The Dakota/Lakota story is a bit more elaborate. The deer, elk and buffalo declared war on all other animals. Takuskanskan – the spirit of motion and change, and according to Walker the first name for the Great Spirit (*Wakan Tanka*) – came to earth and set up his teepee. Then he called all the animals to him one by one. Takuskanskan punished buffalo by making him ugly and clumsy. To elk and deer were given cumbersome horns to weigh them down, and all animals lost the ability to communicate between the species. For if they could not get along together, they were condemned to remain forever apart.

The Buffalo Society of the Mandan was the most prestigious of the age-graded warrior societies. The female equivalent was the White Buffalo Society. Members wore headdresses of albino buffalo, topped with feathers. It is believed that the origin of the tale of the White Buffalo Woman of the Dakota/Lakota came from the Mandan. Her capture was a historical event depicted in Standing Bear's winter account when it was declaimed: 'the capture of the Wakan Tanka woman and the presentation of the pipe'.

The Mandan buffalo dance mimics the mincing, wallowing steps of buffalo wading through snow. The dancers raise their legs progressively higher with each step and sway heavily from side to side.

The type of medicine the buffalo bestowed on an individual could vary. Thus, some ended up as medicine men who specialized in setting bones; others became members of Buffalo Warrior Society. The buffalo dance of the brave was also imitative. Eight men were elected. They dressed in buffalo hides and painted themselves red, black and white. They carried a rattle in the right hand and a six-foot rod in the left. Each dancer wore a crown of willow branches, for the return of the buffalo occurred at the time the willows attained full leaf.

Another Mandan buffalo dance required four participants – one man for each of the four points of the compass. Two men, dressed as grizzlies, guarded the rite from the interference of others. The grandfathers of the tribes beat on drums. On the fourth day, a demon (a man painted black) entered the village and chased the women. He acted the part of a buffalo in rut. The object of the ritual was to bring a plentiful supply of bison; thus, they summoned fertility through this symbolic act. Young men then came in to expel the demon of hunger, and the hunt was assured.

The buffalo figured largely in many other ceremonies, such as the Mandan *O-kee-pa*. The neighbouring Hidasta tribe used the sexual act to transmit the ability to call buffalo to the next generation. The buffalo also played an important part in the Sun Dance performed by all the Plains tribes, along with the calumet ceremony of the Omaha and Poncea, Lakota and Pawnee.

Most tribes had buffalo dance societies. The Arikara buffalo society's medicine lodge was always located in the southwest, since this is where the buffalo held sway. The Arikara even claimed to have been born of buffalo. It was said that at one time buffalo looked just like man except for the horns and the tail. Aided by a buffalo woman, the first warrior created the bow and arrow to arm humanity to defend themselves against buffalo. The buffalo woman married the warrior and their descendants were the Arikara tribe.

For a Lakota woman to become a Buffalo woman was a mark of distinction and honour. It assured her chastity until she was wed and conferred upon her certain powers, one of which was the ability to call buffalo. The related Blackfeet believed that women, like the buffalo, controlled the fertility of the tribe.

The Lakota word for the active and dynamic power of earth is *Ina*, or mother. The buffalo and the earth were regarded as one and the same. Therefore, buffalo had associations with feminine creative powers.

Adding buffalo horns to an eagle-feather headdress meant that the individual had developed buffalo's powers of strength and endurance. The Cheyenne believed that when they placed horns on their headdress they became bullet proof. Many tribes thought if they treated the bones of buffalo with respect, it would be reborn, reclothed in flesh so it could be hunted again.

During drought the members of the Omaha's buffalo society filled a vessel with water and danced around it four times. One would drink and spit it into the air. Then he would spill the water on the ground, and all four buffalo dancers would get down on their hands and knees to drink. So the buffalo is thought to be the giver of all life, and its aid is sought even in matters of rain.

## MEDICINE AND POWER

| | |
|---|---|
| DIRECTIONS | North, West |
| ELEMENT | Earth |
| TRAITS | Strength, determination, endurance, stubbornness, generosity |
| ASSOCIATIONS | Fertility, fidelity, prosperity, potency, vigour, power |

The names of buffalo are too numerous to list; the most familiar is the Lakota name *Tatanka*, or bull buffalo. James Walker believed that the term was a combination of *ta* (a root used for all ruminant animals) and *tanka*, the modifier to the phrase Wakan Tanka, which literally translated means 'Mystery (Spirit) Great' – since the Lakota put the adjective after the noun. Hence, *tatanka* meant great ruminant.

The bison was giver of sustenance and provider of all things, from the hides for clothes and the home to sinew for thread, and food. The native peoples used the bladder for water storage or as a cooking pot. Inflated it became a ball that could be used as a child's toy, or in one of the seven sacred rites, the ball game. The hooves were boiled to create glue. So buffalo bestowed plenty in what would have otherwise been a barren environment. Thus the buffalo became the primary manifestation of the divine for all the Plains tribes.

The arrival of buffalo always signalled a time of abundance, and so it remains till today. The appearance of buffalo often initiates a period of prosperity.

When seen in a vision, the bison imparts its special medicine to the individual. The medicine men who had buffalo as their mentor had the ability to heal injuries and wounds. The appearance of buffalo during a vision quest gave a man the right to paint the buffalo on his shield. It portended that he would be a successful hunter and get the woman he desired for his wife, for it was believed that the spirit of buffalo controls matters of the heart.

The buffalo was thought to be the *kola* or *koda* (friend) of the sun. The white buffalo was most sacred, and the belief in it universally held throughout the Plains. According to prophecy, the birth of four albino calves heralds the beginning of a new age of prosperity for the red man.

The spirit of the buffalo remains in everything; even dried buffalo chips were treated with reverence and respect. Laid on a fire, their smoke carried prayers to the spirit buffalo. Skulls, too, were treated with honour and used in many ceremonies. The holy man would blow smoke from the pipe into the nostrils and then stuff them with sage so the prayer would remain inside the head to be heard by the Great Spirit. The skull contained buffalo's spirit until the horns dropped off. Once a second set of horns were put on the skull, the spirit would return.

Depending on the tribe, the buffalo is associated with the power of the north. Others linked it to the west. Yet its significance remained constant. Buffalo was prayer, gratitude and praise for all that has been received. It symbolized abundance, fertility and growth.

Representative of earth, bison medicine can be invoked for getting in touch with the resonance and rhythms of the great mother. It can be called upon during times of want, but thanks must always be given for the gifts received. Buffalo teaches stillness and encourages feelings of inner quiet and calm.

Buffalo people may appear stolid and stodgy, but they have the ability to move quickly when necessary. Buffalo is unpredictable, so are buffalo people. Bison may look placid and so ugly they're cute. However, these beasts can trample, gore and kill a wolf with ease. The buffalo individual will be stubborn and, once his eye has been set upon a goal, it is better to stay out of the way.

## USE OF BUFFALO PARTS

EATING Meat and marrow, tongue, intestines, liver, other organ meats, blood; dried jerky, fat and marrow

TANNED HIDE teepee, moccasins, leggings, dresses, breechcloth, robes, bedding, belts, caps, mittens, bags, pouches, dolls, items to sell

RAWHIDE containers, sheaths, shields, rattles, drums, saddles, bridle and tack, lariats (rope), masks, bindings, snowshoes and ornaments

HORNS cups, spoons, ladles, fire carriers, powder flasks, toys, headdresses, rattles

BONES knives, arrowheads, shovels, hoes, runners for sleds, saddle trees, war clubs, scrapers, awls, paintbrushes, games, ceremonial objects, tool handles and other 'household' utensils

HAIR headdresses, padding, stuffing, ropes, halters, often woven into jewellery or other ornamentation

HOOVES glue, rattles

TAIL ceremonial objects, medicine switches, often attached to headdresses, whips

BLADDER, PAUNCH, STOMACH cooking vessels, vessels for carrying water, basins, pouches, buckets and cups, toys and ceremonial ball for the ball game

SINEW thread, bowstrings, bindings, bow backings

BRAIN hide tanning

CHIPS fuel for fire, incense for ceremonies

# BUTTERFLY

*Lepidoptera (papillonoidea)*

## BIOLOGICAL INFORMATION

The butterfly can have a wing span of up to 240 mm (9 inches). Most, though, are about 5 cm (2 inches) in length. The wings are covered with a double layer of scales. The category of papillonoidea includes both moths and butterflies and covers over 140,000 species and 70 families. Yet the moth and butterfly differ in looks and habits. The butterfly is a creature of the sun, while most moths fly at night. The moth has a thick furry body. When at rest, its wings lie flat. The butterfly is slender; it is colourful, and when resting the butterfly holds its wings in a vertical position. The butterfly makes the hard-shelled chrysalis; the moth the silken cocoon. The myths and traits associated with moth are something quite different from those associated with the butterfly. Therefore, we will discuss moth under a separate heading (*see page* 233).

### HABITAT

The butterfly is specially adapted to feed on nectar. The *glossata* (tounge) has a long proboscis; and the butterfly can be found wherever there are flowers. There are more species of butterfly in Europe than in the Americas. They, like most insects, have spread far and wide and can be found as far north as the tundra regions of Canada.

### CHARACTERISTICS

Each butterfly goes through three distinct stages – the first two being the caterpillar and the chrysalis – before they reach final winged maturity. The butterfly is a migratory animal. The monarch butterfly of America covers thousands of miles from its winter resting place in Mexico to its final destination in Canada. Sometimes this trek can take generations. A breeding female will lay her eggs, die and the hatchlings pick up the trail as soon as they are physically capable. The path seems to be genetically implanted.

The delightful colours are often a warning of danger. The monarch's orange-and-black colouring announces to any would-be predators that it is poisonous. Therefore, many edible species mimic the colours of a poisonous counterpart to avoid becoming prey themselves.

Romance is often connected with butterfly, although scientific studies seem to repudiate this association. For example: the delicate flight of two butterflies circling, swerving and darting is not a mating dance, but dog-fights between males over territory. One breed of butterfly will lie in wait for the mature female until she emerges from her chrysalis. Then each male will rape her repeatedly before her wings have had the chance to dry enough for her to fly away. Butterfly mating behaviour and courtship are completely dependent on pheromones; thus, they are linked with the sense of smell.

## LEGENDS AND TRADITIONS

The butterfly was particularly revered by the tribes of the American southwest. Its dance is performed by both Navajo and Hopis. Its medicine deals with balance and is associated with flight and air. The single women of these tribes often wear their hair in such a way to mimic the wings of a butterfly to advertise their availability. Even today the women of the southwestern tribes still perform the butterfly dance, wearing their traditional brightly coloured headdresses.

As often seen, the same phenomenon witnessed by two cultures (the European and aboriginal American) gave rise to two different interpretations. For native peoples, butterfly emerging from his chrysalis was a symbol of resurrection. The exquisite creature was considered a miracle of transformation and resurrection.

In the Old World, the connotation was negative. For the ancients and in later European traditions the butterfly was thought to be the spirit of the dead. In Gnostic art, the angel of death is depicted crushing a butterfly underfoot. Its attraction to flame and light symbolize purification by fire. Sailors believed if they saw a butterfly before embarkation, they would die at sea. In some areas of England it is still thought that butterflies contain the souls of unhappy children who have come back to life. Elsewhere in England, a person is supposed to kill the first one they see or face a year of bad luck. If the first butterfly that arrives in the spring is yellow, sickness is in store for the family. Only in Scotland and Ireland does the appearance of a golden butterfly near the dead signify something good, for it is believed that the butterfly ensures the soul's place in heaven.

## MEDICINE AND POWER

| | |
|---|---|
| DIRECTION | South |
| ELEMENT | Air |
| TRAITS | Flight, the aerial dance, colour, metamorphosis |
| ASSOCIATIONS | Transformation, regeneration, life, beauty, and sensitivity, love |

Butterfly is the power of air, the ability to float upon the breeze. Butterfly is known for its darting flight; therefore, it represents the mind and the ability to change it when necessary. Butterfly is the art of transformation. Butterfly represents the never-ending cycle of life, 'symbolic' death and rebirth; hence, its medicine bestows not only the capability, but the clarity of mind needed before any self-transformation.

The lesson of butterfly is letting go of old, outmoded behaviour and expanding into the next phase of existence. It can be called upon to support someone in times of emotional and spiritual transition. Butterfly, then, imparts feelings of lightness and grace. Its medicine allows one to weather the winds of change and trust in the process. Butterfly also can be used in love workings.

The butterfly person is quick-witted, intellectual and an aerial acrobat. As an individual, this person attracts others. Yet the butterfly's flights of fancy soon leave the ordinary mortal behind, and its flitting ways can frustrate others. Trying to get the butterfly person to settle on a single task is often futile. They are viewed as fickle, and one author associated them with the birth month June and the sign of Gemini.[1]

# CAT

House cat: *Felis cattus*

## BIOLOGICAL INFORMATION

The average length is 75 cm (2½ feet), with a tail between 22 and 23 cm (about 9 inches) long. The cat can weigh up to 10.9 kg (21 lb), although some have been recorded at 13.9 kg (around 30 lb). Cats come in many sizes, colours and fur-types. Unlike dog, the cat was not bred to suit a purpose but rather to create a look.

Its brain is relatively large compared to its body. The olfactory centres overlap one another. The feline skeleton reveals a body designed for leaping. Historically, the first cats were the sabre-toothed tigers. Those without the extended canine teeth developed in the Pliocene period.

In the present day, the line between the domesticated and the feral cat is a thin one. Scotland boasts one breed of wild tabby-type cat that cannot be tamed. Similarly, a domesticated cat left on its own soon reverts to the wild.

### HABITAT

Wherever there are people, and a quite a few places where there aren't, cats can be found.

### CHARACTERISTICS

The house cat, like most of this group, tends to be a solitary animal. Hence their reputation for independence even within a home environment. Modern domesticated cats are cases of arrested development, for the main difference between the feral and the domestic cat is the fact that the latter, who never has to depend on hunting for food, never matures beyond the kitten stage of development.

When wild they exhibit similar characteristics to those of their feral and larger cousins. They are ferocious and effective hunters of small animals and rodents. Domesticated cats gone wild are more likely to band together than their truly wild counterparts, possibly due to the city environment in which they find themselves.

## LEGENDS AND TRADITIONS

GODDESSES Mafdet, Sekmet, Bast (Egyptian), Bubatis (Greek), Freya (Norse), Shasti (Hindu), Anu (Irish), Brighid (Celtic)

Although not part of Native American tradition, no book on animal wisdom would be complete without a discussion of the cat. The Oglala refused to have anything to do with any feline, from mountain lion to the common house tabby. Cats, it was believed, had powerful magic and the ability to hex. Any who harmed or partook of the flesh of a cat would be cursed.

Meanwhile the cat, having been domesticated the Old World, has wound its way inextricably into its myths – starting in Egypt. Bast, the cat goddess, is the most well known. She was a gentler version of Sekmet, the lion-headed goddess, who was yet another manifestation of Hathor. Archaeologists believe that Sekmet was introduced from the Sudan. Ironically Sekmet, who drank blood lustily, was also associated with healing. The priests of Sekmet were the doctors of the time.

The Egyptians generally preferred to worship Sekmet in her milder form, Bast. Bast was not the only cat goddess. There was another cat goddess who predated Bast. Mafdet represented the feral Egyptian cat.

The domesticated cat was introduced into Egypt about 2100 BC during the Middle Kingdom. They were used for hunting; a medical book of the time recommends putting cat grease on things to keep mice away. 'Little cat' and 'pussy-cat' became terms of endearment, specific to little girls. Therefore, the connection between feline and female is an old one. If a pet cat, an honoured member of the family, died, the owner shaved his eyebrows and went through all the formalities of burial and mourning.

Another reason for the popularity of Bast: hers was an orgiastic religion, similar in some ways to the worship of the Roman Bacchus or Greek Dionysus. The festivals were frenzied affairs where people danced, drank and made love.

The Celts connected the cat to the goddess Brighid. It was both friend and companion. They observed cats' stealth and sensitivity and tried to emulate them. Cat-magic was invoked by the Druidic priests and priestesses to enable them to walk between the physical and spiritual worlds.

This association of cat with the 'divine', especially the old gods, has continued into the present day. But as with many things the Christian church inverted the old ways to make way for the new. So the names of the gods and goddesses became the demons of the Christian hell – not losing their divine status, only their benevolence – and their worshippers were not simple pagans any more, but followers of Satan, witches. It is not surprising that the status of the once-sacred cat was perverted also, to become equated with evil and witchcraft.

Cats were long-favoured familiars, often hung with their masters and mistresses once the latter were convicted of the crime of heresy. The black cat is a symbol of good luck in England; for the American it means bad luck. The difference reflects the historical view. In the UK it is based on Celtic tradition, while the American view is based on Christian beliefs. Fables of unnatural white creatures abound in Wales and England. Arthur followed the white deer to the magical well. Thus animals of former pagan reverence, those that were white, bode ill in the UK. When the superstition was transplanted to the States, it was 'Christianized' in such a way that black presaged death and evil.

# MEDICINE AND POWER

| | |
|---|---|
| DIRECTION | South |
| ELEMENTS | Fire, sun |
| TRAITS | Independence, playfulness, ferocity |
| ASSOCIATIONS | Healing, childbirth mystery, magic |

Like the other gods/goddesses, the cat didn't relinquish any of its magic – but its meaning became corrupted by the church. However, this has not changed the affection people feel for the creature. In fact, more people have cats in England than dogs, while in the US there are an estimated 60 million cats living in American homes.

Cats have many characteristics humans admire – independence, grace, curiosity, cleverness. Additionally, other attributes have been thrust on them, including the concept of rebirth and resurrection (nine lives).

Cats, along with pigs, toads and crows, were among the most common witch's familiar – spirit inhabiting the body of a given animal. This spirit helps in the casting of spells and contacting the 'other planes' of consciousness, or old-world gods. Not unlike the concept of the spirit guide of mediums, who rarely manifests physically. If one believes in guides, the former idea suddenly doesn't seem so far-fetched.

Cats are female medicine. In India, the goddess of childbirth is associated with a cat. As nocturnal creatures, they are equated with darkness. The dark is the seat of human fears, the unconscious, all things hidden or occult. This is further emphasized by their aloof nature. Therefore, cat speaks of mystery and, vicariously, of magic.

Cat people reflect this. They are introspective and listen to their own intelligence. A cat person is unlikely to heed other people's advice, no matter how good it is or well-intended. Indeed, they appear a trifle self-indulgent and extremely self-absorbed. The cat person tends to be slender, graceful, well turned-out and vain.

# CATTLE

*Bos Taurus*

## BIOLOGICAL INFORMATION

As with many animals that have become domesticated by man, it is difficult to discuss one 'generic' cow. A member of the family *Bovidae*, cows share certain characteristics with other species. For example, goats, sheep and cattle all have an even number of toes. Many, but not all, cattle have horns. Some have thick coats which enable them to survive winters in the far north. The Brahman has a large shoulder hump, similar to that of the bison.

### HABITAT

Prairies and plains, plateaux, open grassland or open woodland. The cow has adapted to as many environments as selective breeding will allow.

### CHARACTERISTICS

All cattle are grazers and grass-eaters. They move in herds, with males generally separated from the females and young, except during the breeding season. Cattle are ruminants, with four stomachs which enable them to digest food that other animals might find indigestible.

Cattle fulfilled the same basic function for the European as buffalo (bison) did for the American and the Yak for the Asian – as provider of food, clothing and leather.

# LEGENDS AND TRADITIONS

The Native Americans were not impressed by cows, which they sometimes referred to as 'smelly buffalo', although the Lakota name literally translated means 'spotted buffalo'. Native Americans didn't like the taste of the meat and only became willing to eat it after the buffalo were effectively destroyed.

Yet for the Old World, cattle, like cat, is an animal whose influence is interwoven throughout the history of human worship. It was revered throughout ancient cultures – including the Hittites, the Sumerians and the Babylonians. The Bible speaks of Jehovah's rage when the Hebrews danced before the image of a sacred calf. This practice was more often attributed to Egypt or Canaan. Most of the cultures of that time had some kind of cattle or bull god/goddess, for example the Sumerian Dumuzi, Sheger of Canaan, and Ishtar, goddess of Babylonia.

The bovine was as important in the Old World as the buffalo was to the Plains people of America. No discussion of them would be complete without a breakdown by gender, covering both the sacred cow and sacred bull. Each will be treated separately within this section.

Egyptian worship of the sacred bull is the most well known, and a multiplicity of gods/goddess were associated with, representative of, or living incarnations of either the bull or cow. In Dynasty II the worship of Osiris replaced that of Ra, particularly among the common people. One of the first manifestations of Osiris in Heliopolis was *Mer Wer* or the Mnevis Bull, which was believed to be the living soul of the sun. He had two wives, both cow goddesses, Hathor and Iusas.

*Kem Wer*, another bull god from a different nome (district), was later transformed into Horus. Since the ancient Egyptians considered the bull to be a symbol of procreation and virility, the bull also became associated with the creator god, Ptah.

Montu was another version of Horus, the falcon-headed god, which originated in the upper Nile some 32 km (20 miles) south of modern-day Luxor, where it was worshipped in the form of sacred bull. Montu represented strength, war. The Bukhis bull was a living animal, Montu incarnate. It was worshipped in four different Theben cities. This bull was thought to be able to cure disease. Its worship reached its peak in Dynasty XI; after the arrival of Ptolemaic kings, animal worship was revived, along with the cult of Montu.

The head of the cow was the symbol for wisdom, while the hieroglyph that depicts a cow lying down meant sacrifice. The foreleg of an ox represented variously strength or offering.

Nut, the granddaughter of the sun and Egyptian goddess of the night sky, was often depicted as a cow with stars on her belly. Nut was mother of Osiris, Isis and Horus the elder, all later affiliated with either bulls or cows.

Isis wore the crown of cow's horns encircling a solar disk. Hathor is the most well-known of the cow goddesses; her worship dates from predynastic times. She was known as the Great Mother, symbol of fecundity and fertility. Votive offerings were given to her in supplication for a child. Hathor was a sky goddess and was regarded as the Eye of Ra. Hathor was also depicted as a cow or a woman with the horned solar disk which was later adopted by Isis. Hathor was described as the beautiful one, the golden one, the lady of drunkenness, song and myrrh.

The conquering Greeks associated Hathor with Aphrodite. Their cattle goddess and great mother was Hera, wife of Zeus. There were two other cow goddesses from Egypt: Mehurt and Neith, the latter of which was also associated with the bee. Further east, the Syrians' cow goddess was Anat.

Later cultures, the Greek, Minoan and Roman, each in their turn, had their sacred bulls – the minotaur of Crete, Baal of Phoenicia, Dionysus and Poseidon, and Neptune and Jupiter, who disguised themselves at one time or another as a bull for purposes of seduction.

Northern cultures and religions were not exempt from cattle worship. Thor was associated with the bull. The Irish had Aine, the Siberians Ajysyt – both cattle goddesses. As a part of their rites, they paid homage to both bulls and cows. The Slavs' cattle god was Volos.

The Celts believed the white bull was sacred. It was a form of god walking abroad on earth, just as the Native Americans have the blessed white buffalo. The white bull was sacrificed to Taranis to return him to his own world. The bull's gift was wealth, fertility and happiness. The cow represented Brighid and, to a lesser extent, the Celtic gods Manannan and Dagda. The Celts rated an individual's worth by the number of cattle he maintained. They were also used as a medium of exchange.

The Scandinavian cow goddess was called Audhumbla. Boann and Damona were Celtic versions of the Irish Dil and Bridgit. The Romans are represented by Bubona and Epona, and the Hindus have Prithivi and Surabhi. Suki is another cow goddess from the Indian subcontinent, but she is not Hindu. To this day cow dances are performed by the Dinka and Shilluk tribes of Sudan.

## MEDICINE AND POWER

| | |
|---|---|
| DIRECTIONS | East, West |
| ELEMENTS | Earth, Air and Sun |
| TRAITS | Bull – virility, strength; Cow – fecundity and maternity |
| ASSOCIATIONS | Cow – fertility, prosperity; Bull – war |

The gods and goddess represented by the cow have been listed previously, and when it comes to direction or element there is more than one possibility. As the Eye of Ra, the cow, in the form of Hathor, has solar associations. As Nut, cow forms the heavens. With the Celtic Brighid, the cow represents both earth and moon.

With its milk and its meat, cow provided the sustenance of life. It was symbol of wealth in Ireland and among the Celts. Some tribes in Africa still measure an individual's value by the number of cows possessed.

To call upon cow is to ask for the good things of life – fertility and prosperity. Cow represents mother and family. Interestingly enough the revival of paganism and Wicca has led to a resurgence of cat worship, but not so much so for the humble cow, although the goddesses Hathor and Isis are two of the most popular with many covens. It is rare to see them represented as a cow, however. Perhaps because urbanized society has divorced us from our farming roots, humanity tends to see cattle as dumb, stolid creatures to be protected against carnivores, not as the bringers of all life.

Cow people, if such exist, would resemble buffalo people. They would appear slow moving and thoughtful, but anyone who has ever been charged by either a bull or cow knows that this is a misperception. Cow people are physical and sensual by nature. They prefer to be able to ruminate over a decision and don't like to be stampeded or rushed.

# COUGAR

*Felis concolour*
also known as Mountain Lion, Puma, Catamount and Florida Panther

## BIOLOGICAL INFORMATION

The cougar is the largest cat in the North America, measuring 1.5 to 2.74 m (2 – 9 ft) in length, with the tail adding another 53 to 92 cm (21 to 36 inches). It weighs between 34 and 125 kg (75 – 275 lb). Its coat is tawny yellow, with a white or buff chest and belly. It has no spots, although the long tail and the ears sport black tips. The whisker patches on the upper lip are slightly darker then the rest of the fur, giving the vague impression of a moustache.

### HABITAT

Once this varied, but now the cougar has been pushed back to the mountainous regions. It is best adapted to hilly northern forests, semi-arid terrain, and subtropical and tropical forest. Its range is northwest American, from British Columbia to Alberta in Canada and Montana and Wyoming in the US. There are pockets of cougars found in California and Texas. What is known as the Florida Panther is a smaller version of the cougar which lives in the Everglades and the marshy regions of Louisiana and Alabama.

### CHARACTERISTICS

Like most cats, the mountain lion is solitary and territorial. It feeds primarily on wild animals, such as deer, coyote, porcupines, beaver, mice, marmots and hares. In recent years it has been known to attack man.

The mountain lions pair only during breeding season. For two weeks, the male and female sleep and hunt side by side. The cougar has no fixed mating season, but usually breeds only once per year. Litters number up to six, which stay with the mother for the first year and sometimes two years.

The cougar/puma is an excellent hunter who can sit still for hours on a perch to ambush its prey. It is one of the few cats to hunt during the day. A male can cover up to 40 km (25 miles) per night. Then it will wait until the prey comes within 9 metres (30 ft) before making its move.

## LEGENDS AND TRADITIONS

The name 'cougar' indicates its origins. The word comes from South America, while 'puma' is derived from the Quechua language spoken by the Incas of Peru. Meanwhile the most common name used in the US, 'mountain lion', resulted from a joke played on the Dutch by the native peoples of New York (then New Amsterdam), perhaps in return for cheating the tribe out of their island home. When the braves brought in the fur of the cougar, the traders thought that this was the female of the same species as the African lion, and they asked what became of the maned male. The native peoples claimed the beast was so ferocious it could not be hunted. It lived in the far-off mountains; from that time on, the name stuck.[11] 'Catamount' is a name most often used by southerners.

The cougar can kill animals far larger than itself, including bears and wolves. This was reflected in the story of 'The Puma and the Bear'. Bear ran off with puma's wife, and boasted that he was so strong he had nothing to fear from puma. As night fell, bear didn't bother to prepare. He took off his slippers to relax, confident in his superior size; but he was surprised and overcome by puma, who was more than his match. With bear dead, puma's wife was banished for her infidelity. As always, the story reflects much about the teller's opinion of the animals in question, including the promiscuity of the female puma, which mates with more than one male. The lesson is many-fold. It teaches of preparedness, warns against over-confidence and shows what happens to the duplicitous wife.

The Florida panther features in the Seminole creation story. The grandfather of all things made the earth, and he desired to put many animals upon the planet. Grandfather creator especially liked Coo-wah-chobee (crawls-on-four-legs, close-to-the-ground) or panther.

He gave to each certain healing powers, but to panther he said: 'You are strongest and most patient. You are majestic and beautiful. I would like you to walk abroad on earth before any of the other animals.'

When the creator stopped creating, he put the animals in a shell and placed it on the earth. A tree grew next to the shell; a root wrapped around it and broke the shell. Grandfather waited for panther, whom he commanded to lead, to emerge. This time, however, panther was too patient. The wind remembered the creator's command, and it helped panther from the shell. So the Florida panther became linked with the winds.

Then came time for the creator to name all the animals. Again, the grandfather went first to his favoured son and bestowed upon the panther clan the knowledge of making laws and healing medicines.

The Seminole continue to hold festivals during the spring when panther and the wind mix medicines for the world. During these ceremonies the people gather by clan, each knowing their place among the others. The panther (or mountain lion) clan are the rulers and the leaders. They not only interpret the laws, but make them.

Heraldry adopted the mountain lion as a symbol of liberty, vigilance, foresight and courage. Meanwhile, the Lakota have accorded the mountain lion the same respect, even fear, which they give all cats. No cat should be beaten or hurt, and it is forbidden to eat the meat of any feline.

Down in the southwestern United States, where cougars are more numerous, they have been observed to be good mothers. Coupled with female element of all felines, cougar has come to mean power, the feminine and the intuitive. Also, strength as exhibited by women in the defence of their young. As the largest cat on the North American continent, the cougar speaks of leadership and assertiveness.

## MEDICINE AND POWER

| | |
|---|---|
| DIRECTIONS | South, Southwest |
| ELEMENT | Fire |
| TRAITS | Stealth, strength, grace |
| ASSOCIATIONS | Invisibility of the hunter, assertiveness, leadership, balance, maternal energy and power |

Calling upon the puma endows the seeker with the animal's incredible stalking ability, the capability to move in silence, hence stealth. Puma provides balance between power and intention, physical strength and grace. This translates to the balance of the body, mind and spirit.

The panther of the Seminole is a leader – but, as an animal who prefers solitude, a reluctant one. According to legend, panther was graced with the learning of all other species, so he knew the secrets of each animal, along with his own. This indicates the power of the psychic or the seer.

Cougar often warns of lessons that come in the terms of a trial, for the young of the mountain lion learn to hunt by experience which includes more than its share of failures. Mountain lion energy presents a chance to perfect skills and abilities, usually in the form of a challenge. This is the time to assert oneself and pounce on opportunity. Cougar teaches decisiveness and imparts resolve.

Puma's appearance can portend coming into one's own power, for catamount brings the cat's intuitive ability, sensitive hearing and night-vision; some say its medicine includes clairaudience or clairvoyance. It can be invoked when seeking something hidden. It imparts patience and silence, which can be used as an aid to meditation. If under attack from a formidable enemy, cougar medicine can use guile to balance any difference in size.

The person with cougar medicine is the unwilling leader who has responsibility's mantle thrust upon him or her. Other individuals recognize mountain lion's qualities and strengths, its wisdom and knowledge. Thus, they tend to lean on the person with cougar medicine who in turn can become snappish. When it's time to defend territory, the puma person goes for the throat. The mountain lion is a capable parent who will go to any lengths to defend its young.

# COYOTE

*Canis latrans*

## BIOLOGICAL INFORMATION

Although similar in appearance to the wolf, the coyote is about one-third the size. It measures 81 to 94 cm (32 – 37 inches) in length. The tail is between 28 and 40 cm (11 and 16 inches). The coyote weighs from 9 to 22 kg (20 – 50 lb). The coyote does not reveal as many colour variations as wolf. It has a reddish grey coat, with rust-coloured legs and a buff or white chest and belly. Unlike the dog or the wolf, the coyote holds its tail down while running, giving it something of an abject appearance.

### HABITAT

Plains, open woodlands, farms, brushland and boulder-strewn areas. The coyote's range stretches from the west coast as far north as Alaska, down to Mexico and east across the prairies and into the mountains and woodlands of the northeast. They are absent only from the far southeast – in the area around Florida, Alabama and Georgia.

### CHARACTERISTICS

Unlike wolf, the coyote is not a pack animal. It stays in small family groupings of parents and offspring. When the young are grown, they leave to find mates of their own and create new territories. Where the ecological balance has remained undisturbed, coyote is a true scavenger, like vulture or crow, who comes along behind wolf to finish the remains of its kill. Possibly for this reason, coyote has been treated with less respect than the wolf. Yet this so-called shortcoming has also been its salvation, because coyote has been much more adaptable to the advance of man than wolf.

However, coyote and wolf share many of the same characteristics. Both are extremely loyal. Coyote families exhibit similar social structure, posturing and communication skills as their larger cousins. Coyote likes to sing, enjoying a night chorus as much as the wolf. It indicates its placement within the family group with the same gestures, ducking the head or tail to signify subordination.

Where the ecological balance has been disturbed, coyote has become top predator, but it has neither the strength nor the bulk to bring down large animals as wolf does. It hunts small mammals such as rodents or rabbits; coyotes have also been known to eat fruit and even vegetable matter.

Coyote mates in January to February. The young are born in April or May after a gestation period of 60 days. The eyes open after 14 to 16 days. They are gentle, caring parents.

## LEGENDS AND TRADITIONS

Coyote is credited with creation by several tribes. The Shoshone believed that coyote created the world, along with brother wolf, and in the afterlife the human spirit went to the land sacred to coyote. In one Miwok legend, the silver fox and coyote sang the universe. The Salish described the first human, made of clay, as so clumsy and stupid that the Old One (creator) sent down coyote to educate bumbling humanity.

The Karok of the American northwest honour coyote for the gift of fire. It is said that coyote stole fire from the fire beings, using trickery and guile. The angry spirits chased him, grabbed his tail and scorched it, and that is why the tip of coyote's tail is white.

The native peoples of California, some 50 tribes, refrained from eating coyote, along with grizzly bear. Coyote bestows 'tough' wisdom in a Pierce Nez (*Nee-me-Poo*) story from the Clearwater River (*Tse-me-na-kem*) region of Idaho. Ant and yellow-jacket had an ongoing rivalry. Each had a favoured boulder. One day ant happened upon yellow jacket upon his rock. Ant picked a fight with yellow jacket until coyote happened along. Three times coyote told them to stop. Three times coyote told them it was silly for animals to fight amongst themselves, for man was coming who would hunt them all. They ignored coyote. Finally, he turned them to stone, where they remain today, locked in a pose of battle – a monument to stupidity and envy.

For the Lakota, coyote was an animal representative of Wakinyan, the thunderbeings. The coyote was *Heyoka*, which meant 'contrariness' or 'backwards-doing'. Those who saw a coyote in a vision were considered Heyoka. The initiation ceremony included sticking their hands in boiling water and declaring it cold. They wore robes in the summer and little more than loin cloths in the winter. Some walked backwards all their lives. Others found different ways of fulfilling their calling. Although it would seem logical that the cross-dressers of the tribe were Heyoka, not all of them were. Therefore, one assumes that cross-dressing inferred a different kind of calling.

The Heyoka were the jesters of a tribe. They taught by example, albeit the wrong one. They found their reflection in the sacred clowns (tsukawimkya, paiyakyamu or kossa, and piptuyakyamu) of the Hopi tribes. It was their job to teach with satire. By doing things backwards they revealed the reasoning beyond the rules. And coyote was their mentor. If one saw coyote or lightning in a vision, one was designated as Heyoka. Thus, coyote is both jokester and trickster. It is keeper of wisdom, for only by knowing the right way can they illustrate the wrong.

*Mica* was another Lakota name for the spirit of the coyote. However, this view of coyote attributes theft, cowardice and all mischief of a malevolent kind to the animal.

In the southwestern US, coyote was not only the keeper of wisdom, it was also the bringer of both wisdom and the sun. One legend credits coyote with the sun's creation. Thus, in territories where wolves did not range, it appears that coyote was given the same attributes as wolf.

## MEDICINE AND POWER

| | |
|---|---|
| DIRECTIONS | South, Southwest |
| ELEMENT | Fire |
| TRAITS | Loyalty, adaptability, sociability |
| ATTRIBUTES | Clown, joker, trickster (*Heyoka*); wisdom-keeper, creator, bringer of fire and light |

Despite all the creation stories and legends that reveal coyote as a benevolent creature, the image that seems to have stuck is that of Heyoka, perhaps because it reflects those of the white ranchers and farmers in the prairies and the west. So coyote has been much maligned; its modern connotation is one of 'contrariness', as in someone deliberately malicious and rude.

Yet even within the concept of Heyoka there was an acceptance of coyote's innate wisdom. Coyote taught much by example. The Lakota credit to it some of their most important ceremonial songs.

Unfortunately, current definitions of coyote medicine concentrate on the bad: thievery, cowardice and mischief. Heyoka medicine includes people defined as mad. The latter results from observation of a lone coyote at play. Even the adults are playful, and it's not uncommon to see a coyote chasing its own tail (and rolling down a ravine as a result) or pouncing on a particular spot over and over again despite the fact that nothing is there. Coyote is spoken of in some books and predictive systems as the bringer of hard lessons. All of which seems a bit harsh for poor coyote.

There's much more in the lore to suggest that coyote is wise rather than the buffoon or, stated another way: coyote plays the buffoon in order that others might learn and listen. Coyote remembers all, yet coyote also entertains. Most tribes respect coyotes as a sacred medicine teacher. Its wisdom should not be dismissed.

Neither can the concept that coyote sometimes brings hard lessons be discounted completely, for when coyote appears quite often something unexpected and unwelcome will occur. Usually the incident is not a consequence of the person's actions, but the result of some outside influence. Thus, coyote powers do not always work in a person's favour.

Still, coyote can help an individual develop the sense of humour and fun that can make every situation a bit more bearable. It can teach one how to play. If coyote does bring trials, perhaps some of its cunning and guile can be used to advantage. Could it be that coyote is not a precursor of bad events, but the best medicine to call for in time of need?

The coyote individual will have a good, possibly exaggerated sense of fun. This person can be a practical joker, or may turn everything into a game. This may or may not be effective medicine in certain environments.

Before rejecting coyote completely, recognize that of the two, coyote and wolf, the former is the more adaptable. It is the survivor. While the pack-oriented wolf is being slowly driven into ever-more remote areas, the coyote's range expands.

The animal's sense of smell is so acute that it rarely takes the poisoned bait left out for it by ranchers and farmers – for in most places in the US, coyotes are still considered vermin and a bounty is offered for each skin. Systematic slaughter refuses to quell their numbers, therefore it would seem that in modern times, where so much of life is out of an individual's control, coyote medicine might be better than wolf medicine.

# CRANE

Sandhill: *Grus canadensis*
Whooping: *Grus americana*

## BIOLOGICAL INFORMATION

Worldwide there are 15 species of crane, all tall, with typically long neck and legs. The sandhill measures 86 to 122 cm (34 – 48 inches), with a wing span of 2 m (nearly 7 ft). It has red feathers on its brow; otherwise it is grey to rust, depending on the iron content of the tundra waters.

The whooping crane is between 114 and 127 cm (45 and 50 inches) tall. Its wing span is around 2.3 m (7½ ft). The bird is pure white with black-tipped wings. As of 1977 there were fewer than 50 whooping cranes left in the wild. Since then the eggs have been taken from whooping crane nests and placed in the more numerous sandhill cranes' nests, where the young are reared by 'foster parents'. When the eggs disappear, the whooping crane parents replace them, doubling the number of eggs produced.

Cranes are only occasional visitors to Britain.

### HABITAT

Cranes feed in freshwater bogs and winters in coastal areas, prairie ponds and marshy tundra. The sandhill makes its home in Alaska, northern Canada and Siberia, migrating to California, Michigan, Minnesota, Florida and along the Gulf Coast. The whooping crane's range is restricted to a small area around MacKensey in Alberta, Canada. It winters in Texas.

### CHARACTERISTICS

Unlike the heron, which flies with its neck tucked into an S-curve, the crane flies with its head outstretched. Cranes nest on the ground in open country, laying two eggs per breeding season.

The cranes' breeding dance is impressive. Both birds leap with wings outspread and legs out. They then bow and repeat the performance, revolving around each other in circles. The male will present the female with gifts. In northern Japan, male cranes seek to impress their prospective partners with their skills of dung-throwing.

The sandhill crane has been spared the extermination of the whooping crane because it breeds in the Arctic. Both creatures are sensitive to changes in environment; the whooping crane has been greatly affected by the draining of the marshes further south.

## LEGENDS AND TRADITIONS

GODDESSES Pwyll (Celtic), Demeter (Greek)

For the Lakota, *Okaga* (south) was considered the giver of life. Okaga was a direction, a wind and a giant all at once, and cranes were his criers, or *akicita*. The benevolent, helpful nature of crane is illustrated in a Lakota story first published in 1842: A lone hunter stumbled across a single egg in a nest and took it home, thinking to save it from the fate of the others which have been eaten by predators.

The crane grew up with the family and became quite human, and when game was scarce, 'father crane' brought food. One night, as the other family members slept, the mother saw a hand push aside the flap across the doorway, followed by the cry of a prairie wolf (coyote). She knew this to be the signal of a war party. She threw a blanket over the crane and woke her family so they could escape. Crane remained behind, thus disguised. Hours later the family returned to find the crane dead. The bird had sacrificed its life to save the family.

This story reveals one of two attributes ascribed to crane according to Native American tradition, that of giver of life and plenty, as symbolized by the south, for the south brought summer winds, sun and warmth – hence, food.

Another tale reveals crane's diligence. Here, the bird crane shows itself to be a persistent, if not always successful, hunter when it arrives at a pond with many singing frogs. Crane chased one after another, only to have each fall silent or escape at its approach. So intent was the bird on its prey that it did not notice fox as it crept up behind it, attacked and ate it. This story teaches two important lessons: frog boasted too loudly, nearly to its own undoing, while crane lost track of its environment. Both practices are lethal to the hunter-gatherer.

The Egyptian hieroglyph for crane meant 'vigilance'. Therefore, the concept of crane as a symbol of constancy and prudence was common to both Old World and New. Much of the myth about crane comes from the Orient. In China it is a symbol of longevity and happiness. Here too, crane represents diligence and persistence. Mediterranean cultures also shared this belief. For the Japanese, the snow crane was equated with wedded bliss and harmony.

Crane was sacred to the Celts, imparting knowledge and patience. The Druids used crane magic to fly and to call forth a vision from a spirit world. Therefore, crane is credited with divination. Midhir of the Tuatha De Danann had three cranes to represent the triple goddess.

According to Buddhist creed, the crane who is able to stand on one leg in running water is the meditator in the stream of time. Therefore, it represents balance. Crane takes life as it comes. It embodies unworried and unhurried nature. With its mantle of snow, the white crane symbolizes divine wisdom which results in an end to the cycle of death and rebirth – hence, everlasting peace or Nirvana.

Books on heraldry state that when cranes land to roost, they set guards. Therefore, the concept of vigilance has long been accepted in England. Cranes are known for both their circumspection and their benevolence.

## MEDICINE AND POWER

| | |
|---|---|
| DIRECTIONS | North (China/Japan); South (Lakota) |
| ELEMENTS | Air, Water |
| TRAITS | Longevity, vigilance, circumspection |
| ASSOCIATIONS | Divine wisdom, balance, happiness, nirvana, justice, fidelity |

Crane is a much-favoured bird. All told, it represents happiness, prosperity and fidelity. Similarly, crane imparts constancy and industry. As a messenger of Okaga (the south), crane brings the promise of summer sun, bounty and youth. In China and the Mediterranean, it promised longevity. This notion is carried further by both Buddhism and Christianity, where crane becomes the symbol of life eternal.

So it seems crane is the bringer of all good things, and to a certain degree, luck. Call upon crane medicine when lacking energy. Its arrival heralds a time of stability coupled with gain, while crane's circumspection allows one to make the best use of these blessings. Some say the appearance of crane can portend a wedding or a time of renewed of marital harmony.

Crane, as a wading bird, is equated with both air and water. Thus it is in contact with both intellect and emotion, and overwhelmed by neither. It can stir the muddy waters of the unconscious without being touched by them. More importantly it can find sustenance while plumbing these depths. Air has also been likened to spirit; therefore, crane speaks of the successful merging of feelings with spirit.

Crane stands close to the shoreline to feed, a 'tween place associated with faeries. It is this same characteristic that Buddhism equates with mastery of time. Together – the blending of spirit with emotions – crane's gift of straddling two worlds, and its sense of timelessness endows it with the ability not only to look into the future, but to face it unafraid. Crane is sometimes invoked for love spells, but its primary gift is balance.

Crane people are unflappable. They may appear a bit distant or self-absorbed as they keep their eyes on some distant vision. This individual will exhibit a talent for knowing what's going to happen, when. Someone with crane medicine may often be called upon to play the peacemaker. The crane person will bring adversaries together by appealing to their wit and their feelings – using one to combat the other as needed. Sometimes, the mere presence of crane will soothe.

# CROW/RAVEN

Crow: *Corvus brachyrhynchos*
Raven: *Corvus Corax*

## BIOLOGICAL INFORMATION

Every continent but South America has some form of crow. It is a stocky black bird with a stout bill and a fan-shaped tail. It measures between 43 and 53 cm (17 and 21 inches). The raven is larger, a maximum of 57 cm (27 inches). Yet the smallest measures 53 cm (21 inches), the same length as a large crow. Therefore, the two can often be confused.

The only way to tell the difference is to look at the tail, assuming the bird is obliging enough to fan it. The tail of the raven forms a point, while crow's is rounded. The raven also has a shaggy throat and a heavier bill.

### HABITAT

Crows prefer woodland, farmland and suburban areas. In the US, they extend from the northern borders down to the south. The only area exempt from crow is the Rio Grande basin. However, the population density of crow decreases as one moves north into Canada.

Raven is much more shy. It has retreated to remote regions in the western US and northern Canada. It prefers coniferous forests and rocky coasts. In the US it can be located in the western desert. In other words, it lives in places not often frequented by man. Ravens range from the

Aleutians across Alaska and most of Canada and from the Rockies west to the Pacific coast.

In the United Kingdom, a similar pattern is followed. Crow inhabits the area throughout southern England, the Midlands and East Anglia, while raven is mainly found in Wales, the highlands of Scotland and the less-inhabited regions of northwest England. Elsewhere, raven ranges into Scandinavia and Eastern Europe as well as the mountainous areas of Asia and the deserts of the Middle East and North Africa.

## CHARACTERISTICS

Crow is one of the more gregarious members of the *Corvid* family. Crows nest singly as a family, unlike rooks, who form colonies. During the day, however, crows flock together. The crow often sets up sentinels to alert others of the approach of strangers. It is omnivorous and a scavenger.

The crow is a remarkably intelligent bird, able to create and use tools to fish grubs from logs. Some crows have learned to use man's mechanisms for their own gain. Closed-circuit cameras have caught crows dropping nuts before cars stopped at a traffic signal. The bird will watch as the cars crack the nut, and then fly down to the pavement, waiting patiently until the light changes and the cars stop, retrieve its reward.

Still, crow is often vilified despite the fact that it shares few of the magpie's or the jay's less savoury characteristics. Crow is not attracted by shiny objects, and it is generally a tidy bird. Not even the young foul the nest. It tends to return to the same nest site year after year, around March, to breed, after which crow abandons the nest and returns to the flock.

Raven is much less convivial. The raven also breeds as a single family unit, and it lives that way. In other words, it does not form flocks during the day. The raven's nest is made of twigs, usually high up in a tree where it cannot be seen. The cup is lined with fur, feathers, moss and lichen. The raven produces four to seven eggs.

The raven regularly rides the rising air currents, soaring much like a hawk. They perform mock fights, tumbling in the air for their own amusement. Like crow, raven is omniverous and certainly no less intelligent; however, it is more difficult to observe, and much more easily routed from its nest. Therefore, less is known about its habits. It is now listed as an endangered species, while crow is not.

## LEGENDS AND TRADITIONS

GODDESSES Athena (Greek)
GODS Apollo (Greek), Odin (Scandinavian)

Just as the raven and crow are sometimes confused, similarly the medicine attributed to each is mixed. In other words, in those places where the territories of the two overlap, a distinction is made between them. Elsewhere, though, where crow predominates it picks up attributes of raven. Where raven has supplanted its smaller cousin, raven takes on the traits originally assigned to crow.

A specific example would be shape-shifting. In those places where both raven and crow roost, only raven is ascribed this gift. Further south where raven does not fly, crow is both shape-shifter and magician.

Simply stated, there's very little to differentiate between the two birds and the medicine and power they are supposed to supply. Even the names can become confused.

The Inuit people of the Arctic credit crow, not raven, with the gift of light, day and sun. Yet crow does not live this far north. In the Inuit tale, crow (raven) stole light from another tribe, but it was heavy and crow could not fit much in his bundle, so the Arctic gets sun only half of the year. Still, the Inuit honour the bird and never hurt it for fear it will take back the gift of light and they will be plunged into darkness for ever.

Interestingly enough, the Chinese made a similar association between crow and light. They worshipped a three-legged sun crow.

The Haida, who lived in the islands of Puget Sound, assigned creation, first man and first woman, to raven. There are some interesting parallels between the Haida story and the Biblical one. For example, in one version of the Haida story, men and women were moulded from clay. In another, the tale begins with a great flood. When the waters receded, raven was left alone. After he'd gorged himself, raven became bored. For raven was the trickster, and there was no one to play jokes on. Eventually, he screamed. A clamshell appeared. Its halves split apart and strange furless, featherless, wingless, two-legged creatures were revealed, cowering inside the shell. Raven put on his most soothing voice and coaxed the animals from the shell. So, raven found the first man, and he was entertained by their antics. For a little while. Then again, raven grew bored. He thought and thought. His eyes glinted as he realized that wherever there were male creatures, there must also be females. Wouldn't it be a clever trick to put the two of them together and see how they act? Raven searched until he found some giant chitons (mollusks) clinging to a rock. He opened one and then another. In each was a woman. He persuaded them onto his back and took them to the men. Since that day raven has never been bored again, although few thank him for playing this prank on humanity. To raven's credit, he also brought the sun, moon and stars, fire, salmon and the sacred cedar to the Haida people.

The British Columbian Niska tribe considered raven as important as eagle, bear or wolf. As a new member was brought into the clan he was ritually 'killed' so he could be resurrected with the spirit of the raven. Meanwhile, the Tlingit of the same region were divided into two basic 'moieties' (societies or clans): the wolf and the raven. The Native Americans of one northwestern tribe fed the afterbirth of their sons to ravens so that the boys would learn the birds' speech.

On the opposite side of the Americas, the agrarian Seneca took the opposite view. They grew corn, beans and squash. They held the Spirit of the Plants in special esteem. Each autumn they held a thanksgiving festival to honour Mother Earth. Crow came to them in the form of misfortune, as the stealer of the beans. The next time the flock arrived the chief ordered the ravaged fields burned, so crows' white feathers were turned black.

A legend of the Sioux crystallizes many of crow's abilities, such as the gift of speech, prophecy and as sentinel or guard. A band was plagued by crows and made war upon the birds, killing all but the youngest. The chief trained this young crow to speak the many languages of man. Then he sent it to spy upon his enemies. As the moons passed, this chief became known as a powerful holy man, for he always knew of an attack before it happened. His tribe would ambush the war party before it could arrive at the village. Eventually the other tribes stopped trying to make war upon this band. Still the bird flew out, and one day it happened upon some old men who were discussing the imminent death of the chief's brothers. The crow had stumbled across spirits who knew all. The bird returned to the village and informed the chief. Soon the brothers died, struck by lightning as had been predicted.

Like the colour black, crow was identified by the aboriginal Americans with the Great Mystery, the void from which all things emerged. For some eastern tribes, crow was the keeper of the sacred laws, laws that extended beyond society's rules or norms. It represented incontrovertible truths which often appeared inexplicable to man – such as death – and crow medicine was exclusively the provenance of women.

The Cheyenne thought so highly of the bird's medicine that crows' feathers replaced eagle feathers in their warbonnets. Other tribes in the southeastern US believed the bird and its powers to represent pure evil. It was reviled rather than revered, and those who practised its medicine were feared. This distrust of crow medicine carried as far north as Canada, where the Ojibwa still warn people against its medicine.

As carrion-eaters, both crow and raven were a part of Native American cosmology. Scavenging was seen as a necessary part of cleaning, bringing balance to nature. The crow was considered a teacher because of its intelligence. Crow was equated with not only with air (intellect), but with earth (practical application). It is one of the most landbound species of birds in the North American continent. Its habits are almost 'tribal'. It appears to be near-human, and it is easily identified with by man.

In Europe, crow had many of the same characteristics as it did in the Americas, both the good and the bad. It was guardian for the Romans, and as in the Seneca legend, it was originally white. Apollo set the bird to watch over his pregnant lover. The bird brought news of the death of the child to the sun god who, in his anger, turned the white plumage black.

Crow, like jay and magpie, is an excellent mimic. In fact, it can be taught to speak without having its tongue cleaved as recommended by

Pliny. For the Celts, birds often brought information, acting as messengers. Particularly ancient birds knew human speech, and this included crow. Like the Inuit, the Celts credited crow with creation.

Much of European mythology equates the crow with evil and death. It is also widely associated with witchcraft. The Europeans agree with the Native Americans, attributing to crow the gift of prophecy. Many superstitions have arisen around the bird. A crow flying around the house and cawing portends a death. A flock flying from a wood is a sign of hard times ahead. In medieval times, even the placement of a raven or a crow to the left or the right of the road predicted victory or loss in battle. In the US state of Maryland, the Scottish ditty about magpies has been adapted to crows:

*One crow, sorrow;*
*Two, mirth;*
*Three crows, a wedding;*
*Four a birth.*

The raven fared only little better than the crow. Heraldry refers to the raven as bold and capable of flying to great heights. It also attributes to raven an extraordinary sense of smell.

Linnaeus observed that the Swedes looked upon ravens as sacred, and no one killed them. Raven was seen as an emblem of constancy. The Norse God Odin had two ravens, Hugin (thought) and Munin (memory) which he used as messengers. Raven was Odin's companion when he hung upon the sacred tree. The god was rewarded for his efforts with the wisdom of runes. From runes sprang a form of prediction. Therefore raven was also associated with the gift of the seer and with magic.

Another tale of old England relays how Oddune, Earl of Devonshire, killed Hubba the Dane to acquire the enchanted standard *Reafen*. One ancient tapestry depicted a figure of a raven which had been woven with magical incantations. The Danes believed that it prognosticated, by its movements, the success or failure of any enterprise.

Bestiaries referred to it as *nycticorax*, night raven, and said that it liked the darkness more than it liked the sun (*tenebras amat magis quam lucem*).

This is the opposite of the Inuit belief that crow's gift was light. The eating of either crow or raven was proscribed in Deuteronomy. Whiteness was equated with purity, so blackness reflected ritual uncleanliness and ignorance. Yet, in one set of miniatures Christ is shown as teaching the raven. The view of raven was as mixed as that of crow.

Like crow, if raven lighted on the housetop this portended death. In the time of Charles II it was asserted that the British monarchy would collapse if the ravens left the Tower of London; their wings are clipped to this day. In Scotland, hunters believe hearing one caw before a hunt bodes a good outcome and plenty of deer. Rooks carry much of the same power as raven. The Scots hold that a rook's nest near a house brings good luck, but should the bird suddenly leave, the house will fall.

## MEDICINE AND POWER

| | |
|---|---|
| DIRECTION | North |
| ELEMENTS | Air, Earth |
| TRAITS | Intelligence, insight, use of tools |
| ASSOCIATIONS | Witchcraft, sorcery, magic, foresight, prediction, sacred law, the void, shape-shifting, luck both good and bad |

By now the reader should be completely baffled. The bird is benevolent or malevolent. It is creator; it is destroyer. Simply stated, the bird can be likened to the symbol for Tao with its curving halves of yin and yang, for one without the other is incomplete. The dual identification of crow or raven adds to the muddle.

It is this author's opinion that whether crow or raven appears is irrelevant. When viewed in the wild, neither bird would allow anyone to measure it with a ruler, much less approach it with a caliper to check the stoutness of its beak. Unless a person's location furnishes a clue, the two should be considered interchangeable. In vision, a symbol might provide clarification. It may suggest a specific legend or tradition associated with a particular bird.

Yet in terms of power, energies or medicine, they are basically the same. When either crow or raven is about, there is magic. The connection between these birds and sorcery is pervasive throughout North American and European lore.

Like many of the animal mentors, crow had both its positive and its negative sides. However, due to its link with both sorcery and the void, it was believed that the propensity for crow's or raven's power to be misused was magnified, even where the bird was esteemed. In fact, the main differentiation seems to be whether or not this magic is sinister. In the southeast US, the crow was an ill omen. In the northwest, the raven was bringer of the sun and creator of the world.

Partly because of their association with the Great Mystery (void) where all times are one and all things exist *in potentia*, crow and raven are also equated with prescience or precognition. The latter is another good reason why crow and raven should be beheld with both veneration and a certain measure of disquiet, for the future can be a frightening thing. In Central America, people with crow medicine are able to look into the future.

The European view of crow/raven differs little from that of the so-called primitive. Norse mythology held that crow/raven had the gift of vision and prediction. Raven was the most prophetic of birds. In addition, raven was quite often identified with evil. Crow portended bad luck, even death, if it alighted on the left side of the road.

Raven's presence foretells change. Crow and raven are black, the colour of the void. Crow merges light and darkness, seeing both inner and outer reality.

Crow is associated with the sacred law rather than the laws of man. Native peoples have used the crow as a symbolic link between humanity and the environment, and regarded its every appearance as having some message. For example, if a person saw a crow flying close to the ground, it presaged rain.

Both crow and raven are the mark of the shaman. Their appearance signals a time for exploring and enhancing one's power. The birds help man to see deeply into the nature of reality and natural law. They permit man to move between the realms and pierce illusion. To call upon raven is to ask for the courage to enter the darkness to seek the wisdom of the primal unconscious.

Secretive raven, even more than crow, was associated with night, therefore, dark magic. If there was a difference in the medicine between the two, raven was stronger and its magic thought to be bigger, deeper, more profound. Where both birds nest, raven was the magical shape-shifter, while crow was relegated to the master of illusions.

Raven is considered more mischievous, a way-changer. It is the trickster of several Canadian tribes. Sometimes raven is feared rather than respected since it can point people to the wrong path as some kind of prank.

To contrast: If crow is the most man-like of all birds – and therefore the most communicative of the two 'magical mentors' – raven is its mirror-image, the essence of spirit or soul. Crow is the more accessible of the two. Another analogy might be that crow is a conjurer while raven's a wizard.

Raven and crow people are intuitive and clever. People with crow tendencies will prefer the company of others to solitude. The reverse is true for ravens. Both medicine groups are natural sorcerers. In ancient times magic was not thought to be supernatural or paranormal, it was seen as the capacity to bring creative thought into physical reality. The individual with crow or raven medicine exhibits this trait. This person will be inventive, creating new solutions for old problems. Others may have difficulty trusting the people with raven or crow medicine because they have the spooky ability to know what they shouldn't. Used well, raven or crow medicine gives mastery and balance. These people are sensitive to changes in the atmosphere, both physical and mental.

# DEER

AMERICAN
Black-tail (mule): *Odocoileus hemionus*
White-tail: *Odocoileus virginous*

EUROPEAN
Red: *Cervus elaphus*
Axis: *Axis axis*
Fallow: *Dama dama*

## BIOLOGICAL INFORMATION

The white-tail and the black-tail (or mule) deer are approximately the same size – measuring 116 to 199 cm (3⅔ – 6½ feet) long and 90 to 105 cm (3 – 3½ feet) at the shoulder. The antlers spread between 90 and 120 cm (3 – 4 feet) and develop symmetrically. The primary visual differences between the two species are colour and antler structure. The white-tail lacks the blackened tail tip of the mule deer. The antlers of the former have a single main beam, while the black-tail have antlers with branched main beams.

There are three different varieties of deer native to Britain: the Red, Roe and Fallow. The red is the largest. Males may weigh as much as 200 to 250 kg (440 to 550 lb).

The Axis deer was imported from India. Its body measures between 130 and 150 cm (52 and 60 inches); the tail is around 20 to 30 cm (8 to 12 inches) long. The axis stands 85 to 95 cm (34 to 38 inches) at the shoulder.

The fallow deer is about the same length and height as the axis, but its tail is shorter. Each are about the size of a large dog. Both axis and fallow deer sport white spots, even in maturity. They also share a black stripe running down the back. The protective spots recede in the adults of the larger species. Fallow deer can be differentiated from axis by their antlers. The former have antlers with a flat plate-like structure, similar to that of a moose, while axis deer's antlers are delicate, like those of the red deer.

## HABITAT

The two American species – mule and white-tail deer – cover the entire continental United States and the lower 320-km (200-mile) strip of Canada. The white-tailed deer is found from the Atlantic coast to the Rockies, the black-tail from the Pacific seaboard to the Tetons and western Plains. The two territories overlap along the continental divide.

The black-tail or mule deer prefers the dryer, mountainous areas, while the white-tail is more often located in forested or marshy regions.

Deer is probably one of the most successful families. Deer can be found on every continent except Australia, where that ecological niche has been taken over by the kangaroo. Deer thrive in the United Kingdom.

Some deer are kept in farms and parks in England, Ireland, Wales and Scotland; they are also found in the wild, although they have retreated to the more remote and wooded regions of the Peak and Lake Districts in England. The tiny roe still ranges throughout the Midlands and the southwestern counties of Somerset, Dorset and Wiltshire. Elsewhere in Europe, deer stick to the Pyrenees, the Black Forest region of Germany, and the wooded areas of Italy, Switzerland and France. The Carpathian red deer is larger than the English.

Likewise, some form of deer is found in abundance in Russia, India, China, Indonesia and South America.

## CHARACTERISTICS

The American black-tail (or mule) deer is adapted to rugged terrain. The black-tailed deer does not run, but bounds or hops in a peculiar stiff-legged, four-footed gait. A territorial animal, the black-tail has glands located on the back of the legs to mark its range. During the summer months, these deer live as solitary animals or in small groups that consist of a mother and her fawns. Because of this, mule deer are much more combative than the white-tail. Like the elk, mule deer gather in groups during the seasonal rut, when males fight to maintain a harem.

The white-tail deer is a woodland creature. Unlike the mule deer, it stays in small herds year round. During the summer months the groups are separated by gender, while in the winter the two merge to form one large herd.

Deer are nervous creatures, with ears that move individually and constantly. A more social animal, the white-tails have a system of alarm signals which includes stamping, snorting and raising their white tail as a flag when a predator has been spotted. White-tail do not form harems; several males may mate with a single female.

Both species are active at dawn, dusk and night, although deer may forage at any time throughout the day if the need presents itself. Their diet includes grasses and leaves in the summer months, along with berries. During the winter they eat the soft branches of cedar, fir, aspen, willow and yew. Acorns and apples are also eaten.

The original home of the red deer was the wooded steppes of Russia. However, it has migrated or been transported throughout Europe and into America. There it is found primarily in the south. The red deer sticks to the woodlands, only visiting the fields to forage. In central Europe the rut occurs from September to the middle of October. In terms of behaviour, the red deer are closer to the black-tail or mule deer, gathering their does during rut. One, occasionally two, offspring emerge after a gestation period of 34 weeks.

The fallow deer is a herd animal who collects a harem. The habit patterns of the roe resemble those of the white-tail, where the male practises serial monogamy, staying with a single doe while it is the mating season and then moving on the next.

The axis deer, coming from a warm climate, does not have a specific rutting season. Mating and birth can take place at any time during the year, and every six months in good years.

## LEGENDS AND TRADITIONS

GODDESSES Artemis (Greek), Diana (Roman), Saysan (Kiowa)
GODS Apollo (Greek), Hercules (Greek/Roman)

Deer symbolism was basic in Mayan art. The number of times it appears indicates its importance. The double-headed dragon often appeared with the cloven hooves of a deer. This dragon god was associated with water, for the water lily often appeared as part of the motif. The rectangular bases of Mayan stelae always have human faces carved into them, usually a stylized representative of significant priests or noblemen of the time, along with one animal, usually a deer. This suggests a link with royalty. Examples of pottery also reveal deer at their base, as if the animal was the foundation upon which the society and religion were built. One archaeological find included the skull of a peccary carved to show a deer standing erect as though human. Indeed, a human with a deer head or headdress was a common illustration.

The Ojibwa tribe used special powers to track deer. It was believed that if they put a medicine bundle in the deer's hoof print, the hunter would soon find the creature even if it was several days' hunt away. The charm would compress the time of travel from days into hours.

All across the globe, deer has been one of the most important prey animals. The Native Americans valued its skin for clothing. Its antlers were fashioned into tools to eat or scrape hide with, or even to smoke with (as pipes). The hooves were used as rattles by the Miwatani society of the Mandan.

A legend relating specifically to fawn comes from the Lakota. When the world was new, a friendly spirit gave to each animal the means to protect itself. To the buffalo the spirit gave horns; to the wolf he gave teeth, and to deer he gave speed. One day a doe came walking past with her ungainly young, and the spirit watching the wobbly fawn realized that in giving speed to deer he had forgotten fawn, so the spirit bestowed spots upon the young to camouflage it until it grew into its legs.

Although the skin and meat were valued, the Oglala Sioux viewed both white-tail and black-tail deer with so much suspicion that they rarely discussed the animal aloud. It was believed if a man shot a deer, without performing the appropriate rites and ceremonies, that his rifle would cease to function and the hunter himself would go mad.

Deer was associated with female sexuality and seduction. One species was supposed to have the ability to shapeshift into the form of a beautiful woman and lure men to their doom. If a man succumbed to the seduction, he was condemned to languish and die as a result of the liaison. If he somehow managed to survive, it was said he had special medicine.

The two main recorders of Lakota history – Joseph Epes Brown and James R Walker – disagree as to which characteristics were attributed to which species of deer. According to interviews conducted by Walker in 1849, it was the white-tailed (woodland) deer that was the seductress, able to transform itself into a beautiful woman and entice young braves to lie with them. Meanwhile, the black-tailed (mule) deer caused guns to misfire. Writing in *Animals of the Soul* published in 1997, Joseph Epes Brown contends that the reverse is true. The seductress is the black-tail or mule deer. White-tail deer, with its ability to endure thirst, was the man's helper during a vision quest.

There are two factors which suggest that Walker's version could be correct. Writing in the 19th century, it might be assumed that Walker was closer to the original story than Brown. The second has to do with the behaviour of the two species during the seasonal rut. The mule-tail deer's habits more closely approximate those of the elk; the male of the species gathers his does and guards them. Meanwhile the white-tail doe may mate with up to seven males during a season. With the Lakota views on fidelity, such behaviour would have been considered immoral. However, if the Oglala made this connection because of the perfume exuded in the deer tracks, then the black-tail must be the culprit, for only it has the gland at the back of the leg directly above the hooves; the white-tail does not. Suffice it to say that deer medicine is primarily women's medicine. Deer dances were women's dances, although a deer woman might be asked to participate in an elk medicine dance. However, the Lakota viewed all animals with forked antlers, including the antelope, as duplicitous.

The Kiowa, another Plains tribe located in southeastern Kansas near the present-day city of Wichita, seemed to hold deer in slightly higher esteem. According to them, deer was one of the first born, created before light came to warm the earth. Deer, fox, magpie – and to a limited extent, prairie dog – all participated in stealing the sun from a tribe which was keeping it. Fox, as most fleet and cunning, stole the glowing orb and ran until he could run no more. Deer then took over, carrying the sun until she could run no more. Magpie was next in the relay, and finally, Saynday,[1] who bore it to prairie dog's nest, where they kept it. So the world had light, but the earth grew parched and Saynday in his wisdom threw the sun up into the sky so everyone could share it.

The dual nature of the deer is preserved in the American southwest. Here, though, the idea of both suspicion and seduction is mental, and control is obtained though the use of words. For the Pueblo tribes of New Mexico, deer was the storyteller – a concept which when taken to its worst extremes also meant liar. Thus, deer was the medicine of a poet or bard, prevaricator or fraud. The former included at least some element of wisdom. However, because of the latter and deer's duplicitous nature, deer people were viewed with mistrust.

In the Pacific northwest, the deer was the bringer of wealth, prosperity and wisdom. As in Europe it was considered a noble animal, and it was known for its strength and endurance. The area west of the Rockies, blocked by the mountains, was one of the few areas in the continental US where buffalo did not roam. Thus the deer took over much of the revered position that was held in the Plains by the buffalo. It sacrificed everything to the wealth of the people, and its ceremonies were used to mark the great events in the calendar, the New Year and female pubescence. Deer gave rejuvenation and renewal to the tribe, as did women with the children they bore.

The Hupa and the Tolowa tribes of northwest California, like the Lakota, used hoof rattles in a girl's coming-of-age ceremony as a symbol of attaining her womanly powers. Meanwhile the White Deerskin dance was one of the two most important rites, along with the Salmon festival, marking the two great turning points of the year – spring and autumn.

This connection with female sexuality and seduction was maintained by at least one of the tribes of the east. The Natchez, located in Tennessee, were hierarchical city-builders and city-dwellers, in some ways atypical of other Native American groups. Like the Egyptians they practised incest within the royal family to keep the blood-line pure, and they were the only North American group to practise human sacrifice as part of their regular rituals. Therefore it would not be unexpected that their view varied slightly. For them, deer taught man how to seduce woman. It was believed that anything that would attract a deer would also attract a woman. Courtship was equated with the hunt. Men were instructed to use the same charms to lure a deer – notably things that sparkle and shine, along with flute music – as he would to persuade his beloved to become his wife.

The deer is absent from the Egyptian pantheon. The Greeks honoured it, though. Deer was linked with the twin god and goddess Apollo and Artemis. These children of Zeus and Leta, born at Ortygia, were the epitome of male and female beauty. Like the Arcadian Artemis, the Greek goddess was associated with the hunt, as was her brother, and deer was one of their creatures. A month, loosely translated as 'deer-shooting', was named after Artemis. Later, the virgin huntress of the Romans, Diana, became linked with the deer. So rather than being regarded with distrust, deer were esteemed and considered a symbol of purity.

Another contrast was that deer were associated not with female sexuality, but male. For the European, the deer was masculine energy, virility, the very essence of maleness. Not surprisingly it was the male deer, hart or stag that received the most attention in Old World religions.

The first symbol of pagan virility was the antlered god or Green Man. Thus, two cultures regarded the same creature, witnessed the same behaviour and came to diametrically opposed conclusions. Celts linked the white hart with Arthur and the legendary hunt that leads the king to the magical well of Pellinore. Meanwhile the same beast lures the knights and their dogs into a trap. Thus, Arthur's and his knights' quest for the white hart were metaphors for man's search for God. Arthur, the chosen, was worthy; the knights were not.

Christianity preserved the view of deer as divine purity. According to Alferic, a hart was responsible for the conversion of the Roman soldier Placida to Christianity. Placida followed the beast into the woods. It turned and Placida saw a golden cross embedded between its antlers. The animal spoke, urging Placida to accept Christ as his saviour. For his piety – and possibly his sportsmanlike behaviour in not killing the deer – Placida became Eustace, patron saint of hunters. In *Livre du Roy Modus*, Queen Ratio (reason) compares deer with virtue and boar with vice. Eventually the hart became regal, while the female hind was the recognized symbol for the human soul.

In medieval times these ideas evolved into a stiffly codified structure. Attributes varied not only between species, but differed according to the stages of growth and development within a species. The randy stag, for example, was distinguished from the noble hart. The latter had magical powers, along with the ability to rejuvenate itself. The former had sexual prowess.

The fallow buck was held in much less esteem and had no specific tales or myths attached to it. Like all male deer, the fallow deer was given different names according to its age – second year, preket; third year, sowrell; fourth, sowre; and after that, buck, which was then graded according to the number of antlers.

The tiny roe buck was called rascal, and it was viewed with amused affection. The stages of development include: year one, kyde; second year, gerle; third, hemule; fourth, roebuck; then roobuck after the fifth. The roebuck, unlike the royal hart or randy stag, represented abstinence or chastity in medieval art.

Books of heraldry report that stag was admired for its elegance and beauty. Deer's senses are remarkably acute. Therefore, the deer has become the emblem of prudence, which is the principle of all virtues.

# MEDICINE AND POWER

| | |
|---|---|
| DIRECTION | East |
| ELEMENT | Wind |
| TRAITS | Swiftness, cunning, grace, beauty |
| ASSOCIATIONS | Sexuality (Europe male, American female), duality and duplicity, storyteller, keeper of wisdom, divinity, purity, prudence, royalty, soul |

At first glance it would appear difficult to rectify the two divergent philosophies regarding deer. It becomes easy through the process of simplification. Thus, deer represents sexuality, both male and female. Deer is a pretty creature, while the buck prancing about in full rut is the very image of maleness, the battles for supremacy symptomatic of testosterone run amok.

The fact that deer can epitomize both male and female sexuality is suggestive of duality, which tends to confirm Native American beliefs about the animal. In truth, the same trait for which deer was admired in Europe made it less popular in America, and that was its ability to dupe the hunter, to leave false and misleading trails for the dogs, and this seems more indicative of the society than the animal. The deer's ability to deceive could be applauded in England because deer were the special reserve of the king, who did not require a successful hunt in order to eat. Therefore, he would view with admiration the same behaviour which the Native American saw with consternation. For the aboriginal American, when a deer disappeared with a false sign, he and his family would often go hungry.

Therefore, both cultures acknowledged deer's duplicity, only their reaction to it differed. This was governed by necessity, for in Europe it was a laudable trait for a prince to fool his enemy. This ability was not totally disregarded by the Native American, who adorned his bow and arrow with deer fur to attain not only deer's wiles, but deer's sight in hunt and battle. Deer make rapid changes of course during the chase in order to confuse the hunter. Similarly, it can vanish into dense undergrowth.

All peoples observed the deer's ability to seduce. Arthur is enticed to the well; his knights lured to disaster. The deer-storyteller of the southwestern Native American tribes can either educate or deceive with its tales. Royalty must be duplicitous, under the guise of diplomacy. It would appear the reaction to artifice depended a lot upon personal opinion.

For the plains Lakota and the woodland Dakota, who placed a high value on female fidelity, deer was suspect. The southwestern tribes were more matriarchal in social structure. Deer was linked with the feminine. However this, in and of itself, was not negative. Their ideas on fidelity were more lenient, so the trickery of deer became the provenance of words. Pueblo peoples merged the northwestern image of deer's wisdom, also a provenance of words, and the duplicity ascribed to deer by the Plains' peoples.

Deer's medicine or power is, as always, an outgrowth of its characteristics. The deer not only sees well, it hears well. The deer is ever alert to danger. It is swift and is able to endure thirst for long periods. So it was called upon by Native American peoples to help during the four-day vision quest, where the brave must do without food and water.

All this is to say that there is no reason why deer cannot encompass the attributes credited to it. It is seduction, for who isn't entranced when they spy a wild deer on the edge of a forest or a field? The tiny roe deer inspires as much awe as any of its larger counterparts.

Seduction suggests sexuality. The female sexuality of deer further implies maternity, love, nourishment and sustenance. The male sexuality in the form of the buck represents aggression, mastery, authority, protection – all things that were considered a part of nobility. The concept of purity and love is in keeping with fawn who, weak and helpless, must be protected by its elders and betters. So, fawn brings out the best in people, the divine.

The interpretation of deer medicine can, therefore, be a much more personal thing than, for example, magpie medicine. It is dependent not only on the gender, but the age of the animal involved. The Native American name 'Little Deer Comes Dancing' or 'Prancing Fawn' is indicative of one deer, while the name 'Black Deer' (found in the 1880 Red Cloud Reservation Census) reveals another facet of both the animal's and the individual's personality. Black, being the colour of mystery, suggests that the latter had a connection with the wisdom of deer, while the former implies joy and playfulness.

The doe is maternity, sexuality, coming of age for a woman. It is the time of renewal and the beginning of new life. As a mother, deer protects her fawn to the best of her ability. Since she has no great bulk and often no horns, she does this through cunning and guile, hiding her child and avoiding it during daylight hours, and taking convoluted paths home in order to baffle any potential predators. Deer as mother is also nurturing. She provides nourishment and sustenance for her young.

However, the male deer is probably most celebrated for his ability to protect his harem. He bellows to mark his domain and his authority over the does. He fights to defend them and will exhaust himself during the rut, even to the point of starvation and death. Many top-ranking males never make it to the next season. His masculinity is also his undoing.

Finally, fawn is innocence, altruistic and unquestioning love, gentleness of spirit – many of the same traits attributed to hind in Christian religion: purity of spirit, hence soul, and to a certain extent naivety. It can also be associated with playfulness and joy.

The deer can be invoked for all these reasons. In a time of trouble the hart will give strength and endurance, and help those who ask for its help whether the best response is to fight or to run. The hind grants defensive cunning. Both doe and buck impart speed and agility, and their magic can be called upon to help the supplicant disappear in a cloud of dust or fade into the background. Likewise, deer has the wit to decide which reaction is the most appropriate. Ever-vigilant and watchful, deer medicine can help keep the individual alert and out of harm's way. Its ability to vanish in the underbrush can be used to confound one's enemies.

Like the buffalo, deer gave its life to feed the people. It can indicate the coming of prosperity and plenty. Conversely, it may indicate some sort of sacrifice is required in order to resolve a problem.

As woman's medicine, it symbolizes coming into one's own power. The beginning of a woman's menses is a sign of fertility and a time of rebirth that contains within it the promise of new life from which all true wealth arises. Therefore, it is logical to assume deer should be invoked during any ceremonies specific to women.

Deer was often used in love medicine. It gave the power to bewitch. Sometimes, ground-up antlers were placed in love potions or medicine bundles. The deer rattle magically endowed, or confirmed, a young girl's ability to bear children. Thus, one can assume that its energies maybe used in another way, to repel sterility or release one from infertility. Which animal is petitioned – doe, stag or fawn – would probably depend a great deal on the individual performing the invocation.

Generally, though, deer medicine allows one to move with deliberation, great awareness and speed. It encourages gentleness and peace. Deer enhances one's ability to change directions quickly without losing one's centre. It deepens awareness of the present moment. Deer allows one to see with great clarity what is going on around and within oneself, which can be used for cultivating surrender, humility and trust in gentle ways. If deer has appeared in someone's life, it may be time to review one's attitudes.

The preferred modern interpretation is the European one, although some of the other traits are still observed. Therefore, deer is also known for its nervous, lively nature and it has become associated with attentiveness.

One must not dismiss or discount the storyteller or the trickster, however. The deer person has the medicine of the bard. This individual can captivate and enchant both with his/her wondrous words and beautiful physique. Others hold high expectations of the deer and are often disillusioned when they discover the deer individual suffers from nervousness and high temper. The same words and wisdom that can entice and educate can also be used to dupe and defraud. Few people are forgiving enough to recognize this as a defence – words to hide behind. Deer can blend into the environment if they desire. Deer people have especially sensitive hearing and do not like loud noises. They are intuitive and often sense the feelings of others.

# DOG

*Canis familiarus*

## BIOLOGICAL INFORMATION

As the Latin designation suggests, dogs are one of the most familiar species to man. With so many breeds, there's no one fixed size or weight. Some breeds stand no taller than 15 cm (6 inches) at the shoulder, while the Great Dane can often exceed 1 metre (3 ft).

The domestic dog has no specific breeding period. Despite this diversity, dog shares more than 97 per cent of its genes with wolf and coyote. The relationship is close enough that the three species can interbreed.

### HABITAT

Worldwide, dog is found on every continent. In Australia, although, the species were introduced by European settlers where they ran wild and are now known as dingo. The dog population there became a threat to many native species.

Like cat, dog resides wherever man can be found. Some dogs still live wild on the African plains, although the true African wild dog is now considered an endangered species.

### CHARACTERISTICS

Dogs share many characteristics with their lupine predecessors. Dogs are pack animals, the domesticated dog having substituted a human family for the animal pack. Left to their own devices, dogs still form packs with other dogs. They display all the social posturing of wolves. In the wild, they have an alpha male and female who are the only members of the group allowed to breed, although all members participate in caring for the young.

Dogs were probably one of the first animals to be domesticated by man, although some archaeologists contend that the reverse is true: Wolf *cum* dog domesticated man. The safety provided by wolves who attached themselves as scavengers to a human camp hastened the transition to village life; for the women could be left alone in relative safety with the pack to raise the alarm when necessary. The women, therefore, often picked an individual dog to take into the home, choosing the ones that they felt they could trust, the ones with the softest features. Thus, the evolution of dogs began simultaneously with that of man.

## LEGENDS AND TRADITIONS

GODDESSES Hecate, Lyssa, Artemis, Scylla (Greek), Lares (Roman), Mahakh (Native American), Nehalennia (Celtic), Ninkharak (Mesopotamian)

The Mayan had domesticated dogs, and pictures of them were found in more than one Mayan temple. The dog had ceremonial significance and often acted as an offering to placate the gods. It appeared bound and ready for the sacrificial table.

The native peoples of North America sometimes associated dog with the powers of thunder, as they did the coyote. The dog-soldiers of the Cheyenne were not only warriors, but they were charged with the protection of the village. As such, the *Hotam iau iu* (dog men) received special privileges, always being the first to arrive for the Sun Dance and setting up their camp on the right bank of the river selected as the ceremonial site, where they could act as the watchdogs of the tribe and territory.

The Crow had a no-retreat society which was called 'Crazy Dogs Wishing to Die'. At the start of battle, these men would pin their sashes to the ground, and there they would stay fighting until they had either won or died trying.

Despite the male association with wolf, kit fox and fox or dog warrior-type societies, it was the women who chose and raised most dogs. They were selected for their gentleness and trained to carry firewood on a travois (a simple vehicle consisting of two trailing poles serving as shafts and bearing a platform or net for the load). Later, after the introduction of the horse, dogs supplemented the pony-borne travois during camp moves.

Dogs were often used as a part of healing ceremonies where a holy man would transfer the illness from patient to animal.

Dog meat was a special delicacy for the Dakota, and like many other animals its bones and skin were treated with great respect so that others of its species would know that the people meant no disrespect by consuming it.

Sunka, the dog spirit, presided over friendship and cunning. Dog was mysterious. The Native American sign for dog (index and middle fingers extended) is almost identical to that for wolf and that of Great Spirit, or medicine. With the latter, the hand moves towards the heavens, showing the direction from which it comes. Wolf was differentiated from spirit or medicine with a forward motion, while with dog the hand swept sideways. It was as if to say, wolf as teacher and pathfinder to man moves ahead of him, while dog as friend and companion moves beside him.

In the Old World as in the New, dog's protective properties were emphasized. Dog was celebrated in many stories as the sentinel. Homer was the first to mention, in *The Iliad*, the dog guarding the underworld. Later this imagery found expression in the Cerberus. Hesiod calls him the son of Typhon and Echidna, and attributes to him 50 heads. Most people, however, settled for three.

According to Celtic traditions, dog was friend and protector. Cuchulainn was the hound of Ulster, while the authorship of the Ogham poem *Cad Goddea* is attributed, at least in part, to Whelp or dog.

Dog was an emblem of steadfastness and faith. In Christian symbolism, dog was the shepherd of the flock. In alchemy, a dog devoured by a wolf equalled gold purified by the property of antimony.

Old World and New also shared the belief in dog as the companion of the dead. In Mexico and Peru, dogs were sacrificed at funerals. Some historians think that the Egyptian god Anubis (guardian of the underworld) was actually a dog, rather than a jackal. Others associated dog with Set, bringer of chaos and brother and enemy of Osiris.

During the 14th century, the appearance of a black dog in a village was a precursor to the arrival of plague. Dogs were believed to have the ability to see ghosts and smell death. A dog howling next to a person's door – particularly if it howled three times and fell silent – was an omen of death. Even if a dog was seen to dig a hole in a garden, a death was indicated.

Still, heraldry waxed poetical on the subject, observing what seems to be the commonly accepted view now. '... To no animal is mankind so much indebted for services and affection as the dog: among all the various orders of animal beings, no one has hitherto been found so entirely adapted to our use, and even to our protection, as this. His diligence, his ardour, and his obedience, have been truly observed to be inexhaustible, and his disposition is so friendly, that unlike every other animal, he seems to remember only the benefit he receives; he soon forgets our blows.'[1] Clark referred to dog as the emblem of love, gratitude and integrity.

## MEDICINE AND POWER

| | |
|---|---|
| DIRECTION | South |
| ELEMENT | Earth |
| TRAITS | Loyalty, love, friendship, intelligence |
| ASSOCIATIONS | Protection, service, war, guardian, integrity, self-sacrifice; death and the underworld |

Even though the dog has been equated with the male medicine of war, most of the divinities associated with dog are goddesses. Only Cerberus, guardian of the gates of Hades, was male.

Dog has long been considered the servant of humanity. It has acted as beast of burden, helped both commoner and king with the hunt, provided affection for countless generations. Dog protects its own. It is associated with the charity worker, the philanthropist, the nurse, counsellor, minister and soldier.

Dog is the guardian of ancient secrets and treasures. So it represents knowledge. It is wise not only in the ways of animals, but in the ways of men. Dog imparts cunning. It can be called upon for defence. In the past, dog has fed body, mind and spirit. Its loyalty to and love of its master is unswerving, even if it is oft-times undeserved. Invoke dog when resolve is fading.

Dogs are one of the few species that are truly purpose built, and it is best, when studying dog medicine, to learn about the specific breed, because there are so many different breeds, each bred for a specific reason. The terrier exhibits different characteristics to the collie, for example.

Even language reflects the traits of dogs. Until one has been followed around by a dog whose dinner is late, that person doesn't really know the meaning of the expression 'hang dog'; no animal can look so starved after completing its meal and its master's too. So, dog also means determination, even stubbornness, and the ability not only to communicate but to manipulate.

Dog people are friendly and companionable. Like the crows, dogs prefer to live and work in groups, and the individual with dog medicine will be happiest when involved with other people. This person is the perpetual volunteer, who always means well despite the actual result of their services. They are loyal to a fault.

# DOLPHIN/ PORPOISE

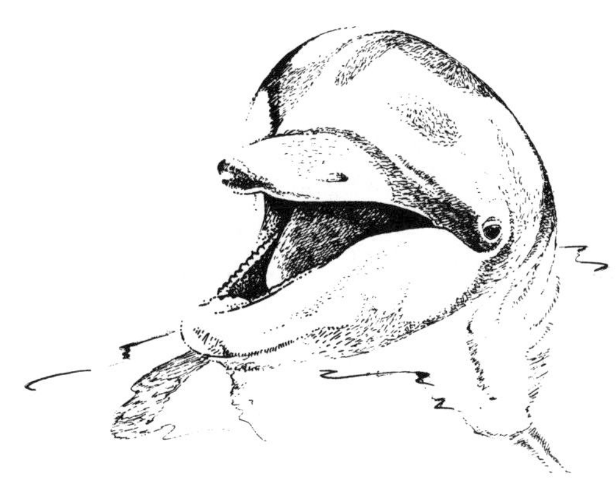

Family: *Delphinidae*

## BIOLOGICAL INFORMATION

This group consists of the smallest members of the *Cetacea* family. As with any group, size varies from about 1 metre (3 ft) to an excess of 9 metres (30 ft). Likewise, colour varies. Some are mottled white, others grey; still others are a silver blue. The Killer Whale, or Orca, is actually a dolphin and not a whale at all. It has distinctive black-and-white markings. All porpoises and dolphins have a notched tail fluke, and the dorsal fin is well developed.

### HABITAT

Except for Orca, dolphins and porpoises usually inhabit warmer waters than the whale. For example, the spotted dolphin is found along the South Carolina coast, down into Florida and west to Texas. The Pacific bottle-nosed dolphin swims in the waters along the California coast and farther south. However, porpoises are not completely absent from northern waters. Some inhabit the Irish and North Seas and the colder waters of Patagonia. More are found in the Mediterranean. There is even one species of freshwater dolphin that lives in the Amazon River.

### CHARACTERISTICS

Porpoises and dolphins are social creatures, like the whale. They converse using a series of clicks, whistles and laughing-type calls. Studies on their ability to communicate are ongoing in Florida and California. Scientists have actually been able to isolate and translate the meaning of some sounds, and claim to have talked with the animals by mimicking their calls.

Dolphins and porpoises are carnivorous and one of the most ferocious hunters of the deep. They can be likened to lions of the sea. Yet, with man, dolphins are friendly. Many sea fables end with a dolphin or a porpoise helping a drowning man to surface or leading a foundering boat to land. There are documented cases of these feats of valour.

Dolphins are curious by nature. They are attracted to boats and to humans. It is said that their intelligence rivals that of man.

Dolphins and porpoises will travel in groups of 50. They are sensuous creatures; sexual advances are a regular part of their social interaction and play, even between a mother and her offspring. Unfortunately, they are not the gentle animals that we believe them to be. Males form gangs of two or three, and they will herd a female until she is in such a state of exhaustion she can no longer resist their advances.

Yet the mothers are caring. They raise their young up to the surface soon after birth to let them breathe. Both dolphins and porpoises have been witnessed pushing a wounded or sick pod member to the surface and keeping them there until they are capable of swimming on their own.

## LEGENDS AND TRADITIONS

GOD Ea-onne (Sumerian), Poseidon (Greek), Neptune (Roman)

Most of the Native American lore relating to dolphin comes from the

Pacific northwest and pertains specifically to Orca. The Haida people of the Queen Charlotte Islands in British Columbia were master boatmen. Most of their food came from the sea. They considered Orca the king of the sea. The Haida used its image in heraldic designs on their boats to give them protection from the elements.

Without doubt, the native peoples of the Gulf and the Caribbean must have had legends about the porpoise or the bottle-nosed dolphin. Certainly the Polynesian islanders did. They considered the porpoise a god in its own right.

The Europeans thought of dolphin as a fish, even as late as 1810. Heraldry called dolphin the king of fishes. Dolphin was an emblem of friendship. It also was a symbol of prudence, since at the approach of a storm, it swims for the shore.

Two dolphins swimming together was used as a symbol for equipoise and balance. However, if they were swimming in opposite directions, they represented involution and evolution. A lone dolphin was an allegory for salvation.

In pagan times, the eroticism of dolphin was celebrated. When it was shown twinned and wrapped around an anchor it symbolized speed arrested: hence caution and circumspection.

## MEDICINE AND POWER

| | |
|---|---|
| DIRECTION | South |
| ELEMENTS | Water, Air |
| TRAITS | Community, friendship, speed |
| ASSOCIATIONS | Guidance, communication, song and harmony, controlled breathing |

Dolphin and porpoise leap, bursting from the sea as they play. As mammals, they must return to the surface in order to breathe. Thus they merge air (intellect) and water (feelings), finding joy in each. Native peoples believe that dolphin's first medicine is the gift of breath, the breath of spirit and of life. Dolphins show us how to enliven every cell using air.

In water, dolphin teaches us about emotions; in play, it shows how to release our emotions in a healthy way. Therefore, dolphin's second gift is one of delight and unconditional love. Dolphin bestows feelings of joy, laughter and light, as well as compassion for one's own pain and that of others.

Breath, and vicariously dolphin, are carriers of consciousness and healing. For both, oxygen and laughter heal.

To call upon dolphin is to call upon the power of healing and transformation. It is the ability to love and live life to the fullest. Dolphin medicine, in its connection with air, equals meditation. It heightens dream-recall, reinforces psychic development, and augments telepathic communications and understanding between people and animals.

The dolphin individual is difficult to keep up with, particularly in their element. People with dolphin medicine see emotions which other people would prefer to keep hidden. Understanding feelings, they make good counsellors and advisors. Sometimes the dolphin person can annoy, since they do not take things too seriously, turning everything into a game. This individual may be something of a flirt; however, the dolphin sees flirtation as just another form of socializing and will have a difficult time grasping the concepts of either fidelity or jealousy.

# DOVE

Family: *Columbidae*
Stock dove: *Columba oenas*
Turtle dove: *Streptopelia decaoctos/risora*

## BIOLOGICAL INFORMATION

The turtle dove *S. risora* is a sandy pale colour with a ring around its neck. The *S. decaoctos* has a brown tail that ends in black, and brown wings. Its breast feathers are a pinkish-buff and it has a black half-collar on the back of its neck.

There are 290 species of *Columbidae* globally. The American species tend to be drab, while the Old World birds are more colourful. The dove measures 30 cm (1 ft), while the pigeon dove is larger.

### HABITAT

The American bird is primarily a city dweller. It lives in parks, gardens and yards wherever trees are present. The European bird, the collared dove, is also becoming a city bird, although it prefers access to some open country. The turtle dove has greatly expanded its range, crossing the Channel. It now breeds in Britain.

### CHARACTERISTICS

The American *S. risora* places a bundle of sticks and twigs in a tree or perched precariously on a window ledge. The European *S. decaoctos*, too, weaves a dish-shaped nest rather carelessly. They lay two eggs in May or June, although sometimes the female will only lay one. This is a rare occurrence.

Once established, the dove will stay close to the nest and will use the same one year after year, one generation after another. To watch a mated pair and their chicks is to view a scene of domestic bliss. Their call is soothing to the ear.

## LEGENDS AND TRADITIONS

| | |
|---|---|
| GODDESSES | Aphrodite (Greek), Atargatis (Aramaic), Astarte (Canaan), Isis (Egyptian), Venus (Roman) |
| GOD | Hachiman (Japanese) |

The Native Americans thought dove contained the soul of a lover. Anyone who hurt or killed a dove would be cursed. The meaning was similar in the Old World. Dove was representative or messenger of both Aphrodite and Venus. Therefore, doves, particularly turtle doves, meant love and marital fidelity. Early pagans associated it with yoni or the female sexual organ.

Certainly there is more information to be found in European tradition than American. It has long been a symbol of peace. Raven was the first bird sent by Noah to find signs of land after the flood, but it never returned; thus, it was cursed by god. Dove was chosen next. It was successful, returning to the ark and leading it back to land. So, dove was blessed by the divine.

In Christian tradition, dove was the messenger of the Heavenly Host – God, the Holy Ghost and various angels. Therefore it is not surprising that angels are portrayed with the wings of a snow-white dove. Catholics often depicted the bird with the annunciation of Mary and with the flame of the Sacred Heart. The Slavs believe that when someone dies, the soul is transformed into a dove. Christian tradition also states that the dove is the only animal that Satan cannot impersonate.

Similarly, superstition equates dove with the soul and death. If a dove flies into a sick room, or bumps into the window, it presages a death in the household. Also to see a dove near a mine shaft meant bad luck for the miner, a cave-in, injury and possibly fatalities.

## MEDICINE AND POWER

| | |
|---|---|
| DIRECTIONS | South, East |
| ELEMENTS | Air, Fire |
| TRAITS | Domesticity, fidelity, calm |
| ASSOCIATIONS | Love, soul, spirituality and sublimation, and marriage |

The first medicine of dove is love. The pagans saw the dove as all things feminine – home, maternity and nurturing. It was the symbol for Astarte and Isis, along with Aphrodite and Venus – the latter being hatched from the egg of dove.

The dove has been used in many oracles. Alexander consulted the oracle of Dodona, founded by a dove. The priests and priestesses of the various goddesses consulted with it. Therefore dove imparts the gift of prophecy to those it visits. It speaks of purity and clear vision.

The alchemists equated dove with sublimation. Sublimation as a chemical process consists of heating a substance so it will turn to a vapour, which then upon cooling hardens to a crystal, or uncontaminated version of the original substance. Thus, dove is purification. The word 'purity' eventually devolved to the word sublime, as something higher or culturally superior.

Dove's appearance indicates a time of plenty and the possibility of a new or a renewed love interest. In the less physical domain, it can signify a spiritual renewal, self-examination, and a trial by fire which leads to purification of soul.

Dove energy can be used for love spells. However, its greatest gift is the ability to nurture feelings of peace, calm and stillness. Dove quiets the mind and allows one to experience the glory in the present moment.

It imparts the sense of the divine and heavenly blessing. Dove allows one to honour and appreciate the beauty of domestic simplicity.

The dove individual gives the impression of serenity and calm. This person may appear complacent, even bland. People with dove medicine tend to be homebodies. This person's idea of a good time is a cup of hot chocolate, a good book or a night spent with the family. No matter the gender, dove people will exhibit a strong maternal instinct which, at its worst, could turn mothering into smothering.

# DRAGONFLY/ DAMOISELLEFLY

*Calopteryx haemmoroidalis*

## BIOLOGICAL INFORMATION

The European 'damoiselle' male measures between 35 and 42 mm (1 1/2 to 1 3/4inches). Its body is a metallic blue-black. The hind wing is 25 – 32 mm (1 – 1 1/4 inches), narrow and brown. The female is slightly smaller. Its abdomen measures 34 – 42 mm (1 1/2 – 1 3/4 inches) and is iridescent green. The hind wings may be marginally larger than the male's, between 28 and 32 mm (1 1/8 – 1 1/2 inches).

An insect of the order *Odona*, the dragonfly is larger. Both have bulbous eyes and membranous, translucent and heavily veined wings. They are known for their ability to hover in a single spot for a long time, along with a capacity for darting flight.

### HABITAT

Dragonflies and damoiselleflies live and breed near water. Therefore, they are found around ponds, pools, lakes, rivers, streams, even bayous or swamps. Access to running water is not only preferred, it is essential. Eggs are laid in the water and the entire nymphal (infant) period is spent there.

### CHARACTERISTICS

The dragonfly leaves the water to enter the adult phase sometime between April and August. They reach sexual maturity after 10 days of fine weather – longer if the weather is bad or cool.

Like butterfly, frog, and even toad, the dragonfly is a creature of transformation which begins its life as an aquatic animal and culminates it as a creature of land and sky.

In flight it performs a wondrous aerial display. Its wings move so fast that they are little more than a blur to the human eye, and their acceleration is phenomenal, from a standing – or in this case, hovering – stop up to 144 kph (90 mph) in a few seconds.

## LEGENDS AND TRADITIONS

GOD/GODDESS Yumni (Lakota/Dakota)

Dragonflies are equated with mirage or illusion. Its wings beat so rapidly that the human eye cannot perceive them. It appears to hang in space without moving, but its wings are, in fact, quite active. One minute it is there; the next it's not.

The Lakota believed that the dragonfly, butterfly, lizard, turtle and swallow all had magical powers which allowed them to evade hailstones, for the hunters observed that they never found these creatures dead or injured after a storm. The warriors transferred these powers to their robes and shields with pictures, in the conviction that this defence could be conferred to them so that arrows and bullets would pass right through the warrior, leaving him unharmed.

The ephemeral dragonfly was also associated with cobwebs and spider's webs. These too were related to protection, for webs survive mainly intact even after they have been pierced by an arrow or a bullet.

Both the dragonfly and cocoon were affiliated with the mystery Yumni, who was the whirlwind and had no fixed abode. Variously known as Yumni, Yomni or Yum, this is the god (or goddess) of chance, love and games.[1] Yumni lived in the teepee of his brother, Itokaga (Okaga), the south wind.

Whirlwind and dragonfly were the essence of illusion, to be invoked to cloud the mind of the enemy. The Cheyenne also used the dragonfly symbol of the whirlwind to impart protection to their warriors. Dragonfly was venerated because of its power to escape a blow. It was swift-flying and elusive. According to other traditions, dragonfly held powerful magic of changing forms. It could play in space and time. The metamorphosis is one of transformation and maturation, rather than that found with the shape-shifting of raven and crow.

According to Jamie Sams and David Carson in their book *Medicine Cards*, dragonfly was once a dragon, who was challenged by coyote into turning into a dragonfly. Once dragon had achieved this shape-change, it found that it could not change back. Thus dragonfly is symbolic of the winds of change, the messages of wisdom and enlightenment, and of communication from the elemental world.[2]

The dragonfly of Europe has had long associations with the world of faeries. The 'wee ones' of Ireland used dragonflies as their steeds – birds, such as robin, being reserved for drawing their coaches. One fable suggests that dragonflies are actually faeries who when looked at in a certain way can be seen for what they truly are. It was said that one way to accomplish this was to rub primrose on one's eyelids. Another tradition recommends following dragonflies in order to find out where the faeries live.

Therefore, the link with magic and illusion is preserved. On a more pragmatic level, dragonfly served as an omen for fishermen (if they were chaste and prudent), for wherever it hovers fish are plentiful.

## MEDICINE AND POWER

| | |
|---|---|
| DIRECTION | South |
| ELEMENTS | Air, Whirlwind |
| TRAITS | Hovering, darting flight; colour |

ASSOCIATIONS Mystery; mirage, deception and the protection received thereby; magic and the land of the faeries

The dragonfly's nearly transparent wings which catch and refract the light are sometimes likened to the rainbow, which to the Lakota mind was not necessarily a good thing. Because the rainbow usually appeared immediately before the rain stopped, it was believed the rainbow held back the rain.

The mystery of dragonfly is contained within its flight. For the dragonfly, even more than the butterfly, flits, and its pattern is so elusive that as soon as the eye has rested upon it, it has bolted.

Part of dragonfly's medicine is its ability to play among the air currents and to dazzle others with light. Dragonfly's gift is the reawakening of the magic and mystery of life. However, its gift also carries an implicit warning: as master of illusion, those with dragonfly medicine should be warned not to fool themselves.

Dragonfly can be used to travel between the dimensions. Its essence is spiritual energy. It can be invoked to aid relaxing meditation, or on the other hand to recharge psychic energy. The native peoples called upon dragonfly by depicting it, or other symbols equated with it, upon their robes and clothes.

Dragonfly facilitates letting go of the past, which is always the first step in spiritual expansion. It can also be called upon to help someone to pierce the veil of deception or delusion. If dragonfly has suddenly appeared in one's life, then look around. Something remains hidden from view, and dragonfly's arrival admonishes caution.

Dragonfly medicine helps during a transition, or it may foretell a time of change. If uncomfortable with innovation, seek assistance from dragonfly, for such things are within its domain.

In the past, dragonfly was called upon to cast love spells; as a representative of chance and games, it is the sign of the gambler – but, like Lady Luck, dragonfly tends to be fickle.

People with dragonfly medicine are dreamers. They can be perplexing and annoying to others. The dragonfly person may appear almost schizophrenic as he or she rests (or hovers), absorbing light and energy for a time, and then flits off to a new project. As individuals, dragonflies have lots of nervous energy. Intermittently it is good for them to land and get grounded for a while.

# DUCK

Family: *Anatidae*
Mallard: *Anas platyrhynchos*

## BIOLOGICAL INFORMATION

The average length is 45 to 68 cm (18 to 27 inches). Colouring differs between breeds. The mallard is common to both Old and New Worlds. The male has a green head, iridescent blue and purple feathers and a drab brown body. The female is a dull brown which acts as protective camouflage when she sits upon the nest. The wood duck is crested and coloured in green, purple and blue; it has a red bill.

Including swans and geese, there are 150 species of the family *Anatidae*.

### HABITAT

Ponds, lakes, rivers, streams, marshes and swamps, both wooded and not. Ducks are aquatic. Generally they prefer fresh water. However, they may winter in salt-water estuaries and bays. As a group, they range throughout the North American continent and Europe.

### CHARACTERISTICS

The wild duck is migratory. It forms large V-shaped flocks. Some travel from Alaska as far down as the Gulf Coast, while others make an east–west trek. Ducks eat aquatic plants.

Both parents share in child-rearing. The male mallard goes through an eclipse phase during the summer, when its colourful plumage becomes muted. It does not leave its mate, but stays behind to help rear the young; hence the need for temporary camouflage.

Ducks are kind and loving parents. If the nest is approached by a predator, the parents will try to lead the animal away by feigning injury. Ducklings are immediately imprinted at the time of hatching.

The mallard is the ancestor of the common domesticated duck. It travels far and wide and will often interbreed with other species to create a whole new breed, such as the Hawaiian duck.

## LEGENDS AND TRADITIONS

GOD Geb, Amun, Re (Egyptian)

Duck revealed itself to be a foolish creature in one Native American story where the drake narrowly eluded the falcon. The next year when drake and his wife returned, he preened over his bravery and skill. Falcon overheard him boasting and became so enraged that he killed duck. The moral – one repeated often in Native American lore – don't gloat over victory in front of the enemy.

Duck figured largely in the Native American calendar. Its appearance was such a regular event it qualified as a month, or moon. For the Megwanipis of the subarctic, duck represented middle summer. July was 'the moon when ducks begin to moult feathers', and August 'when young ducklings take flight'.

The Dakota commemorated the month of May as the moon during which 'flying game return'. A later version of the Dakota dating system refers to April as 'the time of laying eggs'. For the Chippewa, October was 'the moon of migratory game'. Many of these listings are loose translations of the original, many of which included geese.

Duck features in the Iroquois creation story. Long ago before the advent of man, all was covered with water. Birds flew in the air and monsters swam in the deep. One day, the ducks saw a woman falling from the sky, and they flew to her and spread their great wings to break her fall. Tortoise let her ride upon his back. This woman became the mother of good and evil who later created humanity.

The ancient Egyptians associated duck with marshland, which was both mysterious and dangerous. Through the element of water, the duck was bringer of life and fertility to the land. Its god was Geb, the grandson of Atum. Geb was an earth god; his sister was Nut (sky). Geb is credited with the laying of the great egg from which the sun emerged at the dawn of time. Thus, the god is linked to both duck and goose.

Through marsh, which was both a place of peril and a source of water – thus, giver of life – the duck became associated with evil at the same time as it provided protection from it. Two ducks walking together was the hieroglyph for 'washermen', hence cleanliness. Duck was also used for symbols such as hover, fly, alight, and other more diverse concepts like tremble, shake, enter and fat.

The hieroglyph of the pintail duck when combined with the one for the sun was a determinative in the birth name of the kings of Egypt. Literally translated it meant the 'son of the sun' and expressed the king's divine status. It proclaimed his direct descent from the god Re (Ra), along with the other representative phases of the sun, Amun (Amen) and Aten. Therefore, the duck dealt with lineage and royalty.

Goose – and to a lesser extent duck – is often depicted as foolish or silly. Its waddling gait on land is comic. Yet Old World superstition states that brown duck eggs foretell misfortune, and the duck who produces such eggs should be killed and hung head-down to ensure that all evil spirits run away with the blood.

## MEDICINE AND POWER

DIRECTION South
ELEMENTS Water, Earth, Sun (Egypt)

TRAITS Femininity, procreation, fertility
ASSOCIATIONS Domesticity, plenty, warmth, abundance, maternity, birth

Despite the feminine association of duck, only Geb, a god, is linked with it, perhaps because goose tends to get top billing most places. Much of the historical information about duck comes from Egypt. It was equated with the Great Earth Mother which would have had associations with the Canaanite Astarte and later with the Greek goddess, Hera.

For the Egyptians, duck was beneficent, even if the marsh it inhabited was a dangerous place. Interestingly enough, the marsh was the final resting place of the dead, who have passed into the Field of Reeds. Thus, marshes represented the afterlife – its promise and its dark secrets. To reach the Field of Reeds, one had to know the appropriate formulas, to battle serpents and demons and to have one's heart weighed against the feather of Maat, or truth – an awesome prospect. Suddenly the obscure association of duck to trembling becomes clear.

Duck provided food for the people of the Nile. Its plumes furnished decoration and ornament. It was equated with the plenty (fat) and the beginning, in both the egg and in the hieroglyph 'to enter'.

Duck medicine, therefore, means plenty in both Native American and European cultures. However, for the later European and for the Native American, duck also acquired a certain sense of silliness. Certain Native Americans refused to partake of it for fear of acquiring this trait. Therefore, duck can indicate a time of fun. Certainly it represents a time of fertility, which may be literal or figurative. When duck appears, expect increase in some form.

Call upon duck as a symbol of birth when embarking on a new enterprise or relationship. It is said if duck comes at such a time, then it assures that the enterprise will be successful. Duck can assist after a period of turmoil, for duck helps release emotions through the element of water. However, duck moves under its own steam; it is not thrown about by the currents. Duck can lift the landbound individual into the air, or ground those who need it.

The duck person tends to be broody. Even more so than the dove, duck (either male or female) will be a homebody with a strong nesting instinct. They may appear indolent or clumsy to the outside observer and have problems with their weight. Yet, the duck individual is big-hearted and generous, unlike goose, who tends to be irritable and territorial.

# EAGLE

Bald Eagle: *Haliaeetus luecocephalis*
Golden Eagle: *Aquila chrysaetos*

## BIOLOGICAL INFORMATION

The golden eagle is one of many variations of the black eagle. It is 76 to 110 cm (30 – 41 inches) tall and has a wingspan of 2.1 metres (6½ ft). Its feathers are dark, with a pale golden cast in the area around the neck. The bill is shorter and darker than that of the bald eagle.

The bald eagle measures 30 – 31 inches (76 – 79 cm) long; its wingspan is 1.8 to 2.3 metres (6 to 7½ ft). The bald eagle is a large black bird with a white head and tail. It is marginally smaller than the golden eagle in height, but its wingspan is greater. Its closest relative is the South African fish eagle, although it bears a relationship to the British sea eagle, as it does to all fish eagles. The young of the bald eagle look like golden eagles. In fact, the adolescent bald eagle can only be differentiated from the golden eagle by its heavier bill.

### HABITAT

A fish eagle, the bald eagle stays close to water, near lakes, rivers, marshes and coastal areas. Formerly it was found throughout North America. Now its breeding area is restricted to the Aleutian Islands, Alaska, parts of northern and eastern Canada, the northern United States and Florida.

The golden eagle prefers mountain forests, although it can often be seen cruising the wind currents along the western Plains of the United States. It ranges throughout northwestern and northern Canada and from the Rockies westwards in the US.

Recently, the sea eagle – a near cousin to the bald eagle – has been reintroduced to Great Britain, in Scotland. Previously they had been hunted to extinction by herdsmen and farmers, who considered them a danger to their flocks. Now not only are the birds protected, but their nests and eggs are too.

## CHARACTERISTICS

An eagle weighs about as much as a large cat. It is only when one considers that the eagle's wing span can be more than 2 metres long while the bird itself is almost 1 metre tall standing upright, that one realizes it is relatively light and fragile for its size. Birds are able to achieve flight because their bones are extremely porous.

As much as man would like to attribute nobility to the eagle, it is as much a scavenger as the crow. The bald eagle can often be seen picking up dead fish off river banks. It is this trait which has led to its demise, as the bird picks up pesticides from the dying fish and then cannot produce enough calcium for its eggs. Similarly, the eagle is not above a little robbery, taking the kill from smaller birds or animals. The golden eagle, like its cousin the bald eagle, scavenges when it can and will steal the prey of other animals.

However, these birds cannot be blamed for being opportunistic. The eagle's vision is eight times stronger than that of man. In the act of hunting, the eagle must sight its prey from hundreds of feet away, identify it, line it up and assess the distance, and dive in less than a second. The velocity the eagle must achieve to accomplish this means that a single mistake or miscalculation in aim, braking or trajectory could disable the bird or even kill it.

The mating dance of the bald eagle is a breathtaking aerial display. The two birds dip and dive in flight, until at the end of the rite the two clasp each other's feet and plummet spinning to earth.

The female lays one or two eggs a year (three in the case of the golden eagle), but usually only one of the brood survives – as the young battle for supremacy and one sibling is sacrificed for, and eaten by, the other(s).

## LEGENDS AND TRADITIONS

GODDESS Juno (Roman)
GODS Zeus (Greek), Jupiter (Roman), Great Spirit (by whatever name), Wakinyan/Thunderbeing (Lakota)

The Mayan worshipped both the Feathered Serpent and the Serpent Bird. Often this bird is presented with the features of a parrot or macaw, yet in Copan and Quirigua sites the bird bears more of a resemblance to the eagle. The Aztecs created a strikingly realistic headdress of jaguar and eagle. A complete eagle costume was worn by priests for festivals.

The anthropomorphism of eagle was common; evidence of this has been found in pottery located in the present-day southern state of Georgia, while copper-plate masks of eagles have been excavated from the mound region of Peoria, Illinois. Several mounds with an eagle's image carved at the apex have been located in southern Wisconsin. These pictorial representations have been dated to around 2000 BC.

The Fox and Sauk tribes of Illinois wore eagle feathers attached to a deertail-style turban as a symbol of rank. The dress of the woodland Dakota resembled that of the Fox tribe, including the turban headband.

The later preeminence of eagle and its association with the sun are no place better illustrated than with the evolution of the Native American headdress, which had many forms and embellishments particular to a tribe or an individual's medicine.

The Blackfeet developed a headdress where the feathers went straight up and down and, although they later adopted the flared design of the Sioux, the Blackfeet still consider the original design the most sacred. It could only be worn by members of the Bull (Buffalo Bull) Society.

Eventually it came to be reserved for the women who performed in the Sun Dance.

It is believed that the Crow peoples developed the flowing headdress seen in popular representations of Native American life. The design was carried to the Arikara, Hidatsa, Mandan and Dakota peoples. The tail feathers of the immature golden eagle (white with a brown tip) were preferred.

Often eagle feathers were used as a medium of exchange. In the Plains, 12 feathers could be traded for a horse; in Missouri, 15 feathers was the price asked. The Mandan exchanged two horses for a single eagle-feather headdress; the Assiniboin likewise gave two horses for a war-eagle feathered cap.

Eagle feathers weren't as highly prized by the northwestern Yurok. An entire skin was equal in value to a single seashell, while the bride's price was three strands of shells. A redwood canoe was purchased for 24 dentalium shells, or two strands of 12.

The Omaha required the consent of all warriors before a headdress could be created, much less worn. Each feather in the bonnet stood for a man. The tip of hair fastened to the feathers and dyed red represented the man's scalp lock; a ceremony accompanied the making of the bonnet. Each feather was blessed and the story behind each feather was told.

Eagle was also linked with the mystical thunderbird by many tribes. One description of the Dakota/Lakota Wakinyan (thunderbeing) includes the body, wings, tail and claws of an eagle and the horns of a deer. The tribes used whistles made from the leg bone of an eagle in their sun dances to call the blessing of thunderbeings for the proceedings.

When the earth was being created, it was said that a dark cloud appeared in the sky. With a flash of lightning and a crack of thunder, the cloud swooped towards the tree tops. It vanished and in its stead stood an eagle. The bird glided to the ground, and when its feet touched earth, it became a man. So eagle has been linked with creation. Likewise it has been recognized as the messenger of the divine since the beginning of time.

When a Blackfoot trapped an eagle, it was taken to a special lodge. Here the hunter would place the bird with its head propped up on a stick. Then he put meat in its mouth, so that the spirit of the dead eagle would tell all living eagles how well the Blackfoot treated their relations.

The eagle clan was one of the four most important to the Niska Indians of British Columbia, along with bear, raven and wolf. Their initiation ceremony enacted the ritual killing of the adolescent initiate, who was then reborn as both adult and eagle.

The Old World myths surrounding eagle took a similar view to the Native American one. Eagle represented the sound A, or aleph, in the Egyptian alphabet, symbolizing its predominance over all other birds. The night owl and the day-time eagle pictured together represented the sound *sma*, which was used in such words as 'unite'. Thus the predators of the night and day became a symbol for totality and togetherness. The hieroglyph for eagle is found without owl in words like 'morning star', 'star', 'hour', 'prayer', 'underworld', 'world' and 'land'.

The Romans used eagle as their tutelary bird. It was the insignia of the military. Eagle was considered both a celestial bird and the messenger of Jupiter.

The Celts linked eagle to the sun and the oak. The eagle's offerings were courage, wisdom and strength. Similarly, it held the sun's gift of rejuvenation. As a solar bird, the eagle was celebrated at Lammas, or Lughanasadh, on 1st August.

In the traditions of the medieval hunt, the eagle was the most noble of all birds. As such it was the king's bird, and thus protected. It was an act of treason or *lese majeste* to kill one – an act punishable by death.

Bestiaries emphasized eagle's ability to rejuvenate. It was said that eagle burned blindness from its eyes by flying towards the sun. It then plunged to the bottom of a well to quench the flames and remove any burnt feathers. When it finally perched in a tree, it had been completely renewed. Therefore, eagle is equated with phoenix.

The eagle, as an emblem, was used to call both Christians and Jews to baptism. 'Your youth shall be renewed like the eagles.'[1] Probably because of this it was believed that anyone who stole eagle eggs would never have peace of mind thereafter.

This opinion continued into Victorian times. Heraldry refers to the eagle as the king of birds. It was considered a symbol of magnanimity and fortitude ... 'who seeks to combat with none but his equals. He disdains the possession of that property which is not the fruit of his own industry.'[2]

Not everything about eagle bodes well, however. According to superstition, an eagle hovering over the plain and screaming portends death.

Eagle feathers had different uses and meanings for Native American peoples:

## THE SYMBOLISM OF EAGLE FEATHERS

### PONCA

- Upright feathers at the crown showed the number of captures made in battle.
- The number of feathers inclined towards the right represented the number of scalps taken.
- Feathers set low indicated war leaders.
- Feathers stripped to the tip meant the wearer was a good scout.

### SANTEE (WOODLAND DAKOTA)

- A single eagle feather upright equalled four *coups* (after 'stroke' or touching the body).
- When hanging downward, this single feather indicated that the wearer had been wounded in battle.
- The feather was trimmed when someone was wounded without 'counting coup' (striking any blows).
- A feather with a round mark represented an enemy killed.
- If the dot was painted red, a scalp had been taken.
- A warbonnet was awarded to the warrior who had been successful in four battles.

### HIDATSA

- An eagle feather decorated with a tuft of horse hair and dyed red was given to the first man to kill an enemy in battle.
- A feather simply dyed red meant the recipient had been wounded in battle.
- A feather with single red stripe indicated the second kill.
- Two stripes, third kill.

- Three stripes, fourth kill.

LAKOTA (PLAINS SIOUX)

- A single red dot showed that the brave had killed an enemy.
- The number of dots varied depending on the number killed.
- A feather painted with a red triangle indicated that the warrior had slit his enemy's throat and taken a scalp.
- A feather with the tip cut off indicated that no scalp had been taken, but a throat had been cut.
- The first 'coup' feather was placed sideways in the hair.
- If a second coup is made, the feather is worn upright.
- A notch indicated that the wearer had been the first person to wound an enemy in battle. A series of notches revealed the second and third men to wound an enemy.
- A feather split up the shaft was given to any warrior who had been wounded many times.
- While porcupine bands on the shaft revealed the number of enemy killed, the number of bands was equal to the number killed.

MOHAWK

- If one holds or wears an eagle feather, the Creator takes immediate notice.
- When one receives an eagle feather, that person is acknowledged in gratitude and love.
- The feather must be smudged by burned tobacco to sanctify.
- The Kahstowa (the traditional feather hat worn by men) had three upright eagle feathers.

Probably the most poignant of all Native American stories relating to eagle feathers occurred in the 1990s. In the US it is illegal to keep eagle feathers unless one is Native American. A good rule in theory to protect the species; however the practice requires not only identification from the reservation, but references from two tribal elders and verification from the Bureau of Indian Affairs, along with official verification of the tribe to prove Native status. Nathan Jim Jr, a member of the Yakima tribe, was arrested for illegal possession of eagle feathers. He spent 14 months in jail awaiting trial and was put on probation. His lawyer appealed under the religious freedom action. Nathan Jim lost the appeal and subsequently killed himself rather than face jail again. Belatedly, the US Federal Prosecutor relented, took some feathers and drove to the reservation for the funeral, but arrived too late for the ceremony; therefore, Nathan Jim Jr never received his eagle feathers, even in death.[3]

## MEDICINE AND POWER

| | |
|---|---|
| DIRECTION | East |
| ELEMENTS | Air, Sun |
| TRAITS | Courage, bravery, flight, vision, speed |
| ASSOCIATIONS | Divine messenger, long-sightedness, vision, fearlessness, male energy, communication |

*Wambli*, spirit of the eagle, was of particular importance for the Plains Lakota. It was known as 'spotted eagle', a reference to one of the phases the feathers of the immature eagle go through. Wambli presided over councils, hunters, war parties and battle. It is representative of (and messenger to) the sun. The eagle is the chief over all the winged creatures.

Eagle conveys the powers and messages of the Great Spirit. It is man's connection to the divine. For the Native American, the heavens were synonymous with the realm of spirit and with spiritual things, and the eagle flies higher than any other bird. So, eagle feathers were treasured because they carry the bird to great heights. Close to spirit, at this elevated angle eagle became detached from the earth and material things.

The eagle is associated with the east winds. East is the direction of the spring, dawn and rebirth. Therefore, eagle brings the message of renewed life. If an individual has been going through a hard time, eagle not only signals a new beginning, but endows that person with the stamina and resilience to endure the difficulties. If a battle is involved, then it provides fighting spirit.

Eagle brings freedom from inhibition. It gives one the ability to look ahead. Eagle lifts people up to the sunlight. If eagle has appeared, it speaks of an opportunity to awaken both inner and outer visions. It bestows freedom and courage.

Eagle is symbolic of the importance of honesty and correct principles. Eagle medicine allows one to soar above the earth to gain perspective and clarity. It assists in transcending the mundane and perceiving the deepest truth at the heart of a given situation. Eagle enhances spiritual and creative vision. It facilitates communication with the divine for creative inspiration. The eagle comes when it is time for a person to connect with the higher self and divine guidance.

Eagle feathers have been used as healing tools by shamans for centuries. Some people use them for cleansing the aura. Call upon eagle during times of trouble. To invoke eagle is to ask the Great Spirit for help. During a conflict, eagle imparts strength. When tied by the minutiae of everyday life, eagle can exalt. Eagle is good medicine to summon when about to embark on a challenge, a massive life change or a creative endeavour. When eagle arrives, this means being touched by the divine. Problems or their solutions which arise now are no accident.

The eagle person will encompass all that is symbolic in eagle. This individual will be a born leader and may become a bit impatient with those who cannot fly as high or as fast. People will gravitate to them naturally, despite the fact that eagle will often hold aloof or retreat to the aerie. Those who have eagle medicine will adhere to the old axiom 'might makes right,' and are not good people to anger. They have a sharp temper and biting wit.

# ELK (WAPITI)

American elk: *Cervus elaphus*

## BIOLOGICAL INFORMATION

The male elk stands 1.37 to 1.5 metres (4½ – 5 ft) at the shoulder. It measures 2 to 3 metres (6¾ – 9¾ feet) in length and weighs between 270 and 495 kg (600 to 1,089 lb). The female is 25 per cent smaller than the male, with a weight of 203 – 293 kg (450 to 650 lb).

The Wapiti or American elk is a large deer with slender legs and a thick neck. Its fur is brown or tan above and darker underneath. Males have a dark brown mane on their throat and chest, and many-tined antlers (up to six when fully grown), with the main beam about 1.5 metres (5 ft) long. The females lack antlers.

The European elk is what Americans call moose. For simplicity's sake, information on the European elk *Alces alces* will be covered under that heading (*see* **Moose**.)

### HABITAT

Primarily high open mountain pastures. At one time, wapiti (the American 'elk') lived in the Great Plains; now the creature has withdrawn completely to the Rocky Mountains in the US, although it still inhabits the southern plains region of Canada.

### CHARACTERISTICS

Elk make wallows by digging in the ground with their hooves and antlers. These wallows are marked with faeces and urine. In the summer they graze on grasses and leaves. In winter they may resort to eating bark from the trees. Like the bison, the elk live in sexually distinct herds until breeding season, the time of which is influenced by the availability of food. The rut is usually held in autumn.

The elk moves silently and swiftly through the forest; the male is able to achieve speeds of 56 kph (35 mph). The alarm call is a short, sharp barking snort, while the 'bugle' call is heard only during mating season. The male will keep a harem of up to 60 females. The young are born after a gestation period of 255 to 275 days. The cow leaves the herd to give birth, rejoining it a week later when the calf is able to keep up.

## LEGENDS AND TRADITIONS

GODS Hehaka (Dakota/Lakota), The Green Man (Celtic)

The bodies of elk, like deer, had to be treated with respect. Their bones were kept from the dogs; their fat was not spilled in the fire. Proper treatment of the carcass ensured that the next hunt would be a good one.

*Hehaka* (Lakota for 'elk') was the perfect warrior medicine since, except for the seasonal rut, the male elk prefers the company of his own kind. With the Oglala, if a young man dreamed of elk he became an elk dancer. The participants wore masks with the horns of either an elk or deer. Stringed hoops with a mirror in the centre were carried – thus the dancers called upon the sticking power and creative energy of the spider (as symbolized by the stringed hoop or web) and the attraction of the mirror. Elk was male sexuality, just as deer medicine was usually considered the female equivalent. If the mirror captured the reflection of a women her heart was lost; therefore, traditionally Oglala women avoided looking in the mirror. The early white settlers found this a curious custom; however, this belief that one's reflection was a mirror to the soul was not exclusive to the Native Americans.

Elks' teeth were a much sought-after commodity. Unlike eagle feathers, they were used primarily as an adornment for dresses and robes and had no great symbolic significance. However, in a decorative capacity they were much valued and traded.

## MEDICINE AND POWER

| | |
|---|---|
| DIRECTION | West |
| ELEMENT | Earth |
| TRAITS | Stamina and endurance; male pride |
| ASSOCIATIONS | Sexual energy, love medicine, strength, speed and courage |

Young men invoked elk medicine during courtship. Elk symbolized male love. The eagle whistle was reserved for special ceremonial occasions, but elk and deer horns made excellent flutes. Usually, the first indicator of courtship was a young man serenading his intended on a flute.

For some tribes in the Pacific northwest, this animal was a bringer of dreams and visions. It brought wisdom and all the same things that buffalo brought to the people of the Plains – such as abundance and plenty. Elk meant beauty, gallantry and protection.

In times of trouble, elk bestows fortitude. Unlike eagle medicine, elk medicine should be called upon when speed and endurance are required. Elk makes one capable of handling the day-to-day worries of life by lending strength.

Elk can be called upon for love magic. The practice includes the use of a mirror while stamping one's feet upon the earth to raise elk's power. Elk, therefore, is sexual magic and can be used to enhance such workings.

A man with elk medicine will prefer the companionship of his own sex; he could be called 'just one of the lads'. Yet this person will be a good provider and a stern defender should the need arise. The female elk will likewise spend more time with women friends than with men. Such people are independent and would rather rely upon their own strength than lean upon another. They have leadership qualities, although they may alienate others if they emulate elk's nose-in-the-air stance.

# FERRET/WEASEL

Black-footed ferret: *Mustela nigripes*
Short-tailed weasel: *Mustela erminea*

## BIOLOGICAL INFORMATION

There are four different kinds of weasels or ferrets that live in America: the least weasel, the black-footed ferret, the short-tailed ferret or ermine (which is the same as the British stoat), and the long-tail. They range in size from the smallest, the least weasel (*Mustela rixosa*) at 15 cm (6 inches), to the largest, the black-footed ferret, at 45 cm (18 inches). All have the characteristic long, slender bodies and short legs.

The stoat is dark brown with a white underbelly in winter. The common European weasel's coat lightens during the winter but does not turn white.

### HABITAT

The short-tailed weasel, or ermine, prefers wooded areas not far from water. The least weasel lives in meadows, fields and open woods. The black-footed ferret remains in the open prairies, usually near prairie dog colonies. It is one of the most rare and is now listed as endangered. The long-tail has adapted itself to all environments as long as there is access to water.

### CHARACTERISTICS

Most ferrets are nocturnal, although they may be active by day. They are predators, feeding on small mammals, rodents, rabbits, mice, insects, eggs and an occasional lizard or snake. They move into the abandoned burrows of other animals. In the case of the least weasel, this means mice nests. They are fast and efficient predators, killing with a single bite at the base of the skull or by piercing the skull of the prey with their canine teeth.

Weasels/ferrets are noted for their stealth and guile, passing into the most well-guarded nests or coops unseen. Their presence usually remains unknown until the damage has been done.

## LEGENDS AND TRADITIONS

The white martin or weasel was a part of the Mediwiwin – sometimes spelled Midiwiwin – Grand Medicine Society that originated with the Chippewa of the Great Lakes region. The basic tenet was that good conduct resulted in a long life, while evil must inevitably be punished. The initiation began with the arrival of four or five medicine men carrying medicine bags of beaver, otter or weasel, each shaped like a snake. The bags were thrown at the candidates with the hope of endowing power upon them and curing their illnesses. This ceremony was adopted by many of the surrounding tribes including the Sauk and Fox of Illinois.

Ermine fur attached to an eagle feather headdress was supposed to impart weasel's skills of alertness and the ability to elude capture. A shape-shifter in the form of weasel was first to set eyes upon the white settlers. It was weasel who returned and warned the people that the newcomers were a danger, telling of their 'thundersticks' (guns) and houses made of stone.

In a Cree tale, though, ferret exhibited all the traits for which they are known in Europe. A contest was held to win the hand of the daughter of a Swampy Cree chief. The contestants had to guess the girl's secret name. One suitor, known as Bitter Spirit, sent a message to spider asking him to spy upon the chief and learn her name. Spider was successful, but unable to get the information to Bitter Spirit in time. Spider enlisted the aid of weasel to take the name to Bitter Spirit, for weasel was so much faster than himself. But weasel thought better of it, keeping the name to himself and winning the girl's hand. Spider arrived too late at the council to stop it, but he told the chief of the deceit. The wedding was cancelled and word went out to find weasel. Hearing that he was to be punished, the weasel ran and ran. That is why weasel is nervous to this day, for he still hears Bitter Spirit chasing him.

Generally, though, the Native American image of weasel/ferret is more positive than the European, perhaps because the Native Americans applauded ferret's skills in warfare, including its ability to move unseen, to track and scout out its enemies. The woodlands and Plains tribes attached weasel skin to their headgear, while the people of the northwest wore the fur of mink or ferret as a headband – each for the same purpose, to seek its blessings and its powers in battle.

In European lore, if a weasel appears near a house and squeaks, death is imminent. Bad luck is also foretold if a weasel crosses someone's path. Both Native American and European lore agree in attributing to weasel the ability to shift shape. In Europe it was believed that witches could turn themselves into weasels.

Heraldry explains that the first user of weasel fur in arms was Brutus, the son of Silvius. Brutus killed his father by accident, but rather than face punishment he fled to Bretaigne in France. Brutus fell asleep, and when he awoke he found this little beast had crept upon his shield. So it is equated with cowardice. Meanwhile, the fur of ermine in its white phase was reserved almost exclusively for royalty; therefore, it became, and remains, a symbol of status.

# MEDICINE AND POWER

| | |
|---|---|
| DIRECTION | West |
| ELEMENT | Earth, and to a lesser extent Water |
| TRAITS | Speed, agility, guile |
| ASSOCIATIONS | Magic, occult, invisibility, stealth, cunning |

The primary ability of weasel is to 'ferret' out secrets. Indeed, language is always a good reflection of the speaker's views. People 'weasel' (wiggle or squirm) their way into or out of something.

Meanwhile, the Lakota phrase *taku wakan* meant all that was mysterious. The ferret, with its ability to move unobserved, was considered particularly *wakan*. Ferret or weasel would be invoked when a scout wanted to move up on an enemy position. Its fur gave the bearer stealth. The warrior would also call upon this medicine when he needed to escape or elude capture.

Weasel has the eyes to see behind the facade, the nose to sniff out the truth. Weasel is camouflage. Weasel often comes in the form of a lesson or a warning. If weasel has suddenly appeared, it could indicate double dealings – either on the part of the individual or others. The appearance of ferret suggests that it is time to examine one's motivations.

The weasel person is a loner – someone who prefers to sit on the sidelines and watch rather than get involved. Weasel energy imparts cunning and guile. It is the essence of ingenuity, yet, like crow and coyote, ferret is much vilified in people's minds. This individual's intelligence is often underestimated. Other people will view the weasel individual as sneaky. This person will rarely be trusted, partly because of ferret's talent for seeing under the surface. Therefore, people will suspect, and rightly so, that the individual with weasel medicine knows their secrets. People will project onto the ferret ulterior motives even where there are none. The ferret's best defence is his or her power to walk unseen and to remain unnoticed.

# FISH/SHARK

Bony fish: *Teleostomi*
Cartilaginous fish: *Elasmobrachii*

## BIOLOGICAL INFORMATION

If not much can be said about a 'representative' dog, even less can be said about a representative fish. They range in size from the 5-cm (1/4-inch) guppy to the huge game swordfish.

Fish as a group also includes sharks with all their many varieties. The largest shark rivals the whale in size.

### HABITAT

Unpolluted freshwater: lakes, rivers, streams, ponds; saltwater: oceans, seas, bays.

### CHARACTERISTICS

Some fish are grazers; others are carnivores. Many can turn cannibal. They may lay eggs or they may give birth to live young. They live in saltwater or fresh. Probably the one characteristic that all fish share is that they swim. This may appear a simplistic statement, but it is worth bearing in mind that there are some species, like the Florida creeper, capable of scooting over land to the next waterhole when theirs has dried up.

The first useful division for fish consists of those that have bones and those whose body is built on the more flexible cartilage. Bony fish have an internal bladder which helps keep them oriented in water, while sharks (which are cartilaginous) do not.

The most notorious of sharks is the great white shark, which is unique in being able to regulate its own body temperature. Because it is able to circulate warm blood to its brain, the great white is smarter than most other sharks and more efficient as a predator. It is gifted with great hearing, a good sense of smell and it can see a 15-cm (6-inch) object from 20 metres' (66 ft) depth.

Most warm water fish are colourful. The great white shark takes advantage of camouflage, being dark (shadowy like the depths) when viewed from above and white (bright as the sun-bleached water) when seen from below. After eating, the shark goes nearly a month before its next meal, while bony fish nibble, eat or graze constantly.

Fish that form schools have a mysterious life cycle. Like herd animals with harems, there tends to be only one breeding male. Once the male dies, the lead female changes sex and takes his place. Thus, some fish are able to bridge the gap that divides the genders and are able to see the world through the eyes of both sexes.

## LEGENDS AND TRADITIONS

GODDESSES Atargatis (Aramaic), Avfruvva (Finnish), Ashtarte (Phoenician)
GODS Neptune (Roman), The Christian Trinity, Ukupanipo (Hawaiian shark god)

Fish were most important in those regions where they were depended upon as a food source. The Shoshoni and Paiute peoples were prohibited from spearing female fish during breeding season as a conservation measure, although male fish were fair game. Among the Tlingit of Alaska, the first halibut caught each season was called 'chief'. It was dressed and feted so its spirit would return to the waters and tell the others how it had been honoured. In the spring, the Karok of northern California danced to entice the salmon to return and ensure a good catch. No Karok could eat salmon during this festival or for 10 days thereafter.

The sturgeon was totem among many tribes along the northwest coast of the US. The sturgeon was regarded as the keeper of longevity because it could survive to a ripe old age. Therefore, it is thought that sturgeon people are blessed with longevity and grow old gracefully.

The Oglala Lakota called the spirit of fish *Hogan*. It was the patron of ablution and presided over the powers of the waters. Surface water was so scarce in the Plains that it was considered mother's milk, a gift of *Maka* (mother earth). Indirectly, then, fish represents all things feminine and the earth.

Any culture in the Old World or New that relied upon fish as a food source tended to deify them. On some Polynesian islands, the shark is a god. One Hawaiian god was half-fish and half-man. In the Pacific northwest, the Orca or killer whale has attained high status. Most people tend to pick a species – either because of its traits or because it is a primary source of sustenance – and attribute to it the same powers that buffalo had for the Plains peoples and cow had for the Europeans of the Old World.

The Egyptians believed that fish were unclean, and as such fish could not be eaten or used as an offering – to the gods, king, priests nor the dead. The reality was different. Many of the poor had no other choice than to partake in fish. As a result not all species were considered bad. For instance, because the *Bulti* (fish) kept its children in its mouth to protect them, it became a symbol of rebirth.

Other Middle Eastern countries did not share the Egyptians' negative attitude towards fish. The son of Atargatis (Syria), the great mother, and of the Phoenician goddess Ashtarte or Astarte was Icthys, portrayed with the tail of the fish. Fish were often seen as symbols of fecundity. As water creatures they were also linked with spiritual knowledge.

Indeed, fish was so important to some cultures that it was depicted as the cosmic fish. The Scythian fish in the Berlin Museum is one example. In this form it was equated with man's progress.

The Celts associated fish, particularly salmon, with knowledge. It is found in several stories. Taliesin is found in a fish weir. Gwyrhr questions all the animals to find out which is wisest, and picks salmon of Llyn Llyw. Cuchulainn is linked with salmon. Fish's connection with wisdom and spirituality found expression in the Grail legend in the form of the Fisher King, who is in turn related to the apostles.

These more positive associations carried forward into Christian times. Fish was *magna mater*, the great mother. It became the emblem of primitive Christians as a result of the anagram (in Greek) I – ησουζ X – ριστοζ Θ – ξου Σ – ωτηρ, linked with Jesus. Fish were the bringers of wisdom and knowledge. To eat its flesh was to acquire these qualities. One wonders if the many days in the Roman Catholic calendar when followers were forbidden meat in favour of fish (Fridays, feast days, etc.) were intended to help grant wisdom to the masses.

## MEDICINE AND POWER

| | |
|---|---|
| DIRECTION | The depths |
| ELEMENT | Water |
| TRAITS | Fertility, mastery of an environment alien to humans |
| ASSOCIATIONS | Mystery, spirit and soul, emotions, femininity, cleanliness, knowledge and wisdom, sustenance and plenty, rebirth and renewal |

Fish is synonymous with water. Water has long been is linked with the emotions, the subconscious, and all things feminine. The sea and the tides are ruled by the moon. Therefore, fish should be invoked for 'female' medicine or workings that are dependent on the lunar cycle.

For the Lakota/Dakota, fish medicine was linked with bathing. Part of the day's routine was to walk to the nearest stream, strip and wash – a 'bad habit' that white man soon quashed. Yet this association with cleanliness suggests also chastity and purity, which leads to the Christian definition of fish.

If fish suddenly appears in one's life, it's time for a good emotional or spiritual cleansing; time to nose into the dank closets and cobweb-riddled crannies of one's subconscious. It could be a warning that we are not acting on logic or reason, but reacting to something that the subconscious perceives as a threat. At the opposite extreme, the appearance of fish could portend that the solution must be based on emotions or that the problem might be motivated by our unconscious desires.

The presence of the fish could also suggest fertility, abundance and prosperity. It always augurs a time of spiritual growth and spiritual realization.

If it is time for a cleansing, call upon fish. It imparts a wisdom that only occurs when emotions and reason become successfully combined. It is good to meditate on fish for aid in spiritual development and attunement with the divine.

Just as it is impossible to describe a universal fish, it is impossible to describe a universal fish-person. If a person has seen fish in a vision or meditation, it is most likely that the individual will have seen a specific species, in which case that particular species should be studied in more detail.

# FOX

Red Fox: *Vulpes vulpes*
Grey Fox: *Urocyon cinereoargenteus*
Kit Fox: *Vulpes macrotis*

## BIOLOGICAL INFORMATION

The red fox measures 38 to 41 cm (15 – 16 inches) at the shoulder. It is 90 – 103 cm (35 – 40 inches) long, with a tail that adds 35 – 43 cm (14 – 17 inches) to its total length. It weighs 3.6 to 6.8 kg (8 – 15 lb). The red has a black phase, a silver phase, a cross phase and a red phase.

The grey fox is slightly smaller than the red. The height at its shoulder is between 36 and 38 cm (14 and 15 inches); its length is approximately 80 to 113 cm (31 to 44¼ inches), with a tail of 22 – 44 cm (8 – 17 inches) and a weight of 3.3 to 5.9 kg (7 – 13 lb).

The kit fox is larger than either of its cousins, with a shoulder height of 38 – 51 cm (15 – 20 inches); a tail between 33 and 43 cm (14 and 16 inches) and a weight of 1.4 – 2.7 kg (3 – 6 lb). The kit fox is a small, slender fox with huge ears. The body is a pale grey dotted with rust, the tail is tipped in black. The kit fox is considered a subspecies of *Vulpes velox* or Swift fox, yet the names are often used interchangeably.

All foxes are small, dog-like creatures. The red fox is something of a misnomer, for it can appear in any number of colours including grey. Yet no matter its colour, the red fox can always be distinguished by the distinctive white-tipped tail.

The grey fox is a grizzled grey above, reddish below. The tail has a black 'mane' above and a black tip. The feet are rust-coloured. The ears of both the red and grey fox are prominent, one of their more noticeable features.

## HABITAT

In the US, the fox has adapted itself to many varied areas: cultivated fields and woodland, and brushland. It has not become the city dweller that it has in the UK, where the red fox has completely adapted itself to life in the city. It lives in gardens, vacant lots, industrial estates and rubbish tips. It is not unusual to see a fox sunning itself next to the tracks of the overland section of the London Underground.

The grey fox prefers well-covered woods and brushland. Thus, it is seen less often. In the US, some form of fox is found just about everywhere. Where grey and red fox have not strayed, the arctic fox takes over. The same could be said for the red fox. It has made itself at home all over England, Scotland and Wales.

The kit fox prefers open, level, sandy ground; the swift fox has expanded its habitat beyond the deserts of the US, moving out into the Plains.

## CHARACTERISTICS

The fox lives in dens. The male helps care for the young, providing food. Like the coyote, foxes stick to a single family unit rather than forming packs. They form a tightly knit group, and the young are ousted only when it is time for the pair to mate again in April or May. Generally, litters number between four and nine, born after a gestation period of 51 days. The pups remain in the den for about a month and then move above ground. They stay together as the parents hunt. Some may leave the family voluntarily – often as a group – in October and fend for themselves over winter.

The fox is clever and adaptable. The fact that it has adjusted to town life reflects this. Fox has also been known to use tools. Native Americans have observed that fox will sink into a stream to rid itself of fleas, holding a stick in its mouth which it uses as a lure. The insects crawl away from the animal's body and a watery death onto the stick, which the fox then releases. The fleas float away on the current.[11]

The kit fox feeds mostly on small mammals, mice, gophers, some insects, grasses and berries. During the winter months it listens carefully in order to isolate the sounds of its victim. Then the fox will dig under the snow to catch its prey. Kit foxes mate in January or February, producing three to five young in March or April. They are great sprinters, able to run at speeds of 40 kph (25 mph) for short periods of time.

## LEGENDS AND TRADITIONS

GODDESSES Innari, KuzunoHa (Japan)
GODS Enki (Sumerian), Indari (Japan)

Fox was one of the primary gods for the Inca. The Inca of Peru were a fatalistic people who worshipped the stars. They named the constellation we know as Pleiades after the fox. This constellation marked the eastern sky at the place where the sun rose during the winter solstice. Fox was one of the first characters in their creation myth. Like many major cultures, the Inca had a flood story; in it, fox clung to the top of the mountain with the rest of the animals. The poor creature was jostled from his perch and almost fell into the water. Only his tail touched the water; that is why the fox's tail is black. This legend reflects an actual event in the night sky, dating back to AD 200 when the Pleiades dipped below the horizon. This astronomical phenomenon heralded a civil war within the Inca culture which lasted some 800 years.

A Miwok tale credits the silver fox and coyote with the creation of the universe. In the time of mists, in the time before time began, there was nothing but water and a single fox. Feeling lonely, the fox began to sing:

'I want to meet someone.' Coyote appeared. The two walked together, and fox suggested that they create the world. Coyote asked, 'How?'

'We shall sing it into being,' fox said, and she thought of a lump of clay. It materialized in her hands. She threw it to the ground, and coyote and fox sang the mountains, the valleys, rivers and lakes. They danced until the earth grew around them, and that is how the world began.

Further east, fox was linked with warriors. Typical policing societies of the Plains included the Kit Fox Society of the Lakota, the Dog-soldiers of the Cheyenne, and the Fox Society of the Crow. The members of the latter group strove amongst themselves to strike the first blow against the enemy. The leaders carried a staff which, when they dismounted, they planted and refused to move from that spot, even when other members of the tribe retreated.

Fox shares many characteristics with ferret, in its ability to move unseen and its cunning. Other common attributes include: camouflage, swiftness, shapeshifting, invisibility – all important abilities for the warrior.

The Inuit recognized the 'magic' of foxes and feared them. After a kill, the fox was hamstrung so that the spirit could not re-animate the body, for if it were to walk again it might take revenge on the hunter.

The kit fox was revered all across the Plains. It remains an important animal to this day. In 1800, the Kit Fox Society was one of the great warrior societies of Oglala Sioux. They were also used as internal 'police' or marshals of the camp. Therefore, they were guardians of the tribe.

The members of the Kit Fox Society painted their bodies, faces and arms yellow. If the leader was to be handling sacred things, such as during the Sun Dance, his hands would be painted red. A yellow fox skin suspended from the right hand was a badge of membership. An eagle feather attached to the fur was the mark of a leader. Red bird plumes and a war club indicated readiness for battle.

The warriors, or foxes, were stake-holders whose duty it was to defend the helpless unto death in case the village was attacked. It was after the death of four of these warrior-foxes, all stake-holders and sons of the chief, that their grieving father sought a vision. He was told of two children who needed him. He sought and found these two abandoned children, a boy and a girl, and raised them as his own. Before his death, he held a feast and told his people that if one's heart was good towards another, they should become as one family. Thus, one of the seven important rites, the *Hunka* (adoption) ceremony of the Lakota, was born from the sacrifice made by Kit Fox warriors.

A person did not ask to join the Kit Fox Society, but was nominated and then invited to join. The ceremony was complex. Once a member, it was believed that the man could not lie. If later the warrior was wounded, it was thought that he must have done something wrong or broken his vows. Otherwise, he would have remained invincible.

Fox was associated with the Sumerian god, Enki, but seems to have been missed by the Egyptians altogether, although some authorities have wondered whether the god Anubis, rather than a jackal, was a fox; others think he might have represented dog.

Fox was sacred to the Celts, who held a ritual hunt. The fox's pelt contained great magic. The animal represented cunning, but without many of the negative associations later linked with it. Fox was considered the master of diplomacy and wise council. Therefore, fox could be invoked as advisor.

The fox was equated with the devil during the Middle Ages. In bestiaries of the period it was said that fox catches birds by playing dead. This wily creature allegedly smeared its body with red earth, lay on the ground and held its breath. When birds lighted upon fox – presumably for a quick snack – they were killed. In the allegories and parables of Christian tradition, the predator is always the devil and his prey the human sinner. Under the title *Vulpis*, Greimas wrote: 'Those who want to practice his works, they need to be fattened with his [Satan's] meats which are: adulteries, fornications, idolatries, poisonings, murders, theft, lies and such like.'[22]

Fox carried his reputation for cunning through to Victorian times. Heraldry said that the fox was full of wiles and subtlety. It represented those who have done signal service to their prince and country in embassies, where there is more use for wit and dexterity than strength or valour.

Besides possibly wolf and swan, no other animal is so often commemorated in folk tales, almost always in the same context, as the elemental trickster, as one who can persuade even a mother bird to release its chicks to fox's less-than-tender ministrations. Occasionally fox appears as hero of the tale, but this is rare.

The Welsh have held on to some of the Celtic views of fox. They believe that to see a lone fox is good luck, but a pack bodes bad fortune. Several foxes running close to a house indicates disaster. All these superstitions are based on common sense. Particularly for an agrarian community, one fox can do little damage if people are alert to its presence; several, though, can wipe out all the hens in a coop. Seeing several can indicate that there are even more in the immediate area; similarly, once foxes have got too close to a house the damage has probably already been done.

## MEDICINE AND POWER

| | |
|---|---|
| DIRECTIONS | South, Southwest |
| ELEMENT | Fire |
| TRAITS | Cunning, dexterity, speed, agility, invisibility |
| ASSOCIATIONS | Subtlety, wisdom, trickery and guile; (depending on tribe and species): protection, family, maternal instinct, camouflage, healing |

The Hopi used fox furs for healing and in shamans' robes. The healing action took place by the holy man placing the fur on the affected part and drawing the sickness away.

Many Native American tribes wore a fox skin or held ceremonies to invoke its power. It was believed that, worn on the head, the skin imparted fox's intelligence to the individual. Meanwhile the tail of the fox often graced the medicine man's spirit poles (the Plains' equivalent to northwestern totem poles, or the Celtic wand or wizard's staff).

Fox teaches subtlety and imparts the ability to run like the wind. These are warrior traits. Fox is decisive and sure-footed in the physical world. It is swiftness of thought in the intellectual.

Fox can move unseen; it often remains hidden in the background, observing what's around it. Thus, it teaches that knowledge is best gained by not calling attention to oneself. Fox represents camouflage and invisibility. Several authors recommend that if a person wishes to remain unseen in a crowded room, he or she should invoke fox.

Fox is much more adaptable than the larger wolf. So, fox represents integration – of thought and behaviour, of the emotional and physical realms. Fox blends the medicine of cat and dog. Solitary like cat, supple like cat, but very much a canine creature.

Fox medicine is also 'women's medicine'. It is the protector of the family unit. Fox is always concerned with the safety of its fellows. Different elements of fox yield different results. Fox can be warrior energy, like wolf; it is stealth, like ferret. In Native American culture there's a fox society that is exclusively for women, and one specifically for men. Therefore, fox bridges the gap between male and female energies, providing mutual understanding.

If secrets are about, call fox. It allows an individual to counter subterfuge with subterfuge. Fox medicine can be used for either the frontal attack or for strategic retreat into the background.

Sometimes, fox appears as a warning of trickery.

Fox medicine brings the gift to move from place to place with ease and without being noticed. It aids one in developing independence of thought and confidence. Fox can be summoned when it is time to break out of social conditioning. It facilitates the recovery of authority.

The kit fox had none of the negative associations of the red fox. It is intelligent, but not identified with trickery or guile. If red fox spoke with a forked tongue, then kit fox spoke straight and true. Kit fox imparts stealth, but this was good medicine to have whether one was a warrior, a hunter or a scout. Kit fox medicine is not exclusively a man's domain, at least not now, for the women of the Oglala also have a Kit Fox Society. For man or woman, kit fox imparts the laudable qualities of constancy, courage and integrity. These women are stern defenders of their families. As an animal, kit fox is a good parent; therefore, women who are endowed with kit fox medicine are conscientious mothers.

The fox personality is basically feminine. Even the male may appear effeminate and petite. Do not be fooled: the fox is an effective hunter, and the fox should never be dismissed as impotent. The person who does this will eventually rue the day. The individual with fox medicine makes a good parent. These people are able to come up with obscure solutions to obvious problems. Often those with fox medicine seem to know what they should not, which makes others distrustful of them.

# FROG

*Leiopelmidae*
*Lepodactylus*

## BIOLOGICAL INFORMATION

From the class of *Amphibia* and the order *Salientia*, frog is another broad category which encompasses the small tree frogs, less than 5 cm (2 inches) in length, to the cannibalistic horned frog of South America which measures a full 25 cm (10 inches). Some – the North American *Leiopelmidae ascaphus truei*, for example – still have some semblance of a tail, while the South American do not go through the polliwog or tadpole stage of development.

Colours can range from red, black and yellow for some of the poisonous tree frogs, to the more familiar green. Many frogs (such as the bull frog) are known for their booming call, while others are virtually voiceless.

The largest frog genus is the *Lepodactylus*, with some 50 species. *Discoglassidae* contains some 11 varieties, including the painted frog of Europe and the Middle East.

### HABITAT

Water: streams, ponds, lakes, marshes. Even the tree frog is limited in its environment. In the tropical rainforest, some frogs live hundreds of metres above the forest floor in a cup of water contained with the crotch of a tree or the base of a flower.

### CHARACTERISTICS

For our purposes we will concentrate on the more familiar species. Frogs are more dependent on water than toads. Usually frogs live immediately around or in water. Toads, on the other hand, are more terrestrial. The toad tends to brown and lumpy, while the frog (in Europe and North America) is green and its skin tends to be smooth. However, even this is a generality. The female is usually bigger than the male.

The male and female go through two different phases of development. In the first, the tadpole (polliwog) has gills and its territory is limited to the waters of pools, ponds, marshes or streams. After approximately six weeks' time the animal loses its tail and is able to move about on land freely. However, they are limited in range because it is dangerous for any amphibian to have its skin dry out. However, dew and a damp hole in which to hide seem to be sufficient for toad, who must return to water only to breed. The same cannot be said for frog.

Breeding time varies on latitude and climate, but all frogs drop their eggs in gluey strings of 30 to 50 eggs. The young hatch 41 days later.

## LEGENDS AND TRADITIONS

| | |
|---|---|
| GODDESS | Heket (Egyptian) |
| GOD | Gnaski (Lakota), Gnaska (Oglala) |

The frog was pictured quite often in Mayan (native Central American) art, appearing in temple carvings and codices (scrolls written in the Mayan pictorial system). Experts tell us that the Mayan word for frog contained the word for mouth. But then even the lowly maggot, frog's prey, was represented in Mayan art, where it was a symbol of death.

In the Karok legend, frog lost his tail as a result of the gift of fire. Many animals have been attributed with the theft of fire from the divines – coyote and fox as well as frog – and all share something in common: they were permanently marked or scarred by their experience. The ordeal speaks of sacrifice in order to provide heat and light for mankind.

For the Oglala, frog was *Gnaska*, god of water and ablutions. This was translated as 'keeper of occult powers'. *Hnaska* was their word for a frog. Gnaska was not the nicest of divinities, for he plotted with Iktomi to shame Hanwi (the moon) and Wi (wife of the sun); for this, Gnaska was made ugly and banished to live on earth. As the four winds went about looking for their places at the four corners of the universe, Gnaska and Iktomi tried to foment contention among them.

In British Columbia, frog meant happiness and was related to water power. Frog was linked to the east, the direction of rebirth and renewal on the medicine wheel. For the Blackfoot, frog was a manifestation of the Old Man who defeated the evil underwater spirits (symbolized by tadpoles). These creatures were the enemies of mankind. Old Man's victory was repeated every reproductive cycle when tadpole crawled out onto land in the form of frog. The holder of the Blackfoot Beaver Bundle was allowed to put a frog on his costume as a badge of office. The eastern Dakota tribes also credited frog with similar characteristics and stories.

In ancient Egypt, frog was a symbol of procreation, fertility, birth and regeneration. The four male gods of Ogdoad, who ruled before the creation of the world, were shown as frog-headed. Frog was sacred to Heket, the goddess of childbirth. Amun, god of creation, was often depicted as a man seated on a throne with the head of a frog. Meanwhile, the hieroglyph for tadpole represented the number 100,000 – another offshoot of its aptitude for procreation.

Christianity adopted the frog as a symbol of the highest stage of spiritual evolution; lumpy old toad was the antithesis of this. In this role, frog was a much favoured character in fairy tales, turning into a rarefied being, such as a prince, after the transformative kiss of love.

The term 'polliwog' is a word for tadpole. It originally comes from Wales, 'pole' meaning head and 'wog', wiggle. The phrase is still commonly used in the US, but has been all but forgotten in the United Kingdom.

European superstition maintains that it is unlucky to kill a frog which, like the butterfly, houses the spirits of dead children. Despite this association with death, if a frog hops into someone's house, it signals good fortune. A frog croaking during the day has long been thought to be an omen of rain. Some Native American legends attribute to frog the ability to call forth the rains.

Frogs, like pigs, cats and crows, were believed to be witches' familiars. Historically, people thought witches had the ability to transform themselves into frogs. Also, frog is an essential ingredient in any number of spells – good for curing any number of ailments, from warts to love sickness.

## MEDICINE AND POWER

| | |
|---|---|
| DIRECTION | East |
| ELEMENT | Water |
| TRAITS | Fertility, productivity, the voice and song |
| ASSOCIATIONS | Happiness, regeneration and transformation; in some places, the frog represented surgery |

The most commonly accepted definition in modern times seems to be frog as caller of rain or as a sign of spiritual and emotional cleansing. However, this is an over-simplification of a complex creature.

For example, through its link with the Egyptian goddess Heket, frog rules over childbirth. Thus it was believed that frog's power could be invoked to ease the pain of labour. Some Native American tribes connected frog with surgery. Only the shaman with frog medicine could work on a patient if any sort of incision was required.

Because of the shift of tadpole to frog, this animal has long been a symbol of regeneration on a spiritual level, represented on the physical plane by frog's cleansing powers. Frog is the totem for transformation because it is a creature which undergoes changes in its development from a tiny, water-based tadpole, more tail than anything else, to a four-legged animal able to adjust itself to the land.

When frog appears, expect change – not the radical change of the butterfly bursting forth from its chrysalis but the slow transformation of the polliwog with its shrinking tail and developing legs to the full-grown frog. It suggests gentle evolution rather than a sudden great leap forward.

The connection with the water element indicates the emotions. Any transition is uncomfortable, especially if it involves plumbing the depths of the unconscious. It could be likened to adolescence, which is a period of life fraught with insecurities but completely unavoidable. Frog honours water in the form of tears, for tears cleanse the soul during a time of transition. Frog signals a time of necessary growth, and can be invoked to make this process less trying.

Frog imparts the ability to cope with change, and can help the individual take change in his or her stride.

Frog also speaks of the use of a 'magical' voice for announcing one's presence and for release. According to the tribes of the southwest, frog had the power to call up the rains. Thus, it was the sustainer of life in this dry region, and here too frog's medicine emphasized transformation. It represented that brief period of time when a rare rain fills the desert with blossoms and turns the barren landscape green.

Frog is thus good medicine to raise when in the midst of any life change – be it a mid-life crisis or a move. It not only links the individual to the emotional strength needed to endure such a shift, but can help control it – turning confusion and disorder into a natural progression. It instills optimism by transforming the mundane of everyday life into something mysterious.

Frog can also be called upon when it is time to confront emotions in a positive way, to bring feelings up from the muddy depths into the light of day. It helps one become aware of the transformative process, at the same time conferring strength and certainty on those undergoing deep emotional and spiritual change.

Frog suggests fertility, both in its ability to call rain and in its reproductive capacity. From this one can infer that, whatever changes or transformations occur, they will be beneficial in the long run. Thus, frog's arrival tells the individual to take heart and accept the process.

Frog certainly initiates renewal and rebirth on many levels. Some tribes used this medicine for healing. As for fox medicine, the medicine man would lay a dead, dried frog on the affected part to withdraw the poison from the body. Thus, frog can be used to deflect the venom of another person's envy and pride.

The frog medicine person may appear remote and inexplicable, even self-absorbed, while sitting on his lily pad awaiting his next fly. This image of coldness is just that: an illusion. The frog individual is in touch with his or her feelings; therefore, he or she has no great need to reveal them to others. At work, this individual will appear a plodder – worse, a non-starter – yet the frog person always manages to get the job done. This person is a homebody, and a prolific (but not necessarily doting) parent. The children generally will be left to fend for themselves, which fosters independence.

# GOAT

Mountain goat: *Oreamnos americanus*
European: *Capra aegarus*

## BIOLOGICAL INFORMATION

The American mountain goat is 98 to 115 cm (3 to 3½ ft) at the shoulder and 1.2 to 1.8 metres (4 to 5¾ ft) long. Its tail measures 8 to 20 cm (3¼ to 8 inches). These goats weigh 46 to 136 kg (102 to 300 lb). The female is approximately 15 per cent smaller than the male.

The mountain goat is a compact creature with short legs. It has a long shaggy coat in winter, which it sheds during the summer. Both sexes have dangerously sharp, backward-curving horns. The horns of the female are about 22.5 cm (9 inches) long; the male's grow to 32 cm (1 ft). The mountain goat is white to grey, with soft, flexible hooves that allow them to perch on the most precarious ledges.

The Old World goat comes from Persia. *Capra aegarus* was the precursor of the modern domesticated goat. Like the sheep, the goat is a member of the *Bovidae* family which diversified to form the present-day divisions of sheep, goat and cow after the Miocene period. The domesticated goat has been so bred that they come in many different sizes and colour schemes. Some breeds have been miniaturized. Others lack the distinctive horns.

### HABITAT

In the Rocky Mountains, the American mountain goat is limited to areas above the timberline. It can also be found in small areas in extreme southeast Alaska, the southern Yukon, British Columbia and Alberta, as well as in parts of Washington state, Wyoming and Montana.

The domesticated goat can be found in country environments, farmland, and in cities. It may be kept as a pet, although most people have to accept the loss of their gardens once goats have been brought in. They will nibble on just about everything. To accomplish this, they get into just about everything. Even penned they can be destructive, eating the bark of nearby trees as far as they can reach. Goats are also escape artists, albeit lovable ones. Many people keep them for their milk. Most people who are allergic to cow's milk can tolerate goat's milk, while goat cheese is something of a delicacy.

### CHARACTERISTICS

The mountain goat is not a true goat. Its nearest equivalent in Europe would be the Chamois, which belongs to the group known as goat-antelopes. The mountain goat is active in the morning and evening. It feeds off sedge grasses in the summer and woody plants during the winter. Therefore it is capable of digesting things that other animals would find indigestible.

Goats are herd animals. Wild goat herds are segregated by gender until the winter rut. The goat raises a single kid, which is born in May or June. Goats are cantankerous creatures and dangerous prey. Only the golden eagle can successfully attack one. Even the mountain lion stands to be injured by the mountain goat's sharp horns and hooves.

## LEGENDS AND TRADITIONS

| | |
|---|---|
| GODDESSES | Artemis (Greek), Hedrun (Scandinavian), Kara Kara (Turkish) |
| GODS | Ningirsu (Babylonian), Zeus (Greek), Jupiter, Saturn, Pan (Roman), the Green Man (Celtic) |

Native American legends about goats are sparse, perhaps because the species lives at altitudes high enough that most tribes rarely came across them. The Shoshone received their name, 'eaters of goats' from the other tribes. Once the Shoshone were driven from the east into the mountainous areas, mountain goats and mountain sheep formed the staple meat of their diet.

Meanwhile, Old World traditions surrounding goats are numerous. The Egyptian hieroglyph of a goat combined with the whip of power was the symbol for nobility, just as the ram stood for royalty. A more familiar association is Pan, whom many relate to the Green Man of Celtic mythology. Pan was the essence of untamed nature. Pan's horns represented the sun's rays, while the fur covering his legs suggested animal instinct. Some believe that it was goat, rather than sheep, which was the basis of the aggressive sign of Aries (the ram) of astrology. Pan is also representative of Saturn and goat associated with Capricorn. Thus it seems that images of the goat and the horned sheep often become confused.

Its horns, strange linear pupils and cloven hooves led the early Christians to equate the goat with Satan. It was sometimes thought to be Satan's messenger; at other times it was believed that the devil himself appeared in the form of a goat. One superstition based on this was that no one could keep a goat in view for a full 24 hours because it had to return to its master once a day to 'report in'.

Ironically, the foot of a goat or hairs from its beard were thought to protect an individual from Satan. One presumes that the devil sensed the presence of goat, hence believed the individual was already a follower and left him or her alone. Goat skins were hung up by sailors to ensure a smooth voyage, relating indirectly back to the legend of Jason and the Golden Fleece.

In parts of Europe and America, goat has healing properties. People are told to drive a goat or sheep close to a sickroom and let it graze. When it leaves, it is supposed to take the disease with it.

## MEDICINE AND POWER

| | |
|---|---|
| DIRECTION | West |
| ELEMENTS | Earth, Air, Sun |
| TRAITS | Agility, sure-footedness |
| ASSOCIATIONS | Abundance, independence, seeking new heights, ambition |

Goat represents two completely opposite convictions. On one side there's Pan, who speaks of nature and sexual energy, which came to mean – in the lore of the Christian church – corruption and baseness, all that was vile. On the other side we have the goat of Capricorn, which represents ambition, surefootedness and scaling the heights.

Goat is affiliated with both the sun (light and life) and Saturn (Chronos and death), and this is its medicine: the ability to blend the base (the earthbound) with the heavenly, to bring together mortal existence with its passing – therefore, the life cycle. Goat utilizes both the valleys and the peaks, migrating from the lower altitudes in the winter to higher altitudes in the summer.

Goat, in the form of Saturn, imparts discipline. Yet its hooves, which are able to grip the most tenuous surface, suggest flexibility. Its coat provides protection and warmth in the harshest environments. Thus it seems that goat gives the best of both worlds – allowing people to reach for the sky at the same time keeping them grounded, firmly attached to the earth.

When goat appears it may signal a time of difficulties when life takes on the aspect of rocky, mountainous terrain. Meanwhile goat provides not only the impetus to clamber over obstacles, whatever they may be, but the ability to do so. It is a good medicine to invoke if the individual is intent on a specific goal, for it provides the drive, zeal and enthusiasm to accomplish one's aspirations.

A person with goat medicine exhibits great agility in difficult situations. They enjoy all the physicality of life and may appear materialistic. Still, the goat person does not lose sight of the stars. This link with the divine seems almost inborn, but it tends to manifest itself in mundane ways. The goat individual follows conventions, the herd, except for those who choose to follow Pan, the mischievous side of goat.

# GOOSE

Snow or blue goose: *Chen caerulescens*
Canadian goose: *Branta canadensis*

## BIOLOGICAL INFORMATION

The white colour phase (with black wing-tips) of the snow goose occurs most often in the eastern part of the US. It measures between 56 and 76 cm (22 and 30 inches). The blue goose – with its grey body and wings, and white head and neck – is found in the western US and along the Gulf Coast.

When people speak of the wild goose, though, they are usually referring to the Canadian goose, which comes in two sizes. There are many geographical variations. The smaller is 55 – 66 cm (20 – 22 inches) tall, while others measure as large as 89 – 114 cm (35 – 45 inches). The Canadian goose has a brownish black body, head and neck, with white cheek patches. The smaller Brants goose lacks the cheek patch.

### HABITAT

The snow goose lives in Alaska and along the northern coastal regions of Canada. It winters along the California coast down to the Baja Peninsula, and from New Jersey in the east to Texas.

It breeds in the tundra and winters in salt marshes, marshy coastal bays and occasionally freshwater marshes adjacent to grain fields.

The Canadian goose prefers lakes, rivers and marshes. In other words, freshwater as opposed to saltwater. It often feeds in open grassland and stubble fields.

### CHARACTERISTICS

The Canadian goose is the one most people are familiar with. It lays four to eight eggs in a large mass of grass or moss lined with down. Sometimes the parents-to-be will take over an abandoned osprey's nest. The goose mates for life. It is a stern defender of both its young and its territorial rights. The goose is not afraid to attack any stranger who enters its turf, even full-grown human beings.

All wild geese are migratory birds, and their V-shaped flocks flying overhead usually herald the end of summer or the beginning of spring. Geese are good, sturdy flyers; some have been sighted flying over the Himalayas at an altitude of 9,600 metres (32,000 ft).

## LEGENDS AND TRADITIONS

| | |
|---|---|
| GODDESSES | Bau (Sumerian), Juno (Roman) |
| GODS | Geb, Atum (Egyptian) |

The Hidatsa and Mandan peoples of the middle Plains region had a Goose Society that was exclusively female. Its members were mature, between 30 and 40 years of age. They conducted rituals to ensure good crops, the most important of which was held in spring when the geese returned. The birds brought the corn spirits with them. Certain women held sacred corn bundles, and when droughts occurred their magic was sought and special rites were performed. Just as geese brought the corn spirits, the geese also took these spirits away when the birds migrated south for the winter. Therefore, the arrival and departure of geese indicated the turning points of the year.

The goose gave its name to many months. A subarctic tribe, the Miskipizun, referred to April as 'Grey-goose month'. The Migiskau of the same region marked autumn by the departure of the snow goose. Barga, an explorer of the American Midwest in 1878, recorded Chippewa (Ojibwa) vocabulary. For them, March was 'the moon of the wild goose'.

The Egyptians associated goose with the Great Egg of Atum, as they did duck. In Europe, some consider goose a better protector than dog. Many country homes have kept geese for just this purpose, as guardians who give an alarm when their territory is invaded.

Goose was sacred of Juno, Roman goddess of the moon and counterpart of Jupiter. Boreas, the north wind (more accurately north—northeast) of ancient Greece, was associated with the snow goose. The last sheaf of corn often took the form of a gander or a goose in Celtic ceremonies of old.

The most modern manifestation is Mother Goose, whose gift was poetry and stories to generations of readers. Goose meant female energy, fecundity and protection. Goosedown is used for bedding in Europe; therefore it is often equated with marital fidelity and fertility.

## MEDICINE AND POWER

| | |
|---|---|
| DIRECTIONS | North, South |
| ELEMENTS | Water, Earth |
| TRAITS | Protection, fertility, femininity |
| ASSOCIATIONS | Storytelling, rebirth, resurrection, prosperity and fidelity |

The direction varies depending on an individual's or tribe's location and where they were in the migrational cycle. Thus, for the people of the north, who saw goose leaving in the winter and returning in the spring, it was a symbol of the south. People who viewed its return from the north during the winter naturally associated it with that direction.

Generally goose is considered a beneficent animal with links to the Great Mother, the Persephone myth, and the descent into hell each year before the return of spring. It speaks of rebirth, the new dawn and new beginnings. It is linked with destiny, representing the fortunes and misfortunes of existence prior to the return to the maternal bosom when one's time on earth is through.

Goose is guardianship and protection. Its medicine is good to invoke when one's territory is being invaded. Goose is a symbol of fertility and fidelity, therefore associated with marriage. Its feathers make mattresses and comforters; thus, geese speak of warmth in winter and the return of spring.

Despite all the mythology and symbolic importance of the high-flying eagle, it is actually goose that achieves the highest altitudes. Its presence has been recorded by airline pilots at 10,000 metres (33,000 ft), and it is able to maintain this altitude for long distances. Therefore, goose imparts strength and endurance. Additionally, this ability to reach heights suggests inspiration. Thus, goose (beyond its traditional association with mother goose) is a keeper of sacred lore.

So, goose is good medicine whether the topic is marriage, fertility, protection or rebirth. It could herald a welcome change, such as the return of spring. If its appearance announces the advent of winter, goose imparts the strength to endure the cold with the promise of eventual spring.

Goose has been laughed at as clumsy, and the person with goose medicine may reflect this; however, the goose individual is not a good one to anger, for he or she can and will bite. The goose person is materialistic and highly protective of his or her young and territory. These people possess an innate wisdom about physical life and know how to make the best of most situations.

# GROUSE

American ruffled grouse: *Bonasa umbellus*
European black grouse: *Lyrurus tetrix*

## BIOLOGICAL INFORMATION

The American ruffled grouse is a brown bird with a fan-shaped, black-banded tail. It measures 40 to 48 cm (16 to 19 inches) in length. It has ruffs on its neck which it inflates during courtship. During the winter, the ruffled grouse grows hornlike protrusions on the bottom of its feet in order to grip the snow.

The European black grouse is a much more spectacular bird. It has a lyre-shaped tail. The male is black with a red cap during the winter months and mating season. It dons more dowdy plumage in other months. The female is grey.

The American grouse family also includes the Prairie Chicken (*Tympanuchus cupido*) – the Latin name *cupido* referring to its rather amorous nature.

### HABITAT

The ruffled grouse prefers deciduous forest with scattered clearings, farmland or overgrown pastures. It is found throughout New England, the Great Lakes region and the lower two-thirds of Canada.

The black grouse lives in moorland and along the forest edge of Scotland.

### CHARACTERISTICS

The grouse is probably best known for its courtship displays. The males collect in a communal ground to show their wares. Each male dances tirelessly and ceaselessly until he has acquired enough hens. Courtship displays include a type of spiral dance, fanning the tail, inflating the feathers, with the males often facing each other off in some form of ritual competition. The females, meanwhile, choose their mate according to his dance. Often they are all attracted to the same bird – the other males don't stand a chance until the first has achieved his quota.

All grouse are ground birds, although the black grouse does roost in the lower branches of trees. Both types make their nests along the forest floor. When frightened they explode from their nests with an ear-popping whump which usually frightens any would-be assailant away.

## LEGENDS AND TRADITIONS

GODDESS The Corn Goddess (Native American)

Grouse's first association is with motion. Its mating dance has fascinated people for generations. The Native Americans of the Great Plains honoured grouse in dance.

In Europe and America, grouse speaks of the sacred spiral. This symbol has adorned temples and stone monuments throughout the ages. The spiral is located in Newgrange in Ireland, and in the Mithraic temples of Italy. However, in England and Scotland grouse is considered a randy little creature; thus it has sexual connotations – understandably, given its courtship dance.

As it dances, the grouse creates a thrumming sound by expanding its chest and expelling air forcefully from its throat. Therefore it controls the sacred breath. The rhythmic sound itself is equated with drumming.

## MEDICINE AND POWER

| | |
|---|---|
| DIRECTION | North |
| ELEMENTS | Earth, Air |
| TRAITS | Sexuality, fertility, independence |
| ASSOCIATIONS | Shamanism, the sacred dance, sacred drumming and the sacred spiral |

Grouse represents all the elements of ceremony and ritual. It dances and it drums. The shape it makes in its dance is a circle, or spiral. The spiral is one of the oldest symbols of personal power. Grouse medicine, therefore, is the medicine of the holy man or woman or shaman, no matter what his or her primary animal affiliation. Its medicine not only should be, but is invoked by any sacred rite that uses the circle as its base.

In some ways, grouse medicine is the most elemental of elemental medicines. During a vision quest, when the Native American seeks communication with the spirit world, the seeker will often paint his body with a spiral. It is a symbol of birth and rebirth, personal vision and enlightenment. After crying for a vision and receiving one, the seeker is reborn and renamed as a result of this rebirth.

Grouse is an expression of all cycles: the seasonal cycle, the lunar cycle, the endless circular procession of the stars in the heavens. Therefore, its appearance promises that the cycle of change is working in someone's life. It suggests the movement of spirit. Grouse is an assurance that no matter how bad the situation, in the natural progression of events things will be transformed – for the better, it implies. It can appear when someone is about to come into their own.

Grouse also speaks of sexual energy and power. It acts as an affirmation of life and again emphasizes the concept of renewal. In some pagan religions, sex provides the basis of initiation from which all magic arises.

On a spiritual level, the grouse person is a natural shaman. He or she needs no training. This individual seems to know instinctively about the cycles inherent in life. On a physical level, the grouse medicine person is independent. A loner. The male will preen and strut until he has obtained his harem, but once his job of fertilization is completed he has little to do with the upbringing of the young. The grouse woman seems quite content to be left alone to take care of the chicks without interference from the male.

# HARE

Brown hare: *Lepus europaeus*
Snowshoe hare: *Lepus americanus*

## BIOLOGICAL INFORMATION

The hare is larger than the rabbit. It has longer ears and more powerful hindlegs. The European brown hare measures between 60 and 70 cm (24 – 25 inches) in length. Its tail is approximately 8 cm (3 inches) long. It weighs 3 to 6.5 kg (6 to 14 lb). The European or brown hare is cinnamon-coloured with lighter flanks and a white belly. It has long black-tipped ears.

The snowshoe hare is 33 to 46 cm (11 to 18 inches) long, with a weight of 0.9 to 1.8 kg (2 to 4 lb). As the name suggests, it has big white feet. Its coat is brown in the summer, but it turns white in winter.

### HABITAT

The brown hare prefers open meadows and farmlands, but it occurs everywhere across Europe except the high mountainous regions and dense fir forests. It was introduced to Dutchess County, New York in 1893, and its range has spread throughout the Great Lakes region and portions of New England and Pennsylvania.

The American snowshoe hare inhabits the swamps, forests and thickets of the north. It finds its home in the tundra regions of Canada down to the northern US plains. The snowshoe is linked so closely with the snowy owl that, when hare populations suffer, the owls cease to breed; many die from starvation.

There are more than a few breeds of 'jackrabbits', another American term for hare, located in the desert regions of the southwest.

### CHARACTERISTICS

The hare is much more combative than the rabbit. It is the more solitary creature. The hare nests alone while the rabbit lives in warrens. Hares inhabit some of the more inhospitable regions of the US and Canada. Unlike the rabbit, hares make neither underground dens nor maternity nests. The young are well developed when they are born and can usually fend for themselves within a few hours. They have three to four litters a year of two to four young.

The hare is fast; it can achieve velocities of 72 kph (45 mph). Their average pace consists of leaps of between 90 cm and 1.2 metres (3 and 4 ft). They can easily clear obstacles of 1.5 m (5 ft), and under duress they can leap up to 3.6 m (12 ft) with each bound.

## LEGENDS AND TRADITIONS

GODDESSES Hecate (Greek), Harek (Germany)

The Algonquin of northeastern America honoured the Great Hare as a demiurge. It was a player in the creation of the world. But for the more agrarian eastern Seneca, hare or *tonedahyen* was the stealer of squash. Caught by the chief of the tribe, hare cried so piteously when beaten that the chief contented himself with splitting the hare's lip so it could never eat squash again.

Hare proved itself a fool through impatience and haste in a legend with spider, who was sent by the moon to bring words of comfort for mankind. Hare met spider halfway and asked her her purpose. Spider replied that the moon wanted to her to take a message to earth. Hare said: 'You are so slow, let me take it.'

Spider replied: 'Man is afraid of dying and the moon wants them to know that they all must die ...'

Hare left before he could get the rest of the message – the words of comfort. By the time spider arrived at the camp, no one would listen. So to this day she spins the moon's story in her web, but none knows how to read it.

The Montagnais and Naskapi peoples used hare in a form of divination called *scapulamancy*. The bones were thrown into a fire where they would crack and burn. The scapula was then lifted from the coals and the scorch marks and breaks on it were interpreted by the tribe's holy man.

In Egypt, hare was the phonetic symbol comparable to 'un', which was a determinative as the concept of being. 'Un' was also a word that meant to do wrong, to commit a sin, to make a mistake or to be completely worthless. This symbol, combined with the symbol of a kneeling man, meant 'sinner'.

Yet the Egyptians also had a legend that associated hare with creation. Eventually it came to represent procreation and, by extrapolation, immorality.

The Hebrews declared hare meat unclean and unfit for human consumption (Deuteronomy XIV:7).

By Gothic times the hare came to be known as fleet and swift. It was carved on sepulchres as a symbol of diligence. This reflects the attitude of the medieval huntsmen, who learned to honour hare for its ability to dodge, dart and make quick changes of direction. It was considered wily and a worthy adversary for the kingly hunt, while poor rabbit was disdained.

Most superstitions see hare as an ill-omened beast. Trouble is in store for anyone hapless enough to have a hare cross their path, and a hare running along the road indicates fire in the vicinity. Few are unfamiliar with the old wives' tale that a pregnant woman who sees a hare will have a hare-lipped child. This belief was shared by the Native Americans. Witches were supposed to be able to transform themselves into hares. Ironically for all this alleged evil, the left foot of the hare is considered lucky – for all but the creature itself, who requires all four in order to survive.

Hare had associations with old harvest traditions. The last sheaf of corn that was cut contained the corn spirit, which sometimes took the form of a hare. The person who scythed the final sheaf was called 'hare' for the next year.

## MEDICINE AND POWER

| | |
|---|---|
| DIRECTION | Varies by tribe |
| ELEMENTS | Earth, Wind or Air |
| TRAITS | Speed, agility, craftiness, cunning |
| ASSOCIATIONS | Irascibility, haste, witchcraft, luck, fertility, immorality |

Hares are territorial. Two males will fight whenever they come across each other. Hare should not be confused with the sociable rabbit. While the Native American attributes for rabbit are not particularly complimentary, hare fairs even worse. It imparts speed and agility, but with this comes impatience. The hare does not listen to the entire message from the moon to mankind; he bungles it badly and mankind suffers for it.

In yet another tale where hare is supposed to carry a message, he keeps the information to himself. Thus, hare is associated with cunning and deceit. Hare is considered greedy and selfish, while the more communal rabbit is associated with love. If there's an animal that could be held up as a bad example, it is hare.

The European view is essentially the same – a grudging respect for its speed, but generally an animal of bad portent. Even when the animal conveys good luck, it must die to do so.

If hare appears, look around; it could be that someone is trying to pull a fast one, or it could mean that the person is fooling him- or herself. Hare imparts intelligence, but not wisdom nor candour. So if hare has entered someone's life, there's trickery and fraud about. It can also indicate that the individual is becoming too self-centred or that messages are being garbled. Hare is a jokester, like coyote.

The hare person is flighty, nervous and unsociable. They may be ill-tempered. Those with hare medicine are quick witted, but not necessarily reliable. They often are victims of egocentric thinking. Hare is a good fighter, but not a good communicator. The hare person will defend his or her territory and if possible take over others', too.

# HAWK

Red-tailed hawk: *Buteo jamaicensis*
Cooper's hawk: *Accipiter cooperii*
Goshawk: *Accipiter gentilis*

## BIOLOGICAL INFORMATION

The red-tailed hawk is 46 cm to 65 cm (18 – 25 inches) tall, with a wingspan of 1.2 m (4 ft). A stocky bird, the red-tailed has dun plumage. Its breast lightens nearly to white, while its tail is rust-coloured. The red-shouldered hawk and Cooper's hawk are similar, but smaller, lighter birds. Generally speaking, though, when the Native American speaks of hawk or 'red-eagle', they are referring to the red-tail.

The goshawk measures 51 to 66 cm (20 to 26 inches) and has a wingspan of 1.1 m (3½ ft). The goshawk is stocky, with a dark blue-grey back, black crown and a pale belly finely barred with grey. There are also pure white colour-phases, but these are rare.

### HABITAT

Mainly deciduous forest near open country side. The red-tailed hawk is found throughout North America. The broad-winged and red-shoulder species live strictly east of the Mississippi. Thus the hawks have taken over the niche once filled by the eagle.

The goshawk prefers coniferous forests. It remains close to farmland and the woodland fringes in order to take best advantage of the available food supply. In North America and Europe it stays in the north or in mountainous regions. In the UK, goshawk was once common. Now it resides mainly in Wales and Scotland.

### CHARACTERISTICS

The hawk's vision is eight times greater than that of man. However, this soaring and majestic bird is not able to achieve the same heights as its larger cousin, the eagle. Hawk makes up for this with its ability to hover. It can suspend itself in midair. In the American prairies it is a common sight to see a red-tail hanging on the breeze as it sights its prey.

The hawk is also more likely to perch for long periods of time and watch for movement in the grass before it takes wing. Therefore, it is a much more 'energy-efficient' bird.

It is noted for its keen vision and insight, along with its ability to dive and hit its target. The broad-wing is the only hawk that migrates from one region to another.

The Harris Hawk of South America has become the most popular bird in falconry. It is unique in that it works co-operatively with other birds of its kind as it hunts.

## LEGENDS AND TRADITIONS

GODDESSES Isis, Hathor, Amenti (Egyptian), Hera, Circe (Greek)
GODS Ra, Horus, Montu, Sokaris, and the triune: Ptah, Seker, and Osiris (Egyptian)

The Pueblo tribes of the American southwest did not differentiate between hawk and eagle. For them the hawk was 'red eagle', endowed with all the same qualities as eagle, and its feathers were used in much the same way. So hawk, like eagle, was a messenger of spirit.

The Lakota, though, did make a distinction. They noted that the hawk did not fly as high as the eagle. Similarly they saw its ability to hover and its downward-looking nature, and decided that if eagle was man's messenger to the heavens, then hawk must convey the tidings from the grandfathers and grandmothers to man. Therefore, it was associated with the 'good, red road' which was the Native American equivalent to the Christian 'straight and narrow path'. The Lakota name for the spirit of the hawk was *Cetan*. They credited it with the warrior's quality of endurance.

Many Native Americans linked hawk to thunder and lightning. Thus, it had ties to both air and fire. Its red colouring meant that it represented the sun. Therefore, for most aboriginal Americans hawk's feathers were sacred and used in various ceremonies.

The black, or Harris, hawk was believed to have certain healing powers. It enabled the medicine man to isolate and go straight to the affected part, thus facilitating treatment.

In Egypt, hawk or falcon was associated with Ra and Heru. It was worshipped as Horus, whose body represented the heavens and whose eyes were the sun and moon. Specific characteristics of falcon were attributed to other gods and goddesses such as Montu, Sokaris, Hathor and Isis – Isis was often shown as a hawk hovering above Osiris. Hawk was also a symbol of the Egyptian triune of gods: Ptah, Seker, and Osiris. When the falcon or hawk was depicted sitting upon the Shen, the eternity sign, or at the end of a notched branch, it represented a year.

The Celts believed that hawk carried the sun in his feathers. Its power was memory and advancement – in other words, sight, the ability to look both forward and back. Two knights of Arthur's Round Table were named after hawk: Galahad (Gwalch-Y-Had, summer hawk) and Gawain (Gwalachmai, hawk of May). Merlin could shape-shift into a small hawk, and he gave his name to a breed.

Because hawk was associated with regeneration in classical history, it was later used by the Christians as a symbol for resurrection. Like deer, hawk had a strict hierarchy attributed to it during medieval times. The *Boke of St Albans* says: 'First an Egle ... There is Gerfawken. A Tercell of gerfauken, and theys belong to the Kyng. There is Fawken gentill, and a Tercell gentill, and theys be for a prynce. There is Fawken of the rock. And that is for a duke. There is Fawken peregryne and that is for an Erle ...'[1] If the Eagle was the bird of kings, then the hawk was the nobleman's bird, with the smallest, the sparrowhawk, reserved for ladies and varlets (pages).

Heraldry referred back to the Egyptians when it described hawk as an emblem of the sun and of light.

## MEDICINE AND POWER

| | |
|---|---|
| DIRECTIONS | East, South |
| ELEMENTS | Air, Fire (sun) |
| TRAITS | Hovering flight, speed, endurance |
| ASSOCIATIONS | Sun, light, perception, foresight; a messenger of the gods to man; regeneration and resurrection |

Hawk brings swift and decisive action, along with foresight. Because of its ability to fly high, hawk is associated with light. As messenger from the spirit-world, it is bringer of knowledge and wisdom. Hawk endows an individual with endurance. Hawk teaches observation and patience. The hawk will sit motionless for hours, waiting for the its prey to appear. Likewise, hawk hovers, sizing up its quarry before it swoops. Therefore it is not just an emissary, it is the right action taken at the right time.

If hawk appears, it could be warning that an individual would be wise to look before he or she leaps. Perhaps a situation needs to be studied a bit more before proceeding. If one sees a hawk on the wing, check its course. The direction itself is interpreted to ascertain the meaning. Thus, if a hawk is flying south, then the message was thought to have something to do with those things attributed to the south: warmth, youth, physical reality, bounty, plenty and all things associated with summer – or, on a more spiritual level, with the path one must walk to achieve enlightenment.

When hawk arrives, the person is put on notice to remain alert to his or her surroundings. The connection with thunder and lightning can indicate turbulent change. This can be in the form of the sudden illumination of insight, or something that is initiated by external circumstances.

To invoke hawk is to invoke the transmuting energy of fire. It can be called upon when one needs strength. Its powers do not so much provide protection as confer upon the individual the courage and fortitude to defend him- or herself in times of trouble.

Those with hawk medicine will be difficult to tie down. This individual is freedom-loving. However, once mated, hawk people are dependable. This person would be a stern defender of family and friends. The hawk individual can also provide profound insight into others and difficult life situations. Their advice is often sought and should be heeded. Hawk, as a smaller bird than eagle, is more often subject to attack. Crows will gang up on hawk, and owls will prey upon the hawk in its nest if they can. So, too, the hawk person may be exposed to ridicule by lesser individuals.

# HORSE

*Equus caballus*

## BIOLOGICAL INFORMATION

Horses vary in size from quite small, such as the Welsh Mountain pony which stands about 90 cm (3 ft) at the shoulder, to more than 2 m (6 ft plus). They come in a variety of colours, from white through various tans, reds and browns to black. Like the dog, many have been purpose-bred. Therefore the traits of specific breeds vary depending upon the use for which they were designed.

### HABITAT

At one time horses were found on every continent, including the Americas. Some of the first horses were small, no larger than a dog. The horse survived the Pleistocene period everywhere, except in the New World. The horse was domesticated around 2000 BC.

The horse is an animal of the grassy plains. It lives at many different altitudes. The sturdy and smaller pony is more likely to be found in hilly, rocky and mountainous terrain.

### CHARACTERISTICS

Left to their own devices, horses are migratory creatures. The herd is headed by a lead female who metes out discipline in the form of banishment. Male horses stay along the periphery of the herd. Basically they are tolerated. Sometimes young males will be driven away by the older males to form bachelor herds until they find another larger group of females to join, providing fresh blood and fresh breeding stock.

## LEGENDS AND TRADITIONS

| | |
|---|---|
| GODDESSES | Hippia, Menalippe (Greek), Hipponia (Roman), Quan Yin (Chinese), Rhiannon (Welsh), Samjuna (Indian), Aine (Irish), Epona (Celtic) |
| GODS | Poseidon (Greek), Mars (Roman) |

To follow the appearance of the horse on the Native American scene is to chronicle white man's influence. The Europeans rewrote the history of the Native Americans with the introduction of the horse. The only other item that was to have more influence was that of white man's diseases. Supremacy in battle and domination of territory can usually be traced to those tribes who had access to horses. Thus, they were able to predominate, strategically, over those who did not. Since the arrival of horses took place from the southern and eastern coasts, the inland tribes were compressed and pushed further back by those tribes who had horses. The influence of the gun cannot be underestimated in this equation, but still it is safe to say that the Plains regions were not fully utilized or populated until the appearance of the horse.

The measure of the wealth of an individual or a tribe was rated by the number of horses he or they possessed. Thus, horses represented power. Many historians have condemned the Native American custom of 'buying' a wife, yet one wonders how this is any different from the 'bride price' of ancient times or the 'dowry' of more modern ones. A woman's price was between three and five horses. Since the horse reflected an individual's wealth and power, this was a compliment illustrating that women were highly valued.

## TABLE OF HORSE VALUES[1]

| TRIBE | ITEM | WORTH IN HORSES |
|---|---|---|
| Mandan | Eagle headdress | 2 |
| Assiniboin | Quill shirt/fur-trimmed leggings | 1 |
| Assiniboin | Eagle war-cap | 2 |
| Assiniboin | Beaded scarlet blanket | 1 |
| Upper Missouri | 15 eagle feathers | 1 |
| Crow | 10 weasel skins | 1 |
| Crow | 100 elks' teeth | 1 |
| Crow | Woman's dress of bighorn with 300 teeth | 3 |
| Crow | Carved pipe bowl | 1 packhorse |
| Kiowa | Muzzle-loading rifle | 1 |
| Blackfeet | Medicine pipes | 9+ |
| Blackfeet | Catlinite carved bowl with stem | 1 |

Horse, with its thundering hooves, was also associated with thunder power. In the Lakota language, horse was *sunktanka*, meaning 'great (or super) dog'. This is not as illogical as it may sound at first, for horse shared many of the same admirable traits as dog – in its ability to haul, its loyalty to man and its courage under fire.

The Old World view mirrored that of the Native American. The domestication of the horse opened up whole new horizons for humanity. It truly was freedom. A man could walk about an average of 15 miles a day. Even the Roman infantry could only cover 30 miles per day. When horse carried man on his back, this same distance could be covered in an hour. The horse was so integral to the history of the planet that the addition of stirrups to saddles has been correlated directly to the fall of the Roman Empire, who did have this innovation.

Horse is fleet. It was often used as an emblem of war. The Romans linked it with Mars, god of war. Therefore, horse represented sexual energy, virility and the physicality of man.

The Celts thought that horse brought good luck and good fortune. One animal of note was the white horse. It was sacred – associated with Rhiannon and Epona, who sometimes took this form. The white horse provided protection from the evil eye.

Again, Christianity perverted the white horse's place and it became a symbol of death. Yet no one would deny the species' nobility. Heraldry attributed to horse courage, pride and tractability. It was called the 'favourite beast among all nations, as being more useful to man than any other of the creation'.[2]

The relationship between the warhorse and nobility was more than spiritual. It was practical. Few outside this social sphere could afford to buy a horse, much less keep one. When horses were used for ploughing, usually they were owned by the lord of the land and borrowed by the peasants.

Therefore the European and the Native American view was similar. The horse was nobility and freedom from restraint. However, the Native American view was a more egalitarian one, except where women were concerned. Any man who could capture a horse could own one. However, it was believed that if a woman rode a fast horse she would ruin it, making it slow and lethargic.

The origin of plaiting braids in a horse's tails comes from the belief that an animal so adorned was immune from attack by witches. Horses were even thought to predict the weather. According to folk wisdom, if several horses are seen standing with their backs to a hedge, a storm is brewing. Studies indicate that this is not superstition, but a part of horses' natural behaviour – they are seeking protection from the oncoming storm. Horses exhibit the same sixth sense that most animals possess; therefore, such auguries should be taken seriously.

# MEDICINE AND POWER

| | |
|---|---|
| DIRECTIONS | All |
| ELEMENTS | Wind, Air |
| TRAITS | Endurance, speed, sociability, matriarchal power |
| ASSOCIATIONS | Strength and loyalty, power, energy and freedom of spirit |

Horse serves but is never completely subdued; thus, it represents independent spirit. Horse embodies both earthly and unearthly power. Certain types meant war. Similarly, horse was a symbol of strength. In the US they still speak of 'horse power' when describing the power of an engine.

Interestingly enough, despite all its masculine associations horse was linked to more female divinities than male, which seems to suggest that the qualities of power, energy, movement, speed, endurance and freedom are gifts of woman rather than man.

Horse is likened to the wind. It was a symbol of thunder and lightning. Therefore, the terrestrial horse's element was air rather than earth. In shamanistic practices it is a spirit horse that carries the holy man to the heavens. Therefore, horses possess not only swiftness upon the land, but the gift of spiritual flight.

Horse speaks of stamina, riches and power. It imparts strength and endurance. Its gift is value as reflected in the physical world – in other words, self-respect and self-esteem, although this 'value' can sometimes be translated literally.

If horse has put in an appearance it can mean an increase on either the physical or spiritual level. It indicates a time of renewed confidence and energy. It speaks of going places, and going there quickly; therefore, it usually signifies that events in life are going to pick up pace.

Horse should be called upon when energies are low or when circumstances in one's life require stamina and strength. Likewise, it should be invoked in order to jump over obstacles or get things moving if they have become stuck. Call upon its warrior spirit and strong heart if confronted.

For many, horse's power suggests the shamanistic path; but all animals impart special medicine to the individual. The horse person is both warrior and leader. This individual evokes confidence in others. Horse people are loyal, especially to those who have earned their trust. As a herd animal, the horse prefers to be in the company of others and is most easily chastised by being ignored.

# HUMMINGBIRD

Ruby-throated: *Archilochus colubris*

## BIOLOGICAL INFORMATION

This strictly American bird is most numerous in South America. All hummingbirds are members of the family *Trochilidae*. The ruby-throated hummingbird is the most common in the US. It is a tiny bird, 9 cm (3½ inches) long, with brilliant green dorsal feathers and white below. The male is further adorned with a bright red throat patch. Its most distinctive physical characteristic is its needle-like beak.

### HABITAT

The ruby-throated hummingbird inhabits city parks, urban and suburban gardens and woodland.

The rufous hummingbird lives in the temperate rainforest of the northwest Pacific coast from Washington state through British Columbia and into parts of southern Alaska.

The buff-bellied hummingbird prefers the warm. Its range stretches from the far southern tip of Texas down through Mexico to Guatemala.

### CHARACTERISTICS

All hummingbirds are known for their unique mode of flight. Their wings beat so fast that they are invisible to the human eye and emit a characteristic hum, from which the bird gets its name. Like the hawk, they can hang in space. They are the only birds capable of flying backwards.

Hummingbirds rarely perch, even to feed. The female will perch to watch the mating dance of the male, which consists of pendulum-type swings back and forth. The nests are woven, like hammocks, hanging between the two branches of a tree.

The hummingbird is a nectar drinker. Their peculiar flight pattern and long beaks were developed specifically for this purpose. Some are so specialized that they can feed from only one plant. They are attracted to long, tubular flowers, especially those with bright colours like orange or red. The ruby-throated hummingbird particularly likes the nectar of petunias, trumpet creepers and bee balm.

## LEGENDS AND TRADITIONS

GOD Tezcatlipoca (Mexico)

The Nasca were an agrarian community in southern Peru who lived in the fertile valley just outside the Pampas Colorado, between the Pacific shore and the Andes. The Nasca predate the Inca by thousands of years. It is now believed that the tribe achieved semi-divine status to its cultural successors, the Inca. The Nasca carved some 18 bird shapes into the soil, on a massive scale. Although not the largest figure, hummingbird figures prominently. The shape is recognizable from the ground, but only truly appreciated from above. It measures approximately 25 metres (82 ft). Like all the Nasca pictures, it is made of a single uninterrupted line. One expert, Dr Reich, contends that the images and lines mark important points in the heavenly map and were used as a sort of calendar to mark the planting season. Later studies indicate that the figures represent certain clans or village communities. They were maintained for processional purposes, when the groups would walk the animal's outline on special holy days.

In Mayan teachings, hummingbird was connected to the black sun – the sun when it was eclipsed – and the fifth world. In both Toltec and later Aztec cultures, the blue hummingbird was the southern form of the god Tezcatlipoca, the smoking mirror. The smoking mirror was the black obsidian used by priests for scrying. Tezcatlipoca was the spirit of war and darkness, symbol of the Jungian shadow side of human nature. It was the primary god of the Aztecs. Tezcatlipoca battled eternally with the feathered serpent, Quezalcoatl. Both gods demanded sacrifice: the latter was satisfied with fruit and flowers; the former, the human heart. In other words, of the two (the feathered serpent and the hummingbird), the serpent was the more benevolent. Indeed, the smoking mirror – and vicariously hummingbird – was equated with war, conquest and death.

Hummingbird was also associated with the ghost dance, an exclusively Native American form of Christianity that originated in western America. A Paiute holy man, Wovaka, saw himself in a vision as the messiah for the red man. In his vision he was told that if the tribes got together in peace to dance, then the ancestors and the buffalo would return and the white man would disappear from the land.

The ghost dance did not call for active resistance to the white man, in fact it advised against it. Yet this new faith struck such terror in the hearts of the white citizens that Native American religion, art and dance were outlawed for 100 years, until the 1960s. The white reaction to the innocuous ghost dance left its final mark, and shame, at the massacre of Wounded Knee.

In the southwestern United States, hummingbird had another meaning entirely. It referred to love. Its feathers were used to invoke love magic or added to love charms. The hummingbird was linked to the rainbow, hence colour. Pueblo women performed the rainbow dance; therefore, the hummingbird was beneficent and female energy, which is illustrated by the following story.

The Hopi people lived in the southwest, on land dry at the best of times. Their living was precariously balanced, and during extended periods of drought the tribe had been known to flee rather than face starvation. So, one day a young boy and his sister were left alone in the village as their parents went in search of food. The little boy fashioned a hummingbird from the pith of a dry sunflower stalk to keep his sister entertained. He told her as he gave it to her, 'Just as the spider fashioned man from clay, I have made this hummingbird for you. If you throw it in the air it will fly.'

The little girl was delighted with her brother's gift. The boy then left her to find food. She threw the toy in the air. The great spider woman, who had heard the boy, granted the bird life. It flew – up, up and far away. The boy returned empty-handed. The next morning when they awoke with empty bellies, the bird had returned with maize.

They thanked the bird, who now lay in a pithy heap upon the floor. For the next four days, each morning the girl threw the bird into the air, and each evening it came back with food. Then, on the fifth day, it returned with nothing. It lay on the floor lifeless, as if its magic was spent. The boy asked his sister to try one more time, but this time he asked the bird to find their parents.

Stalwart hummingbird went off in search. First, though, he found the god Muiyinwuh, who had dominion over the rains. Boldly the bird demanded why the god had hidden in his kiva[1] when people were starving above. Muiyinwuh disdained the hummingbird's censure, but invited the bird to take as much food as he should need.

After taking the feast to the children, hummingbird continued his search until he found the parents, who were on the verge of death. The hummingbird brought this news to the children, who immediately gave away their fine meal so that their parents might live. Meanwhile Muiyinwuh thought about what hummingbird had said and decided to visit the earth to see for himself. He discovered that things were as bad as hummingbird had said and he relented, making rain for the thirsty earth.

Nourished by the food and encouraged by the appearance of distant rain, the parents returned to the village. Thus, parents and children are reunited, thanks to hummingbird and Spiderwoman, who gave the bird life. The fields once again were rich with corn and the desert bloomed.

# MEDICINE AND POWER

| | |
|---|---|
| DIRECTION | South |
| ELEMENTS | Air, Fire, Stone (obsidian) |
| TRAITS | Hovering flight, vibration, colour |
| ASSOCIATIONS | Joy, music, love, the rainbow, also war |

It is difficult to reconcile such diverse characteristics, except to say that perhaps hummingbird is living proof of the old axiom: all's fair in love and war. Certainly, in the author's personal experience the original meaning of hummingbird as god of war seems most appropriate, for hummingbird's appearance usually presages a crisis.

However, hummingbird is normally accepted as joy, light, music and colour. Its arrival could mean that these elements are missing from one's life.

Hummingbird may be called upon to open the heart chakra. It assists with gentle purification, and cleanses away emotional residue. Therefore, it is useful medicine in times of physical transition. Its warlike aspect brings courage when facing emotional challenges, and provides uplifting support for facing the past and any unresolved issues.

As representative of the smoking mirror, hummingbird is linked with scrying – therefore, with foreknowledge and prediction.

The hummingbird person will be bright, colourful and cheerful, although a bit flighty. A better word would be mercurial, for hummingbird medicine imparts the ability to switch from a buzzing hover to darting flight in an instant – a trait that will bewilder the more landbound. Because of the association with rain, the hummingbird individual can be emotional, or may exhibit two personalities. The Lakota believed that the rainbow held back the rain, since it appeared with the sun. Thus the hummingbird individual can be both passionate and cold; motionless and amazingly quick.

# JAGUAR (PANTHER, LEOPARD)

*Felis (pantera) onca*

## BIOLOGICAL INFORMATION

The jaguar measures between 1.5 and 2.4 metres (5 and 8 ft) in length; with a tail of 43 to 67 cm (17 to 26¼ inches). It weighs 54 to 136 kg (119 to 300 lb). It comes in two distinct colour phases. The first is yellow to tawny with black rosettes which run in horizontal rows along back and sides. It bears more than a passing resemblance to the African leopard (a different species), and was mistaken for it by the Europeans.

The black panther was once thought to be an entirely different species from the spotted jaguar, hence the name. It has now been recognized as a colour variation, for in full light the darker rosettes of the jaguar can be seen even on the darkest coat of the black panther.

'Jaguar' is a Native American name, meaning 'he who kills with one blow.' The word 'panther' comes from the Greek.

### HABITAT

Jaguar originated in North America. Only when the land bridge of Central America was formed did it emigrate to South America, and there it stayed. Jaguar resides in brush, forested areas, jungles, swamps and semi-arid mountainous scrub. Once it inhabited the southwest US in parts of Texas, New Mexico, Arizona and southern California. Sadly, the jaguar has been sighted only once in the US since 1940. However, its range includes all of the tropical and subtropical regions of Mexico, Cental America and down into South America.

### CHARACTERISTICS

The jaguar is the biggest and most powerful cat in South America, larger even than the cougar. Like the African lion, it roars to announce its presence. In this, jaguar is unique – it is the only cat in the Americas that roars. It maintains a territory of 24 square km (15 square miles).

The jaguar is one of the few big cats which actually likes water, and is often seen playing in it. Like most cats it is solitary except during breeding. Some mated couples may stay together, but it is more typical to have them separate after a year.

## LEGENDS AND TRADITIONS

GODS Tezcatlipoca (Aztec), Chac/Rain Gods (Maya)

Even when jaguar was more abundant it did not stretch far into what is now the US, therefore most of the stories associated with it come from Central and South America. In pre-Columbian America, jaguar was a god in Peru, Mexico and Guatemala.

Judging from Mayan art, jaguar was second in religious significance only to the snake. The Temple of the Jaguar at Chichen Itza has a frieze with jaguars in procession, the king had to walk beneath this frieze during his the coronation. The *Chac* or Rain Gods of the Four Corners were jaguars. Altars at Copan Quirigua and Chichen Itzen were carved with jaguars, while the double-headed jaguar figured at the sites of Chichen Itza, Uxmal and Palenque.

Jaguar was the ruler of the underworld. It was symbol of the night sun and one of the major deities in the Mayan pantheon. It was carved into their calendars. The *Balam* were the jaguar priests who officiated at the most important religious ceremonies. They are illustrated in human form, with the markings and claws of the jaguar on their hands and feet.

It was depicted on pots, as noted on shards found around the area of Copan in the Yucatan, and illustrated alongside the water lily; thus, it can be surmised that the Maya observed jaguar's love of water and made a link between the animal and water deities. Jaguar's fur was a symbol of royalty, just as the skin of the leopard was reserved for the chief or holy man of the tribe in Africa.

Elsewhere, the Inca of Peru also erected temples to the jaguar.

The Mexican Aztecs viewed time in terms of the ages of creation. The myth of the origin of the first epoch dealt with the destruction of man by jaguar. This was caused by Tezcatlipoca. Therefore, jaguar was associated with the smoking mirror and with all the things identified with that deity: destruction, war, blood, sacrifice, shamanism, prediction and scrying.

So jaguar represented all those things that the Christians would consider evil. Yet for aboriginal Central and South Americans, destruction was as much a part of life as creation was. Devastation and death were necessary elements in the cycle, just as winter's freeze is required for spring's rebirth. Thus for the Aztecs, the god to appease was not the one of creation, but the one who had the power over dissolution and demise.

Native Americans shared the commonly-held belief in sacrifice, that nothing was gained without loss, concession or renunciation. The first practitioners of self-immolation were the Mandan. Later this gift of blood became common in the Sun Dance as its practice swept the Plains up into Canada.

From the southwestern United States come two tales of jaguar. In one, jaguar shows a young skunk how to hunt. On their first trip out, jaguar kills a stag. Unfortunately he does not take time to explain that a hunter should never take on more than he can handle. The next time young skunk goes out to hunt, he tackles a deer and dies. The moral suggests that the fault lies not with the pupil but with the teacher.

In the second story, jaguar and deer end up sharing a home. Both choose particular sight for a teepee. During the day deer would work on it, clearing the area, and at night jaguar returns to discover someone has been helping him. The next morning deer awakes to find that someone has been helping him too. In the next few days the home is completed. Only then do deer and jaguar learn who the unseen helper is, and they agree to share the space. But jaguar kills a deer and brings it home for their first meal, and deer is sore afraid.

The following day, deer decides to teach jaguar a lesson. He coaxes a bull to gore a jaguar, which he then drags back for that evening's dinner. Now both are afraid. That night, deer's antlers strike the walls and the entire structure shakes. The noise is so loud that both stag and jaguar flee, going their separate ways. And since that time they have never lived together or co-operated again.

## MEDICINE AND POWER

| | |
|---|---|
| DIRECTION | North |
| ELEMENT | Underworld (Night Sun) |
| TRAITS | Night vision, roaring voice |
| ASSOCIATIONS | Smoking mirror, war, bravery, sacrifice, the art of prediction |

Jaguar is power and expression. It is also the gift of vision. Jaguar medicine conveys the ability to see at night and the vision to look into the dark part of the human soul. This cat, both literally and figuratively, knows the heart of man. Hence, jaguar is rarely fooled by people.

Particularly in its black phase, it sees the shadow inside each being. As the smoking mirror, Jaguar imparts prescience. The priests sought warnings of disaster rather than words of comfort. Thus, another animal rather than jaguar should be invoked if one is scrying for reassurance. Jaguar implies: 'Forewarned is forearmed.'

Often, others see jaguar as a threat. Jaguar is born with the knowledge of future events. Unlike lynx, this cat announces its mastery over the future with a roar. Jaguar is warrior, mirroring war with all its component parts: blood, pain, injury and death, the ultimate sacrifice. Its god would be appeased with nothing else than the still-pumping human heart. Thus, jaguar is destruction. Its medicine is not to be taken lightly. Neither is it received without sacrifice. It is a solitary medicine, which makes many others uncomfortable.

When jaguar appears, secrets are afoot – mysteries which pad silently and darkly across one's existence, unrecognized until they roar and ambush from above. Jaguar also gives its gift of sight. It is intuitive and reads people easily. Thus, jaguar is both a shout of alarm and a means of defence. Once exposed, the big cat bestows the strength for battle if battle is required.

In pre-Columbian days, jaguar's sight was invoked through the polished obsidian of the smoking mirror. The area was censed; the priest (often the king) stared into the glossy stone until he was blessed with a vision of the future. The original rite required a sacrifice. The priest's tongue was pierced with a stick, and blood flowed onto the burning coals and the black mirror. This ritual still exists today in the Yucatan region of Mexico. For those with the ability to scry, obsidian can be used, and red wine substituted for blood, as it has been for other rites. If obsidian is not available or if one is unable to find a polished stone, it is said that water (jaguar likes water) dyed black will achieve the same effect.

The jaguar individual is a loner – partly out of preference, largely because others find his or her presence disturbing. This person may be nominated as a leader, but a sacrifice is inherent in the medicine because the jaguar person loses his or her prized privacy. This person can be utterly ruthless as an adversary. Jaguar medicine will not be bested or ignored.

# LARK

American horned lark: *Eremophila alpestris*
Meadowlark: *Sturnella magna/neglecta*
European crested lark: *Galardia cristata*
Skylark: *Alauda arvensis*

## BIOLOGICAL INFORMATION

The horned lark measures 12 to 20 cm (7 to 8 inches). It is the only true American lark. The bird is brown with a black stripe below the eye and a crescent upon its breast. The black 'horns' are not always seen.

The meadowlark is more closely related to the starling (*Sturnella vulgaris*) than the lark. It is much more colourful than either the lark or the starling, and on the average bigger than the horned lark by about 2.5 to 7.5 cm (1 to 3 inches). The back is striped white and dark brown. The stripes extend up to the cap. The chest is a brilliant yellow, and marked with a black 'V'. The throat, too, is yellow; this colour covers the face. The eastern version displays a paler yellow than its western cousins.

The European crested lark is brown with darker markings. It is distinguished from other larks by its crown of 12 feathers which stick up from its head when it is agitated.

The skylark is dull brown, with darker stripes. Its crest is small, and is only visible when it is excited. The outer tail feathers are a tell-tale white.

### HABITAT

The horned lark inhabits the plains, fields, airports and beaches – generally, land that is open. It is found from the Arctic south to North Carolina, Missouri, coastal Texas and northern South America, Eurasia and North Africa.

The meadowlark stretches from coast to coast in the United States. The meadowlark also prefers open fields. It lays three to seven eggs and builds domed nests which are concealed by long grasses.

The crested is common in Europe – in fields and meadows. It moves to town during the winter. The crested lark is rare in England, however, found only when it has been blown off course.

The skylark was once so plentiful in Sussex that it was netted and sold at London markets. Now it is protected. The skylark prefers moors, downs, heaths and meadows, again preferring exposed areas where it can get a good view of the surrounding countryside.

### CHARACTERISTICS

The lark is known for its melodious whistle. It is also an excellent mimic. The lark eats insects, grains and seed. It is a ground nester, and makes its nest with woven grass. The nests may be found abandoned in February once the eggs have been destroyed by snow. Larks raise as many as three broods a year.

## LEGENDS AND TRADITIONS

GOD Itokaga or Okaga (Lakota/Dakota)

Itokaga was the 'giant of the south', one of the four winds and son of the 'mystery'[1] *Tate*. South was the direction of the sun and the bringer of warmth, light and life. It was associated with youth. Meadowlarks are one of Itokaga's *akicitas*, or messengers.

The meadowlark's medicine was women's medicine. It spoke of beauty, fidelity and a happy marriage. If a woman had lark medicine, she was fertile, fecund and sweet-tongued – traits lauded by men.

In one tale originating in the Old World tradition, eagle and meadowlark combine their forces to bring the latter's song to the gods. Eagle had the strength to make the climb to the heavens, but lark had the sweetness of temperament and personality to gain access to the Gods.

One Old World superstition claimed that any person who ate three lark's eggs for breakfast before the church bells rang would sing with a sweet voice.

## MEDICINE AND POWER

| | |
|---|---|
| DIRECTION | South |
| ELEMENTS | Air, Fire (sun) |
| TRAITS | Voice, sweet song, fidelity |
| ASSOCIATIONS | Good cheer, warm weather, spring, sun, happiness, melody |

When lark appears, expect good news. It's the bringer of abundance, plenty and the impending harvest. It could be that some project that has been pending will now come to fruition. Obstacles will suddenly disappear, or perhaps some new opportunity will present itself.

Meadowlarks have long been associated with love magic in Europe and the Americas. Thus, the bird augurs a new love interest. If already married, the meadowlark contains the promise of faithfulness and devotion. In the language of spring, it should bring new bloom to an old bush.

The lark could be considered the diurnal counterpart of the owl. The meadowlark is associated with the clarity of illumination or the sun. It imparts cheerfulness, with realism. In other words, the meadowlark individual does not view the world through rose-coloured glasses, but under the glaring light of day and still chooses to enjoy it.

Invoked during rituals, lark adds its voice. Its sweetness can open doors which would be otherwise closed. Its presence ensures honesty and constancy. Thus it would be good medicine or magic to call upon during a wedding ceremony – assuming one has a tolerant Justice of the Peace or minister.

The lark person has a sunny disposition and a musical voice. This individual is warm and attracts others easily. Meadowlark medicine people evoke love from others because they accept people as they are without question or prevarication.

# LIZARD

Family: *Drac*

## BIOLOGICAL INFORMATION

Lizards can be traced back to the Jurassic period. Like many of the broad groups mentioned in this book, the lizard ranges from as small as the American chameleon, 5 to 7.5 cm (2 to 3 inches) including the tail, to the giant Sumatra dragon which often exceeds 2.2 m (7 ft) in length. The latter have been known to capture, kill and eat children, and adults have often sacrificed a limb to the creature.

As cold-blooded animals, lizards are normally abroad during the day. In the early morning they can be found sunning themselves in order to get their blood circulating well enough for them to move about. Through the use of sun and shade, and sometimes water, the lizard regulates its body temperature. In more extreme climates, where it snows, reptiles hibernate during the winter.

### HABITAT

Lizards inhabit deserts, dry grasslands, rainforests (tropical and temperate), savannah, some mountain plateaux and rocky areas where they can perch and sun.

Lizards have adapted themselves to some of the harshest environments. They prefer warmer climates, and most can be found in a fairly broad band around the tropics. Still, some are equipped with a form of anti-freeze in their blood which allows them to survive in colder environments.

### CHARACTERISTICS

Lizards are primarily egg-layers. The female will dig a nest in an area of warm, soft, loose dirt or sand – in some cases, in the mouth of a large volcano. This keeps their eggs at a fairly even temperature. Like the alligator, gender is determined by the amount of warmth the eggs receive (males require more), which means the female can to a certain extent regulate the gender of her offspring.

## LEGENDS AND TRADITIONS

GODS Quezalcoatl

Lizard was one of the many symbols carved on the Pampas Colorado of Peru, a series of massive drawings created by the Nasca tribe, who predated the Inca by several thousand years. The Nasca farmed the fertile valley between the Pacific Coast and the Andes. It has been postulated that the lines and geometric designs of these drawings appear to be an earthly reflection of important points such as solstices or stellar/planetary paths. Many depict obviously important animals, such as the hummingbird and condor. The largest of all – at some 180 metres (590 ft) – depicts a lizard. The pictures have been linked to village communities and/or family lineage. If the size of the image is indicative of the emphasis the animal received or the status of the clan within the Nasca social structure, then lizard was unrivalled. On important dates, the clan or community would come and trace the animal's image in a procession. The presence of large amounts of pottery shards in the area indicate that offerings were made. Possibly Egyptian-style picnics were held where family members would visit the temple-tomb, or in this instance the sacred site, on a day-long outing to share their repast with their ancestors.

The Dakota believed that lizards conferred strength, since they were difficult to kill. They were considered impervious to hail since few bodies were found after such storms. So lizard could be invoked, or lizard skin worn as a talisman, to protect the warrior against bullets and arrows. It was believed that its scales worked like armour.

To many, lizard was the dreamer who sits absorbing the rays of the sun and conserving its energy until it is time to strike. It is an efficient predator who, when it decides to stir itself, moves swiftly. Therefore, lizard conferred speed, along with protection.

Others saw lizard as a visionary. This view was particularly strong in the southwestern United States where, in the desert climate, lizards were more numerous and much more often observed. Therefore, lizard medicine is that of the shaman.

Lizard's association with the sun also links it to fire, like salamander. This, in turn, suggests illumination of the soul.

Salamander and lizard have often been confused. Bestiaries of old state of salamander: *si casu undecumque inciderit in caminum*[1]: 'Salamander lived in flames.' But traditional heraldry rebuts this: '[saying that] a salamander can live in, and not be burned by the fire, is without foundation of truth, for the experiment has been tried.'[2] One wonders by whom. Still, heraldry made a similar connection between the two creatures, with the salamander often represented as a simple common lizard. Thus, the association between lizard and salamander, sun and fire, has been long established.

The distinguished Hugh Clark, author of *A Short Introduction to Heraldry* (published in 1810), was a bit more sanguine: 'Lizard, a small animal of the crocodile species. It delights in warm countries and is very common in Italy; they are found in trees in summer, where they make a noise like the croaking of frogs.'[3]

# MEDICINE AND POWER

| | |
|---|---|
| DIRECTION | South |
| ELEMENT | Fire (sun) |
| TRAITS | Cold-bloodedness, adaptability, the predator |
| ASSOCIATIONS | Swiftness, dreaming or dreamtime, and visions |

For the aboriginal Americans of the southwest, lizards carried the medicine of the visionary. Almost all tribes had some form of vision quest, during which an individual would try to contact the spiritual fathers – similar in many ways to what the aboriginal Australians called dream time.

Traditions varied, but most included some kind of ordeal. The Lakota would 'lament' for a vision, during which time they could neither eat nor drink. Some tribes made the trial more personal, in which the individual seeking insight dug his own grave and then spent the night in it unattended. Still other groups would have their initiates stand and stare at the sun, until nearly blinded, thus furnishing a blank canvas on the retina upon which the grandfathers could paint a vision.

Lizard medicine not only provided a link to the spirit world, it also imparted the ability to endure thirst, heat, sun – whatever was called for by the rite. The spirit world was considered just as real as our physical one.

Therefore, lizard could be invoked as a portal, or perhaps more appropriately the key with which to open the door. Yet this is an oversimplification of lizard's energies.

Most lizards are territorial. The chameleon is notorious for its colour changes, for reasons of camouflage or combat. The American chameleon, which is not a true chameleon, changes from green to brown to match its background. Other chameleons turn startling shades of red, blue, black, yellow or purple in response to attack. The loser signals its submission by muting its shades.

Many lizards will inflate their bodies, hoods or back spines (if they possess them) when they confront an adversary to make themselves appear bigger than they are. Usually it is the lizard with the best 'posturing' that wins the fight, although many breeds, like the dragons of

Sumatra, will battle till death, with the winner subsequently eating the loser.

This ability to change body size has both confounded and amazed the hunter, as a seemingly large animal suddenly deflates and slips into a crevice or a crack apparently too small to house it. Lizard brings the medicine of flexibility. The Florida chameleon brings invisibility. The other more brilliantly coloured types bestow adaptation.

Therefore, lizard is symbolic of physical transition or transformation as well as of shifting realities. It grants the ability to endure hardship. For the Lakota, lizard was valuable medicine to be called upon by the warrior for protection, and it still can be invoked for this today.

The lizard person may appear lazy until motivated to action, when chances are they will leave all others sitting astounded in the dust. These individuals posture when threatened, often inflating their importance, a trait which can alienate. The true chameleon can be colourful, but this can repel as often as it attracts. Despite their dreamy nature, such people are not to be underrated; they can and will strike, quickly and lethally.

As always when studying any broad group, such as the lizard family, it is best to look up the individual species once recognized and study its particular characteristics.

# LYNX/BOBCAT (WILDCAT)

Lynx: *Felis lynx*
Bobcat: *Felis rufus*

## BIOLOGICAL INFORMATION

The lynx is native to both Europe and America. It measures 74 to 107 cm (28 – 41 inches), with a tail between 5 and 14 cm (2 and 6 inches). The lynx weighs 5.1 to 18.1 kg (11 – 40 lb). The true lynx is buff or tawny, with blackish hairs interspersed throughout its coat. Its belly is a cinnamon brown. The short tail is tipped with black. It has long black ear tufts and large cheek ruffs, with black barring, which form a double pointed beard at the throat.

The thing that distinguishes the lynx from the smaller bobcat, besides habitat, is the lynx's long legs and big padded feet, which act like snowshoes in the Arctic winters. Overall it is a bigger animal and requires a larger territory.

The bobcat is exclusively American. It is 71 to 125 cm (28 to 49 inches) long. Its tail measures 10 cm to 20 cm (4 to 6 inches); it weighs 6.4 to 31 kg (14 1/8 to 68 1/4 lb). The bobcat is similar to the lynx, but smaller and lives further south than its Canadian cousin. The bobcat has a tawny coat, which gives it a ruddy appearance, and sports mottled black spots. The bobcat also has a winter phase, when the coat turns slightly grey. Its short tail, from which it gets its name, has two or three black bars, with a black tip above and white underneath. The face has thin black lines that extend to the cheek ruff.

Many people would have a hard time distinguishing between the two animals, and many mistakenly refer to bobcat as lynx and lynx as bobcat – and both as wildcat.

## HABITAT

The lynx lives *only* in deep forest. It has disappeared from western Europe completely, but can still be found in Poland, Russia and the Slavic countries. Lynx also inhabits much of Canada and Alaska. In the continental US, lynx live in small areas of Washington state, Oregon, Idaho, Montana and the Rocky Mountains. In the eastern US they can be found in upstate New York and throughout New England, as well as the extreme north of Michigan and Wisconsin.

The bobcat prefers scrubland and woodlands, although it can adapt to marshes, farmland and deserts. It is found from coast to coast in North America, and from Canada to Mexico, although it is sparsely distributed and completely absent in the area around the Midwest.

## CHARACTERISTICS

Like most cats, lynx is solitary. It often sticks to the trees; therefore it is rarely seen until it is too late. By day it will rest on a branch or a ledge waiting to leap down on its prey. Its large furred feet permit completely silent stalking. It is also a powerful swimmer. Its primary prey is the hare, so much so that when hare populations drop so do those of the lynx. It will also hunt birds, voles and mice. It scavenges the remains of dead deer or caribou. The lynx stores its kill, covering it with snow or ground litter. It mates in March to April, producing litters of one or two in May or June. The young stay with the mother throughout the first winter.

Likewise, bobcat is solitary and nocturnal. While both cats are good climbers, bobcat spends less of its time in trees and does not require them in order to live. Usually it perches in rocky alcoves waiting to pounce. Its mottled colouring provides good camouflage. The bobcat eats mainly rabbit and hare, although it will also feed on porcupine, mice, squirrels and bats. Males are sexually active all year; females come into season in February or March. Litters number between one and seven young.

## LEGENDS AND TRADITIONS

The Skidi Pawnee who, it is believed, originated in Mexico, worshipped the stars more than the sun. They honoured the cadent points of the compass (northeast, southeast, southwest, northwest) rather than the cardinal points. During the Morning Star ceremony, the northwest was marked with a cottonwood tree which was supposed to symbolize the wildcat.

The Lakota held cats in fear and awe. They believed that to kill or mutilate any kind of cat – mountain lion, bobcat or even the plain old domestic tabby – carried a curse. The culprit would have terrible things happen to him. Therefore, they avoided cats.

There's a rather loose affiliation in Europe between the lynx and gypsies, possibly because of their link with the occult. Some have claimed it is lynx rather than lion who is represented in the sphinx; hence the name. Although this theory has yet to be proven, it would suggest that lynx was once honoured in both Egyptian and Greek cultures.

## MEDICINE AND POWER

| | |
|---|---|
| DIRECTIONS | Northwest[1], North, East |
| ELEMENTS | Fire (Bobcat), Snow (Lynx) |
| TRAITS | Silence, excellent hearing and vision; the predator |
| ASSOCIATIONS | Lynx – stealth, invisibility, independence, mystery and adaptability; Bobcat – secrets, discretion, inner vision, camouflage |

Bobcat and lynx for the most part remain unseen, sticking to the background. The bobcat stays in rocky areas where its coat blends into the background or, like lynx, enters the trees so it can leap down on its quarry from above.

Therefore, bobcat/lynx are the essence of mystery. The lynx is the knower of secrets. According to David Carson and Jamie Sams, authors of *Medicine Cards*, lynx does not guard secrets, it simply knows them, and is reluctant to share its knowledge with others.

The presence of bobcat/lynx means something has been concealed. Lynx/bobcat medicine can impart vision which allows the individual to see beyond that which is immediately apparent.

Both bobcat and lynx spend most of the time alone; therefore, one of the life lessons they bring is isolation. These cats endow an individual with independence, but also loneliness. Bobcat/lynx is inscrutable. If lynx teaches at all, it is by example. These cats cannot be coerced into revealing their secrets.

Some say lynx/bobcat endows the individual with clairvoyance and farsightedness. Others say its medicine can be called upon to confer invisibility. Lynx medicine rather than bobcat is more often connected to the shaman, the holy man or woman of many races – the one who puts knowledge into practical use. This person will pass knowledge on to one he or she finds worthy.

Bobcat is keeper of occult knowledge and guardian of secrets. Thus, the individual who has bobcat as a totem is a mystic rather than a shaman, for this person would prefer to keep such knowledge to him- or herself. This person is a hermit and may be aloof and uncommunicative.

As one of the smaller cats, bobcat in particular often finds itself under attack from other predators such as bear, wolf or badger. Therefore, this medicine carries a penalty of retribution. Birds, jays and crows will attack bobcat if it gets too close to their nests. Similarly, they will raise the alarm when they notice its presence.

Ravens, who share the same regions as the lynx are more shy and leaves the big cat alone; therefore, although lynx medicine also carries the castigation of equals as a penance, it is less likely to be attacked by inferiors.

As knower of occult wisdom and secrets, lynx/bobcat represents both clairvoyance and clairaudience. This animal, once invoked, could allow you to look within people and situations.

Like many of the medicines that carry profound insight, night vision and the ability to see into the soul, lynx/bobcat medicine makes others discomfited, as if they instinctively know that the lynx/bobcat individual can read their deepest, darkest secrets with a single glance and judge them accordingly. And then, worse still, dismiss them as insignificant.

# MOLE

American mole: *Scalopus aquatus*
European mole: *Talpa europea*

## BIOLOGICAL INFORMATION

The American mole measures anywhere from 8.2 to 22.3 cm (3 to 9 inches) and weighs 82 to 140 g (3 – 5 oz). The mole has short, velvety grey to black fur, although it can be brown or even tan. One Mexican species is hairless. Their forefeet are broad; their palms are everted and their toes are slightly webbed. The snout is long and flexible.

The European mole has long, spade-like paws with long claws. It is dark and does not vary much in size, staying within a range of 12.5 to 16 cm (4 to 6 inches) long. It has a plush black coat and a barrel-shaped body.

### HABITAT

The mole prefers open fields, waste areas, lawns, farmland and meadows at both high and low altitudes. The European mole is found just about everywhere in Europe, even into Asia as far east as Mongolia. In the US the most common type of mole has the largest range, from the east coast to the Rockies; where these don't roam, another type fills the ecological gap, for example the star mole and hairy-tail of New England and Canada, or the Townsend mole of California.

### CHARACTERISTICS

The mole almost never comes above ground; it lives most of its life tunnelling beneath the surface where it eats insects, grubs, worms, larvae and roots. As a result its skeleton is constructed in such as way that its legs are digging mechanisms, and not designed for supporting weight.

The mole builds a network of tunnels about 30 cm (1 ft) from the surface, and extends it continuously. The mole uses its forefeet like spades and its hindlegs to shove dirt behind it as it moves along the system. Intermittently it will stop to push unwanted earth out. This results in the typical mole hill.

The creature is virtually blind; the eyes of the common mole can't even be seen. Other species have eyes that are the size of a poppy seed.

The female bears some two to seven young per year. The young leave the nest within 33 days, but remain under their mother's care for some time thereafter.

## LEGENDS AND TRADITIONS

The Tewa of California associated mole with their mythos about the world's creation. In the beginning, people lived beneath the earth. They did not know that their world was dark because they had never seen the light. Eventually, though, man began to wonder: 'Is there something else?'

Mole came along, digging his underground tunnel. The people asked him their question, and mole told them to follow. The tribe formed a line behind mole as he dug his way up to the surface. They emerged blinking into the light. The people had to pass dirt back in order to move ahead. The hole became blocked and they were never able to find their way back below again.

Thus, mole had secret knowledge which it shared with others. It was not only the pathfinder, but the pathmaker. Mole's gift to man was most profound. It was sunlight and illumination, wind and sky.

For the Lakota, mole was the caretaker of the earth. Blind, it perceived through touch, scent and taste all *Maka*'s (mother or grandmother earth's) movements. It was credited with the ability to sense any turbulence within the great mother's breast, such as earthquakes and volcanoes. Therefore, mole knows all mother earth's aches and pains, sorrows and woes. Likewise, this blindness implied that mole views the world without bias. Chief Archie Fire Lame Deer stated that mole never prejudged others.

In its underworld realm, mole was the master (or mistress) of root medicine. Mole medicine was often linked to women rather than men. Mole is associated with spiritual healing or the laying-on of hands, for mole senses affliction through touch. Also it brings with it a knowledge of herb lore.

This ability to exist without emerging into the light of day, except by accident, also astounded the Europeans. Hugh Clark states in his work *A Short Introduction to Heraldry*: 'Mole is formed to live wholly under ground, as if nature meant that no place should be left entirely untenanted ... We should imagine that the life of this quadruped must be the most solitary; but ... we discover no signs of distress or wretchedness in this creature.'[1]

In England, mole is thought to bring good luck, unless it digs up dirt too close to a home. This portends the death of a family member. The person indicated depends on the room in closest proximity. If the mound of earth appears near the kitchen, the wife will die.

Carrying the front paws of a mole is supposed to protect against illness – except perchance for the mole, who would probably be feeling a bit puny after such surgery. The paws are supposed to be particularly good for relieving the pain of toothache and menstrual cramps.

## MEDICINE AND POWER

| | |
|---|---|
| DIRECTION | West |
| ELEMENT | Earth |
| TRAITS | Depth, sensory perception, touch |
| ASSOCIATIONS | Earth wisdom, healing with roots and spiritual healing, self-reliance and cheer |

Mole imparts prescience, the ability to predict the future, through its closeness to earth. This is most likely to come in the form of clairsenscience. People with clairsenscience feel things; their intuition is marked.

Mole is considered the guardian of the nether regions. It has the ability to find the hidden bounties of the earth. Mole exhibits sensitivity to touch and vibration and understands energy fluxes. Some see mole, like bear, as introspection. It has the capacity to regard the world only in black and white. Therefore, mole endows the individual with the knowledge of right and wrong, good and evil.

Mole medicine should be invoked if one needs to feel connected to mother earth. Mole imparts groundedness, and its appearance unbidden indicates that this need is essential for the well-being of the individual.

Mole can confer the knowledge of roots and herbs. In Native American tradition, roots or herbs could not be plucked unless prayers were said to the plant, mother earth and the animal who claimed dominion over the same. Mole's arrival indicates a time of expanded learning in this area. If one has an interest in such lore, call upon mole.

Mole has other abilities, for example the ability to dig things up. Therefore, mole can mean something is about to be unearthed or that something needs to be. It could initiate a period of self-examination – for remember, mole does not judge others. Perhaps it is time to expose anxieties and fears to the cold light of day.

Vicariously, mole might be urging a person to emerge from their hole into the beauty and bounty of the earth and sun. Neither needs be a painful process because mole also gives self-reliance and joy.

The person with mole medicine would pretty much 'hole up'. This individual is a hermit and generally content to stay that way. Mole medicine people will be attracted to alternative therapies, particularly those that include the use of plants – such as traditional Chinese Medicine, herbal therapy and aromatherapy. Blind mole also imparts the healing touch.

The mole knows things without seeing them, but unlike many people who carry animal medicine with predictive capabilities, mole normally does not elicit discomfort from others because he or she keeps these impressions quiet unless they will help a person to heal.

# MOOSE (EUROPEAN ELK)

*Alces alces*

## BIOLOGICAL INFORMATION

The moose's antler spread is between 1.2 and 1.5 metres (4 and 5 ft). Their height at the shoulders is 1.95 to 2.25 metres (6½ to 7½ ft). Males weigh 405 to 630 kg (900 to 1,400 lb), females 315 to 495 kg (700 to 1,100 lb).

The moose is the largest deer in the world. The American moose is the European elk by another name. About the size of a horse, moose have high humped shoulders, a stubby tail and long legs. The muzzle is huge and pendulous with a large dewlap hanging under the chin. The antlers are massive and broadly flattened.

### HABITAT

Moose inhabit spruce forests, spreading swamps or peat bogs, and aspen and willow thickets. In the US, moose are found in New England, around the Great Lakes and in the Rockies; they exist all across Canada. The European elk is limited to the eastern and northern forests of Scandinavia, Lithuania, Estonia and Russia. Since the 1970s, the population has been moving further south as new habitats become available.

### CHARACTERISTICS

The moose is actually something of an aquatic creature. It will stand almost neck-deep in water grazing on water lilies and other aquatic plants. Moose browse on woody plants too. The moose swims well and runs at speed of 56 kph (35 mph) through the forest. It is unpredictable and ill-tempered, and has been known to attack stationary cars or to 'tree' a man (waiting beneath for the person who has run up there for safety) for several hours.

Moose never form herds. The females live with their young and the males travel singly. Not even in winter do they bond together. Unlike most deer, the bulls do not acquire a harem, but will stay with a single cow for a week and then move on to another, in a form of serial monogamy. They breed in September and October. The female usually has one calf – although two are not unknown – after eight to nine months' gestation. At six months the young are weaned. Just before the birth of the next calves, they are driven off by their mother. The male has nothing to do with care of the young and will chase its own offspring off its turf if they should ever meet.

## LEGENDS AND TRADITIONS

Moose was considered one of the most powerful medicines to have. In Alaska, the Athapaskan tribe linked moose with raven. Hunters prayed to the sentinel, raven, to find moose. Each moose that appeared was considered a gift of raven.

The Algonquin referred to moose as twig-eaters, *mong-soa*, which was adapted by the European settlers to the present American word 'moose'. The term has been picked up in the United Kingdom and seems to be almost universally accepted.

The Algonquin carved moose antlers into tampers used to push the sacred tobacco into the pipe. Antlers were also employed as other tools. The woodland Dakota used deer and elk antlers as scrapers for hide, and the Algonquin probably use moose antlers the same way.

It's reasonably safe to assume that in the far north, where moose abound, it replaced buffalo in myth and legend. Elsewhere, it replaced elk. Therefore it was considered to have both male and female energy. The Ojibwa considered moose a great warrior, and its medicine was invoked for battle. Many viewed moose as 'grandfather deer' – the wise older man who could take the younger bucks under his care and guide them. Its wisdom was considered more stolid and more stable than that of either elk or deer because it took a lot to scare moose off; they were just as likely to confront an adversary than run.

The Montagnais-Naskapi of Canada practise *scapulamancy*. The scapula of the moose was often used for this. After being thrown into the fire, the shaman would read the cracks, burns and breaks on the scapula in order to predict the future. So moose can convey prescience and foreknowledge.

## MEDICINE AND POWER

| | |
|---|---|
| DIRECTIONS | North, East |
| ELEMENTS | Earth, Water |
| TRAITS | The only truly solitary 'deer'; serial monogamy, strength and agility |
| ASSOCIATIONS | Male and female energy, speed and stamina |

Moose is linked with both the masculine and the feminine; this varies depending on the tribe. It is linked with the masculine for its size and mass. The male in particular can be aggressive. It has been known to charge a large parked vehicle for no apparent reason. Similarly, it will even attack an armed man.

The male gives a 'bugle' call to announce his presence, much as the Native American men would often announce their arrival home from a war party with a whoop and a song of their exploits.

On the other hand, moose is associated with the elements of water and earth. As receptive and representative of emotions and fertility, it has long been connected with women. The female moose is a good mother. The female bears no antlers, therefore she is unlikely to challenge or charge as the male does unless her young are threatened, when she uses her sharp hooves and lethal kick for defence.

Thus, the associations made with moose are diverse and dependent entirely upon the culture's point of view.

Where elk was not found, then moose replaced elk as male sexuality. In this form, moose endows courage and authority, along with the less lovable trait of unpredictability. As the largest ruminant, it was associated with grandfather warriors, suggesting the confidence born of wisdom and experience which results in self-esteem.

As female energy, moose represents fecundity and fertility. Female moose medicine enables plumbing the depths of emotion to find nourishment. Yet she imparts groundedness. However, moose does not possess a sense of community; even a sense of family is limited to the female of the species. Here we find the negative side of the feminine as the mother. When it comes time to breed again, she actively drives her calf away, to the point of using violence against it.

Moose medicine gives strength and endurance in times of emotional turbulence. As one of the major teachers, its appearance suggests that some sort of life lesson is on the way. Its association with warfare implies this may come in the form of a contest. Moose is a mighty warrior and its courage can be called upon during any conflict. It may portend a time when one will be called upon to defend oneself. However, it may appear as a warning against boasting about one's accomplishments.

If the female appears, this indicates fertility and growth. It can signify a pregnancy. It may be an emotional time, but it will also be a nourishing and productive one. Despite all the positive manifestations, the female may also symbolize the need for independence. Perhaps it is time to kick the youngsters from the wallow.

The moose individual is stubborn; they can be bellicose and belligerent if they find someone annoying. At other times, they can be patient, taking the time to teach the young a new and important skill. They will always be unpredictable about how they choose to react. Thus, others may find this person difficult to approach. Similarly, the moose individual is independent. They will possess stamina and knowledge which they impart to others. They are good parents, but stern disciplinarians.

# MOTH

*Lepidoptera (papillonoidea)*

## BIOLOGICAL INFORMATION

Usually, the moth is a creature of the night. The category of *papillonoidea* includes moths and butterflies. The moth has a thick, furry body to the butterfly's hard shell-encased body. When at rest, the moth's wings lie flat; the butterfly's stay upright. It is the moth, not the butterfly, which makes a cocoon of spun silk. The butterfly's chrysalis is made of a more chitinous material.

### HABITAT

Moths are found everywhere but the polar regions. Both moths and butterflies can be found as far north as the Arctic tundra; however they are most numerous in warmer climates.

### CHARACTERISTICS

There are a few daytime flyers in the moth family, but they are rare. The empire moth is one example of the former. With wings of orange and brown, it is the exception to the normally bland colouration of the moth.

With the night flyers such bright pigmentation would be lost on predators, who must rely on infrared vision or sound. During the day moths sleep. With wings flat against the bark of trees, their dull brown hue provides effective camouflage.

# LEGENDS AND TRADITIONS

GODS Wakinyan, Yum, Yomni or Yumni (Dakota/Lakota), Medusa/Gorgon (Greek)

Moth is included here separately from butterfly because the powers or medicine attributed to it are quite different to those attributed to butterfly. Similarly, it is only the moth that makes a cocoon, which has a special significance of its own.

The whir of the moth reminded the Lakota of the sound of the wind. Therefore, moth was associated with the whirlwind which cannot be contained. The whirlwind was known as *Yum* (Yumni, Yomni), the fifth son of *Tate*, the four winds, and the only one who did not have a direction to call his own. Yum was the lord of games, gambling and love.

However, despite this relationship, moth, or more importantly cocoon, was linked with the thunderbeings and war. Native American warriors often wore cocoons attached to their clothing. It was believed that this imparted protection and conferred the power of the whirlwind upon the wearer. The warrior was transformed into the destructive force of the wind.

Even the swirling silken design of the cocoon of the moth suggested whirlwind. Therefore, a cocoon was often depicted on war regalia, to grant the mystical power of confusing the mind of an enemy. The symbol entailed a diamond or sometimes elliptic shape through which several diagonal crosses or Xs would be drawn, to represent the shifting direction of the wind.

Cocoon as whirlwind was invisible, and one of many beliefs shared by tribes was that carrying the symbol of a cocoon or the actual cocoon itself would make them vanish. An unfortunate belief at times, for on more than one occasion when the Native Americans thought themselves to be so protected, they were wiped out by the 'long knives' – the US Army.

The tribes of the coastal northwest also used the cocoon in their ceremonies and rites. They made rattles of empty cocoons into which they would insert seeds. These they strung into position along a central axis. The rattle sent the voice of the cocoon, and their prayers, unto the heavens.

The European associations with cocoon are comparable, in that the cocoon was seen as a symbol of the sacred spiral; thus, it mimicked the same design as the whirlwind. It speaks of both the stable centre and the unstable exterior. A correlation could be found in mythology between the whirlwind and Medusa the Gorgon. Therefore, the link remained, as it did with butterfly, with transformation, death, rebirth and regeneration.

Superstition reflects these connections with death and renewal, the old and dying, and the new: a moth fluttering into the house portends death in the household in the next year. Moth was also associated with the souls of the dead. In some areas of the Old World, cocoons were destroyed. Elsewhere such an action was taboo. A moth flying out of darkness means a letter or some news is on its way. Thus, moth's attraction to light was seen as both a blessing and a curse.

## MEDICINE AND POWER

| | |
|---|---|
| DIRECTION | Centre |
| ELEMENT | Air (whirlwind) |
| TRAITS | Wind, flight, night |
| ASSOCIATIONS | Protection, invisibility, love, games, darkness, death |

The moth is associated with night flight, the ability to move unseen. It was the wind that rattled through the trees and muddled the direction of sound. In the latter function it worked particularly well, as whirlwind blows in all directions simultaneously.

The cocoon had all the passive traits of spider's web, which allowed bullets and arrows to pass through and still remain more or less intact. It also held some more proactive traits, such as the capacity to bewilder. Its energies are generally destructive and would be called upon in case of battle or attack. In a way, the Old World tradition and New World philosophy meet, because what is war if not death and upheaval?

In its more positive manifestation, moth (cocoon) can be called upon in cases of love. If an individual stands in the centre of the buffeting whirlwind, the object of his affection will be blown to him. So whirlwind was love medicine.

Yumni, and to a lesser extent the cocoon, ruled over games, for games, like love, bring excitement, the rush of blood in the veins and the thrill of the chase. In loss, which shamed the Native American, came the undoing or death. In European hunting parlance, the 'unmaking'. So Yum was invoked for gambling, but appears to be as fickle as our own lady luck.

The main purpose of cocoon and moth is to bemuse, bewilder, allow one to move like the wind – loudly or softly, but almost always unseen. If it appears, something may be veiled from the observer. It may have come to clear away the fog of confusion. The destructive force of the wind is also its cleansing force, which clears the path to spring's renewal.

# MOUSE

Family: *Heteromyidae*

## BIOLOGICAL INFORMATION

The mouse is 10.7 to 14.3 cm (4 to 5 inches) long; its tail measures 4.8 to 6.3 cm (about 2 inches). Mouse boasts a weight of 6 to 10 g (1/4 – 3/8 oz). Usually the coat is darker above, fading to a lighter colour below. The fur may be grey blending to buff or brown to white. Some mice, like the plains harvest mouse, may present a black dorsal stripe, or they may have tufted tails. Such adornments are unusual, though: because of its size, the mouse is not a creature that wants to be noticed. The common house mouse is a dirty black or grey. The mouse family is the largest family of mammals on the planet. They comprise some 19 genera and 70 species in North America alone.

### HABITAT

The mouse is found in every available habitat – desert, grassland, woods and forest, mountain and meadow.

### CHARACTERISTICS

Mice breed throughout the year, and in warmer climates are able to produce between two and seven litters per annum. Mice are good climbers. Most breeds are so similar that the only way to tell one from another is by looking at their bone structure.

Most mice eat grain, fruit and nuts. They construct nests in protected hollows, gathered leaves, underground, inside buildings or inside walls. In other words, they are able to take advantage of almost every possibility.

Some have cheek pouches. They will gather and store grain like chipmunks, squirrels or gophers. Thus, they speak of forethought and pragmatism.

## LEGENDS AND TRADITIONS

The Lakota believed that the mouse, like gopher, nibbled at the moon and therefore was responsible for her monthly disappearance. Thus, mouse reminds us that even the smallest things can be destructive. Mouse and rats can come in plagues and have in the past wiped out entire populations.

Often the young man about to go crying (or lamenting) for a vision quest was enjoined not to ignore the tiny mouse at his feet while searching the sky for an eagle or a hawk. Mouse has a power all its own.

In Europe and North Africa, mice were the symbol of bad times, bringer of pestilence and plague. Indeed, most agrarian societies viewed mouse as a pest. In one Celtic legend, the mage Cwawl sent mice to ruin Manawydon's wheat crops as revenge. The animals were so numerous they devastated the land.

## MEDICINE AND POWER

| | |
|---|---|
| DIRECTION | South |
| ELEMENT | Earth |
| TRAITS | Highly developed senses, reproduction |
| ASSOCIATIONS | Organization, specialization, close scrutiny and examination, plague |

The people of the regional northwestern United States thought of mouse as a messenger. A prolific animal which usually makes its home in the ground, mouse is representative of mother earth.

Many mice are nocturnal, hence they have lunar associations. Indeed, their activities and their reproductive cycle seem to be regulated by the moon. Mouse's time is late summer. It is associated with the harvest because many nests are disturbed during the process, therefore they are more visible at that time of year as they prepare for winter.

For all these reasons, mouse is associated traditionally with plenty and abundance, and their ruination. In its lunar attachment it means fecundity and fertility. However, mouse also contributes to destruction.

Mouse is the messenger of earth. Where the species makes itself apparent, bounty follows. It can also be a harbinger of doom, for when mouse vanishes from an area, it means the place is unhealthy. Likewise, mouse can bring disaster. A single family of mice can consume or contaminate grain that would otherwise feed a human for months.

If mouse is a threat, it is usually an invisible one, for it is rarely seen unless caught unawares. Most people do not know they have mice until they find visual clues – gnawed boxes, the splintered hole in the floorboards.

Therefore, mouse is intelligent, and as anyone who has laid mouse traps can attest, quite often mouse can outwit man and his devices. This leads us to mouse's most current identification: scrutiny. Mouse examines things. Because of its size, it examines things closely. It hoards things, as does squirrel, but it seems better able to keep track of its cache. Thus, mouse has the ability to organize. Mouse might be compared to the specialist of today. This leaves mouse unable to comprehend 'the big picture'.

This latter meaning seems to be relatively new. Reaching back in time, mouse was associated with destruction, often cursed as a plague against humanity. Its productivity – the ability to breed six to seven times a year – was not exactly viewed with favour.

Yet if one wants to get close to an issue, mouse medicine provides the sight needed. If overwhelmed by details and minutiae, call upon mouse. It can help one set things in their proper order. Mouse moves about unnoticed by humanity even when living in the same home.

Mouse comes when attention should be paid to details. It suggests loss, usually through ignorance. Therefore, when mouse appears, see what may have escaped notice. If the pieces all seem to be properly arranged, then perhaps one should step back and see the overall perspective. Since mouse is usually unable to observe the big picture, it could be that individual pieces have been arranged incorrectly.

Mouse people could be good scouts or spies, but they are unable sometimes to grasp the overall view. Therefore, this person needs another to lead. The individual with mouse medicine is happiest when he or she is organizing, categorizing or cataloguing the component parts. As a child, this would be the sibling who decides to take a watch apart to see how it works, but doesn't bother to put it back together again. The destructive power of mouse does not come from malice but from ignorance of how their actions influence others – usually because when mouse goes about its business it is oblivious to other people's presence.

# OPOSSUM

*Didelphis virginiana*

## BIOLOGICAL INFORMATION

About the size of the average house cat, the opossum measures 64.5 to 101.7 cm (25 to 40 inches). Its tail adds another 25.5 to 53.5 cm (10 to 21 inches) to its length. It weighs between 1.8 and 6.3 kg (4 and 14 lb). Its coat appears a grizzled white, with long white hairs covering black-tipped fur underneath. In some areas there are populations of brown and black opossum. The opossum has a long, furless prehensile tail. Its feet have a digit that acts like an opposable thumb, allowing it to clasp things.

### HABITAT

The opossum is adaptable to most environments, but it prefers places that provide some cover such as open woods, brushy wasteland and farmland. The opossum's range covers most of the eastern US, except the far northern states of Maine, Minnesota and Michigan.

### CHARACTERISTICS

The opossum is solitary and nocturnal. Its life expectancy in the wild is about 1 year; in captivity, 10 years. It is omnivorous, eating insects along with grains and berries. When threatened, the opossum will roll up and play dead – the American expression 'playing possum' survives to this day. It even has a special gland that exudes a musk which mimics the smell of death. It is an efficient runner, able to accomplish high speeds in quick sprints. Similarly, it is a good climber. Depending on the size of its adversary, the opossum will also feign an attack. It hisses, arches its back and opens its mouth wide to reveal all 50 teeth.

Often opossum is depicted hanging by its tail, but the tail is not strong enough to support the animal's weight, and would be torn out of its socket if this were attempted. Instead, opossum uses its tail to grasp and for balance, which allows the opossum to extend its reach.

The opossum is the only North American marsupial. Gestation takes about 14 days. The female carries and nurses her young in her pouch until they are about two to three months old; then they are carried on her back for another two months.

## LEGENDS AND TRADITIONS

The Cherokee have a story to explain the opossum's prehensile tail. Once, when the earth was young, opossum had a fine bushy tail, like raccoon or squirrel. But opossum was vain, and soon everyone grew tired of having to admire possum's tail. Finally rabbit decided to trick opossum. Rabbit sent his friend cricket over to style opossum's tail. Conceited opossum fell asleep as cricket brushed the thick hair. When he awoke, his tail was wrapped in ribbon – to protect it for the pow wow that was going to be held later that day, rabbit said. When the dance came, opossum uncovered his tail to reveal something as bald and scaly as a snake's. Possum fainted dead away with shame, which he still does every time he gets surprised or embarrassed to this day.

This story illustrates the Native American view about vanity, pride and cowardice.

The European settlers had a more forgiving attitude towards opossum. They noted its ingenuity and versatility, and its strong maternal instinct. They developed an admiration for the little creature that is reflected in children's stories of today.

## MEDICINE AND POWER

| | |
|---|---|
| DIRECTION | East |
| ELEMENTS | Earth, Air |
| TRAITS | Physiological control, dexterity, the connection with trees (arboreal traits) |
| ASSOCIATIONS | Strategy or strategic retreat, protection, maternal instinct |

Tiny opossum is a master strategist, with more than one way to defend itself. Of course, it is notorious for playing dead and even has enough body control so that, when it drops, it emits the chemical smells of death. When the predator catches a whiff of rot, it backs away. As soon as the predator is thus put off, the opossum escapes.

Added to its repertoire of defences is opossum's speed, ability to climb and art of bluffing with a mock attack. The opossum will try all these strategies before it opts for the death pose. Thus, opossum shows wit and wisdom in immediately assessing the strategy most appropriate to a situation. This is one of opossum's greatest gifts.

Opossum's paws can grip. The tail also acts as another grasping mechanism. This gives opossum balance and allows it to stretch and clutch things that would normally be beyond its reach. Thus, opossum medicine provides agility, equilibrium and stability – and in addition the power to stretch one's capabilities in order to attain a specific goal.

Opossum is probably the best mother of the American menagerie. Not only does the opossum not let its children out of its sight, but it never loses contact with its young.

Call upon the opossum when under stress. Even in the human animal, the body responds with the fight-or-flight instinct. Opossum medicine helps one to evaluate a situation correctly in order to decide what the proper response should be. Opossum medicine will tell the individual whether to fight, flee, or play dead.

In a predicament, and in life in general, possum imparts balance in all its many forms. Its medicine includes the ability to grasp things, both physically and mentally. If a person has been striving to achieve something without success, call upon possum. It helps one stretch that little bit further in order to attain one's goals. All told, this is not bad medicine to have. Invoke possum to gain equilibrium coupled with flexibility, dexterity and sagacity.

The woman with opossum medicine will be a solicitous mother and extremely protective of her young. For both male and female, possum medicine bestows the capacity to understand an event immediately – coupled with the knowledge of how best to cope with it. This person will be well balanced, if appearing a bit slow to react. However, this is a misapprehension. When at rest, possum conserves energy, but once it is time to act, possum acts not only quickly but appropriately.

# OTTER

American: *Lutra canadensis*
European: *Lutra lutra*

## BIOLOGICAL INFORMATION

The otter has a long body and a thick tail that acts as a rudder. It measures 89 to 131 cm (3 to 4¼ ft), with a tail of 30 to 50 cm (12 to 20 inches). The weight averages between 5 and 13.6 kg (11 and 30 lb). The Amazon region boasts the largest otter, at 1.9 to 2.8 metres (6 to 8 feet) from tip to tail. With webbed feet and strong legs, the otter is well adapted for aquatic life. The fur is brown, although it looks black when wet. The sea otter has a yellowish head and neck. At one time it was believed that these were two separate species. Recent studies indicate that they are basically the same breed which has adjusted to different environments.

### HABITAT

Otters inhabit bays and estuaries, river banks (especially in uninhabited areas), and the areas near ponds or lakes in wooded areas. In the US, the 'freshwater' otter is concentrated in the extreme northwest and north-east, and in the southeast. It ranges far across Canada. Its seaborne brother swims in the Pacific down through California.

The otter, after being driven close to extinction in England, is slowly being reintroduced from Scotland and Wales. Similarly, the otter of California's Pacific coast was almost lost through destruction of its native habitat as a result of offshore drilling. The otter is now a protected species, with the oil companies having been forced to revise their procedures to prevent spillage. Consequently, the numbers of the California sea otter are on the rise.

### CHARACTERISTICS

The otter makes its dens in the soft mud of a river bank. It is a playful creature. Often mothers and cubs will be seen romping along the river bank.

Otter is also an extremely energetic creature – it has to be in order to maintain an appropriate body temperature during the long periods of time it spends in cold water. It is a skilful predator, yet it must hunt for most of its waking hours just to maintain its weight.

## LEGENDS AND TRADITIONS

The Chippewa Midiwiwin Society honoured otter, and used its fur for their pouches. The initiation ceremony into the Society was supposed to instill otter spirit power on the initiate. The medicine bags contained a shell that was associated with immortality. Tribes of the American midwest eventually adopted this ritual. Elsewhere in the Midwest, the otter and bearskin cloak was a sign of high rank for the Fox and Sauk tribes of Illinois. It was specifically reserved for the chieftain.

Otter and seal were both hunted by the sea-faring, boat-building tribes of California. The Chumash of the middle region were renowned for their spears and boats which had been adapted for hunting otter and seal. Further north, the Tlingit of British Columbia had two main moiety which were further subdivided into clans, one of which was otter. The Yup'ik believed that otter had *yua*, a human spirit, and could take on human form. This is similar to the Scottish belief about selkies and seal.

Often, otter medicine was considered women's medicine. As a tender and playful mother, otter was to be emulated by women. Otter medicine endowed its holder with the ability to heal. The healing of otter was more gentle than badger's, which was used to dig disease from the system. Most women's medicine relied on herbs. The holy woman whose mentor was otter would carry an object that came from otter – its fur, teeth or claws, and her medicine bag, in which she carried either herbs or a pipe, would most likely be made of otter fur.[1]

Not all tribes thought of otter medicine as strictly female, however. The Lakota honoured otter's courage as a masculine trait. The Ptan was a warrior society of the otter. There was a specific rite to sanctify the otter skin, which warriors would use to cover the sacred hoop, a symbol of the sun and of years. Meanwhile the person who wore a cape of otter skin indicated his mastery over both water and land.

The European view is little different to the Lakota. The hunter knew otter to be a worthy adversary when cornered, and therefore the otter's traits were 'masculine', including bravery, stoicism, loyalty and obedience. Otter was equated with dog. In this instance heraldry must be quoted directly because it seems to crystallize the European perspective: 'The otter, when tamed, will follow his master like a dog, and even fish for him. An old otter will never give up while it has life; nor make the last complaint, though wounded ever so much by the dogs, or even transfixed by a spear.'[2]

## MEDICINE AND POWER

| | |
|---|---|
| DIRECTION | North |
| ELEMENTS | Water, Land (sun) |
| TRAITS | Suppleness, playfulness, excellent swimming, activity |
| ASSOCIATIONS | Joy, femininity, persistence, gentleness; also masculinity, courage, constancy |

The otter is at home in both earth and water. Living in these receptive elements, the otter became associated with women's medicine. The otter has a strong sense of family. The otter is open, yet protective of its young. Otter teaches through play and fun; even work appears jolly when otter does it. This animal is easy and relaxed in its manner even when it is hunting.

Its masculine traits include bravery and stoicism. Otter is an ardent friend and supporter, extremely loyal. Otters of both genders have mettle. Otter will never go out of its way to do battle. Once challenged, though, it is fierce, willing to fight to the death to guard its young.

Otters were also credited with being the organizers of the animal kingdom, perhaps because of their elaborate dens. Their homes are sectioned, like the modern house, into rooms. Food is kept separate from the sleeping quarters and the toilet away from the other two areas.

Lithe, agile otter speaks of the balance between masculine and feminine energies. Otter melds grace with courage. The spirit of fun is coupled with the ability to work hard. Young and old otters both find joy in life. Otter medicine teaches people to share, imparting generosity.

Otter helps one access the inner child. It should be invoked when life turns to drudgery, for otter makes light of everything – especially work. Otter encourages humour and laughter. Otter nurtures the experience and expression of joy. Its power can also be summoned in times of trouble, for along with a sense of fun, otter grants pluck and tenacity when one is confronted with life's struggles.

When otter's around, expect an increasing sense of freedom, lightness, and delight at being alive. Its appearance is often an indication of happier times coming.

The otter person is energetic. This individual has calories to burn. This is the oft-envied friend who can eat anything and still stay slim. To their more lethargic companions they can seem hyperactive and their lifestyle quite frenzied and frenetic. Yet they are more organized than appearance suggests. They also have a sense of humour and a sense of fun. Their jokes, though, do not detract from others. People with otter medicine exhibit healing touch. They love water, and actually prefer to swim beneath the surface rather than over it.

# OWL

Family: *Strigidae*

## BIOLOGICAL INFORMATION

There are 130 species of true owl worldwide. Seventeen of these live in North America. These include the barred, the boreal, burrowing, great-horned, screech, short-eared and snowy owls, to name only a few. The measurements in size range from that of the great horned owl (10 cm/25 inches) to the tiny sparrow-sized elf-owl. The boreal owl has similar dimensions to a blackbird, while the great grey owl has a wing span of 1.5 metres (5 ft). There are no less than 12 species of barn owl, each with the distinctive heart-shaped facial disk.

### HABITAT

The owl is found mainly in forests, but some Old World species have adapted to grasslands. The eagle owl is native to central Asia. The little owl was introduced into Great Britain at the end of the 19th century. It lives in both woodlands and urban environments. The beautiful white snowy owl prefers open country; it is rarely seen perched in trees. Instead it rests and nests on the ground. The burrowing owl lives in the plains and desert. Again, between the various breeds the entire North American continent is covered. Some form of owl can be found throughout Europe, the Middle East, northern Africa and Asia. Very few areas have escaped exploitation by these birds.

## CHARACTERISTICS

Most owls are nocturnal. The snowy owl, however, is a creature of daylight – as is the eagle owl. Some owls, such as barn owls, are equipped to hunt in either day or night. As the name suggests, the barn owl often makes its home in the eaves or rafters of barns or other vacant buildings.

The true owls use the abandoned nests of other birds which they have adapted to their needs, although sometimes they will roost in the hollows of trees or lay their eggs in the crotch between two branches. Despite their lack of engineering skills, owls are good parents, working together to rear their young.

All owls are fearsome predators. They eat small mammals such as mice, rats and voles, and other birds. Farmers sometimes view owls as pests because they eat other birds. However, owls prefer to consume pests and vermin rather than chickens, thus they keep the rat and mice populations under control. The desert species rely on snakes and reptiles for feed.

Owls' feathers are edged in such away to give them completely silent flight. They are renowned for their hearing, able to pick out the location of prey from sound alone. An owl can hear the rustle of a vole under 10 cm (4 inches) of snow from 100 metres (283 ft) away. The entire head is built to receive sound. The bowl-shaped fan of feathers around the eyes and face scoops up noise. The ears are positioned directly behind the eyes in a central location. (The feather tufts of the great horned owl and the short-eared owls do not mark the location of their ears.) The flexibility of the neck allows the owl to face any sound directly. The ears are slightly asymmetrical, with one placed marginally higher than the other, giving owls the ability of echo-location. In an instant, the owl triangulates the direction and the distance of a sound and pounces upon its prey.

The owl's eyes are fixed in the sockets. An owl cannot swing its pupils from left to right. Thus, these birds need this range of motion in the neck and supple spine in order to look from side to the side. They cannot, as superstition suggests, twist their heads all the way round; they just move so quickly that they create the illusion of doing so to the human eye.

## LEGENDS AND TRADITIONS

GODDESSES Athena (Greek), Diana (Roman)

The screech owl of the Yucatan was called 'the moan bird' by the Mayan people. It was associated with death. Both the screech owl and the great horned owl appear in the surviving Mayan codices – scrolls written in the Mayan pictorial system.

The shamans of the Skidi Pawnee wore owlskin headdresses. In so doing they became messengers of the Evening Star during their ceremonies. The Morning Star ritual reenacted the sacred marriage between the Morning Star and Evening Star. So, the holy woman wore the feathers of the hawk or eagle, since she represented the appearance of day, while the holy man dressed as owl, symbol of the night.

The Menominee included the owl in a legend that describes a contest between day and night. Rabbit, representing light, challenged owl, keeper of the dark, to a magical contest. The other animals came to cheer for their champion, for some, like owl, loved night best while others preferred the sun.

The owl cried 'Untipaqkot' (night) to emphasize its power over day. Eventually, as the battle continued owl grew tired and confused. He forgot and screeched 'Wabon' (day). So night lost power over day, but rabbit gave darkness half the day, so the animals who preferred the night might know comfort too.

The Lakota had an Owl Society. These warriors were primarily night fighters. They wore dark rings around their eyes to indicate that they were willing to do battle at night. The dark rings also conferred upon them owl's sight.

The Sioux agreed with the Pawnee that owl was a messenger. As with most histories that come from a verbal tradition, there are variations. In earlier works, those written in the 1800s, owl was *akicita* (messenger) to *Unktehi*, the first of all evil beings, who was always fighting *Wakinyan* (the thunderbeings). Elsewhere it was reported that *Waziya* (North, sometimes also known as *Wazi* or *Woziya*) claimed owl as his *akicita* – specifically the snowy owl, a logical alliance with the north. In more recent publications, owl as wisdom has become associated with the good, red road. It was attributed to South, or *Okaga* (*Itokaga*). With the many species of owl that exist, it's not unlikely that each direction could claim a breed that reflected the appropriate traits.

The Navajo and Pueblo tribes of New Mexico and Arizona venerated owl, and they feared it. They would not enter any building or home where any part of an owl was kept. This respect is illustrated in a Navajo/Apache legend of this region. A boy was born to a human mother. The babe had the wide eyes of the owl and long, tapering fingers like owl's wings. The mother was frightened of her child and abandoned him. The owls picked up the child from the tree where his mother had hung his cradle and raised him as one of their own. The boy learned how to hunt and fly. One night the owl boy returned to his human parents, interrupting a sacred moon dance. He called to his parents, but he spoke only the language of the owls, and they were terrified. They ran, and the boy, in his anger, attacked. This story reminded the people not to fear something they didn't understand.

The eastern river-land tribes believed that owl appeared as an admonition, but not as a harbinger of death. In one fable, owl warned a husband of a cheating wife. Thus, the owl brought unwelcome news.

In both Europe and America, the owl has long been considered a harbinger of death – sometimes for extremely practical reasons. The children of the Dakota were taught to wake in an instant and prepare for escape if they heard the hoot of an owl. Being the bird-call most easily mimicked by humans, its hoot was often the signal given before night attack. Some of the Germanic tribes and the Scandinavian Vikings also used owl's cry. Therefore, the belief was not superstitious, caused by owl's association with night, but quite sensible. If one heard an owl in the dead of night, it could quite literally mean death. Therefore, it's not surprising that in England and America it is still believed that if an owl is seen perched upon a windowsill, one of the occupants of the house will die before the night is through.

Owl has a rich history in the Old World. The Egyptian hieroglyph for owl served as the letter 'M'. It symbolized death, night, cold, and the invisible sun – that is, the sun after it has been carried to the underworld. Combined with a notched line and an eagle, the hieroglyph for owl represented the sound *sma*, which figured in words like 'unite' and 'come together'. In this context, it suggests peace between opposites (day and night).

Originally owl was the symbol for Athena; its image represented her on temples and coins. Eventually, when the Greeks 'humanized' their gods, the owl became her companion. It sat on Athena's blind side, enabling her to see the entire truth. The emblem of the owl was carried by the Athenians as their armorial ensign. Athena later became associated with the Roman goddess Diana. The latter also was a lunar goddess; thus the link between the goddess and the owl continued.

In a legend from the East, Chingius Chan, the first Tartarean emperor, was defeated in battle. When pursued by his enemy, he hid in a bush. As soon as he was safely ensconced, an owl perched on the bush. His opponents, seeing the bird on top of it, failed to search that bush, assuming that a wild bird would not roost so close to a man. Chingius' life was saved by owl, and thereafter the Tartars held owl in great veneration.

The Celts associated owl with many of the same characteristics as fox. It was both diplomat and messenger. Owl guided people during a time of change. Blodeuweed, the maiden of flowers, was transformed into an owl. This bird figured largely in the fable of Culhwch's and Olwen's search for Mabon, the divine child. During his travels, Gwyrhyr encounters owl as one of the oldest and wisest of all animals, and speaks with him.

Heraldry attribute to the bird prudence, vigilance and watchfulness. Later English associations were not so kind. For example, it was believed that anyone who looks into an owl's nest would become unhappy and morose for life. In Wales, the hoot of an owl does not mean death. Its call reveals that a woman has just lost her virginity.

## MEDICINE AND POWER

| | |
|---|---|
| DIRECTIONS | South, North, East |
| ELEMENT | Air |
| TRAITS | Night flight, night sight, stealth and auditory radar |
| ASSOCIATIONS | The moon, telepathy, insight, magic, wisdom, honesty; lies and deceit, darkness, death |

To landbound, sun-loving mortals, owl – with its ability to roam both comfortably and silently in the night – was feared. Owl possessed capacities that primitive man could respect, but not necessarily understand. Anything that man fears – such as darkness and night – is viewed as suspect. So, owl as the conqueror of the night was worshipped, but not always trusted.

Its call could be easily imitated; therefore its hoot was a harbinger of death that resounded immediately prior to an attack. Owl is called 'night eagle' by several tribes, as a sign of respect. Elsewhere it is referred to as the great deceiver, and its silent ruffle-edged feathers are 'deceiver feathers' that lull prey into a false sense of security.

Owl and crow/raven share many traits. Owl, with its ability to locate prey in conditions that kept mortal man blind, is symbolically associated with clairvoyance, astral projection and magic. Certainly the three birds were regarded with the same mixture of awe and apprehension. On a shamanistic level, owl and crow/raven medicines are most likely to be twisted out of true (in other words, put to dark purposes). The magic carries inherent within itself temptation.

Owl is also equated with wisdom. Like the goddess of old, owl allows one to see the truth behind the lie. Likewise, owl is able to hear the words that remain unspoken. Owl notices nuances that others miss, the essence of wisdom. Owl can be summoned to look at the world through another person's eyes, or for distance-vision.

Since there are so many species, here is a brief list of the traits specific to different breeds:

- Snowy owl is the white owl, and messenger of *Wazi*, the old wizard of the north, who is associated with resolution. It is one of the diurnal owls. It instinctively follows, sometimes even precedes, the migrating food supply. It speaks of timing, prophecy and silence. This owl can swim and play dead like possum. Therefore, it is a strategist.
- The screech owl is big in voice and small in stature (about 90 cm/12 inches tall). Yet it is a brave bird, more ferocious for its size than many of the bigger birds. In truth it is only the young who screech, as a defence mechanism. It teaches lessons of courage, voice and defence.
- Great horned owls feed primarily on skunk, so their medicines are linked. Both animals demand respect, albeit for different reasons.
- Short-eared owl also hunts by day, although it is perfectly capable of hunting at night. The short-eared owl is one of the few that is not often mobbed by crows, mostly because this owl takes the offensive and attacks first. It imparts versatility, curiosity, and the blending of fire and air.
- Barred owl competes with the spotted owl for territory. It is one of the most benign of all owls, with few of the negative attributes of the others. It is a vocalist. It imparts grace and charm in addition to all the other positive traits of owl.
- Barn owls are adaptable hunters, although they have the reputation for being soft and gentle, probably because of their heart-shaped faces. The barn owl was invoked by medicine men to instill these qualities in their treatments. In Europe, though, barn owls were often associated with ghosts and the souls of the dead.

Many believe that owl means wisdom. It could be invoked to locate lost objects. To call upon owl is to act with insight. It can also be summoned when one needs to see clearly in the darkness. This can be on a literal level or a more spiritual one. So, owl enables one to face life's problems.

When owl appears, it suggests the individual is being kept in the dark about something. Owl brings warning, along with the night sight to pierce the darkness that conceals. Its arrival suggests that discretion and observation are needed now to fend off an attack. Depending on the species, it may be time to give a warning screech (screech owl), or it may be time to sit back, blend into the environment, and wait to see what will happen next (snowy owl).

The person with owl medicine is a natural seer. Like many others with this power, owl people make others nervous. The owl individual is attracted to esoterica and the occult. The owl person is intuitive. If an owl gives advice, pay heed. The owl is intelligent and compassionate, but may find itself drawn to the dark side of life and magic.

# PORCUPINE

New World: *Erethizon dorsatum*
European: *Hystrix cristata*
Hedgehog: *Erinaceus europaeus*

## BIOLOGICAL INFORMATION

The porcupine is 65 to 93 cm (25 to 36 inches) long, with a tail of 15 to 30 cm (6 to 12 inches). It weighs 3.5 to 18 kg (8 to 40 lb). The American porcupine has a stolid body with a high, arched back and short legs. It is noted for its barbed guard hairs which are found on the front half of the body. These spines are usually yellow in colour in those animals who reside in the western half of the US, and black or brown for those who inhabit the eastern states.

The European porcupine is the crested porcupine. It is similar in size to the American. Its fur is brown with a white crest on its chest. The guard hairs are black, brown or white.

The hedgehog (length 35 cm/14 inches) is smaller and lighter in colour than the porcupine. Its coat appears grey, and it has contrasting hairs of white, yellow and brown. Although its guard hairs serve more or less the same function as the porcupine's, they do not do as much damage.

## HABITAT

The American porcupine prefers woods. It ranges throughout Canada, through the Rockies and parts west. In the east it is located in small areas of New England, upstate New York, Pennsylvania, Michigan and Wisconsin. It was found in the Chicago suburbs as late as the 1970s.

The crested porcupine lives in flat, dry country or at the foot of mountains. Its main range is north Africa. However, some reside in southern Italy and Sicily.

The hedgehog is the most adaptable of the three species. It inhabits almost all of Europe and parts of Asia. It likes light scrub, and if provided with the right environment, such as a compost heap or wood pile, it will happily nest in the urban garden.

## CHARACTERISTICS

Usually the porcupine beds alone except during mating season. Then pairs share the same burrow for a time. Porcupines mainly come out at night. Their diet includes roots, tubers, fruits and berries. The American porcupine mates in October/early November. Its gestation period is seven months, while for the European crested porcupine it is only about eight weeks. One presumes the American porcupine delays fertilization for a time, like many other species. The female gives birth to two to four young, who take a long time to mature. The lifespan of both crested and American porcupines is about 15 years.

The porcupine's preferred defence is to roll up into a ball, protecting its stomach and face. If confronted in its den, porcupine will attack, but not without warning. First it will stamp its feet and shiver its spine. If the invader does not take the hint, it will turn its back on its adversary. Then it will run backwards at the individual. If the barbs touch, watch out. Porcupine cannot, as many think, shoot its barbs at people.

Despite its armoured defence, the porcupine is easy to kill with a single blow to its nose. It is particularly vulnerable to cougar and wolverine, who have learned how to flip it over to expose its soft, unprotected underbelly.

Hedgehog is the nearest English equivalent to porcupine. It nests in dense brush, heaps of loose wood or grass clippings. Before starting a bonfire of an established woodpile, it is always wise to make sure that a family of hedgehogs have not taken up residence there by gently stirring the boughs with a spade or a fork.

The hedgehog eats slugs and other pests, and therefore can be a welcome addition to the garden. One can create hedgehog homes by making a 'V' out of two pieces of wood and covering the structure with glass clippings or logs – remembering to leave an opening for the hedgehog to gain access.

## LEGENDS AND TRADITIONS

GODDESS Nayaa Xatisei (Arapaho)

Normally, porcupine is associated with innocence and child-like wisdom, but one Native American tale illustrates that porcupine was not only playful, but wily – a creature to be wary of, for in this story, porcupine even outwits the great trickster coyote.

Porcupine woke up one fine day and decided to hunt buffalo. He tracked them for days, and when he found the herd they were on the opposite side of a river. Porcupine called to one of them and persuaded it to take him across the river. Buffalo offered to put porcupine on his back, but the creature did not want to get his feet wet. So buffalo swallowed porcupine, not just giving him a free ride, but providing him with the means to kill the larger animal from the inside out. Porcupine slaughtered buffalo with a single swipe of his tail against buffalo's great heart. Porcupine then whispered magic words to emerge from the buffalo's belly whole.

Coyote was pleased to discover a dead buffalo for that night's dinner. Porcupine then enlisted coyote to butcher the meat, offering him a share of the kill. Eventually, though, the two began to fight. Coyote killed porcupine, but porcupine got his revenge, for the magic words he uttered to be released from the buffalo caused a giant redwood to grow. It lifted the meat from the forest floor and rejuvenated the dead porcupine.

Coyote shouted angrily at porcupine to throw down the meat. Porcupine obliged, but not without killing coyote – and his family, who had come to join in this fine repast.

This tale suggests that porcupine had much stronger medicine than simple innocence. It could dupe the powerful buffalo and outwit the wily coyote. With guile it killed an animal several times larger than itself, and with its magic induced a tree to grow.

Porcupine quills were highly valued. They were dyed and used to decorate robes, dresses, leggings and moccasins. Large quantities of quillwork were produced by the Cheyenne and Lakota peoples, despite the fact that porcupine did not inhabit the Great Plains. Quillworking was a highly specialized and honoured craft. There were Quill Societies in Arapaho and Cheyenne tribes. The patterns and designs were considered sacred and the symbolism only known to the members of the Society. It was said that the whirlwind-woman, *Nayaa Xatisei* (Arapaho) created the first ornaments of this kind. The Cree and Ojibwa used similar quill designs as their enemies. The Blackfeet required an initiation ceremony before a woman could do quillwork. From the Micmac in the east, north to Canada and across the Plains, quills were used to adorn cradles, fans, medicine pouches, even bows and arrows.

The European hedgehog, according to Guilim, signifies a man expert in gathering substances. It imparts the ability to grasp opportunity. Hedgehog could best be described by the proverb: 'making hay while the sun shines prevents future want.' The Calmuc Tartars used hedgehogs instead of cats to hunt pests.

Some European farmers believe that hedgehogs suck the milk from cattle lying in the fields. In England the hedgehog replaces the ground hog in predicting the end of winter on Candlemas (2nd February). In *Poor Richard's Almanac* it was recommended that people watch where a hedgehog built the entrance to its den, for that indicated the direction of the wind. The hedgehog would always place the entry opposite the prevailing winds. So hedgehog, too, had its magic. It could foretell the weather and the season.

## MEDICINE AND POWER

| | |
|---|---|
| DIRECTIONS | East, West, Centre |
| ELEMENTS | Earth and Air |
| TRAITS | Prickliness, curiosity, being easy-going |
| ASSOCIATIONS | Sensitivity, tenderness and trust, playfulness (in woodland areas), family, protection and defence, magic (medicine) and prediction, along with cunning; weather sense (hedgehog) |

The direction attributed to porcupine varies by group. An association with elemental air suggests east according to some cultures. Its association with the winds (*Wakinyan*), particularly in the form of storms, implies west. Whirlwind meant centre. For the Plains' tribes, porcupine would have been found either east or west of them, but rarely passed through their region.

Porcupine shares many qualities with skunk. It was rarely intimidated. Porcupine views humans with mild curiosity and not as a threat. Few animals frighten it. Porcupine won't be hurried or pushed around. Like skunk, porcupine backs up for attack and signals its alarm before it takes the offensive.

Porcupine's eyesight is poor. As a forager, it keeps its nose to the ground. Usually, porcupine will ignore any animal that crosses its path unless challenged. Why should it worry? It has an excellent defence system.

Thus, porcupine speaks of nonchalance. Despite its size, it is an animal to be respected. Similarly, it speaks of courage in the face of danger. In the legends of the Americas, porcupine has the power of persuasion and ruse on its side, and it holds powerful medicine in the form of magic.

Because of its many strengths, porcupine is confident and can afford to be a frolicsome creature. Most recent views say porcupine's gift to man is child-like play and innocence. This is a recent addition to the definitions of old, which saw porcupine as a prankster – perhaps influenced by the benevolent view man takes of hedgehog. The latter features in literature, children's classics and today's cartoons. This new, revised image implies faith and trust in the wisdom of the divine.

The old vision revealed that porcupine was skilled in magic and faithful to himself – perhaps this trust is the true meaning of innocence. The animal is a loving parent, playful and relaxed with its young. Therefore, porcupine also contains some of the medicine of otter. Porcupine is another animal to be invoked when life has become too serious.

If trust is an issue, summon porcupine. With its snuffling nose it can scent dishonesty in others, which it can then turn against its adversary. Porcupine can also be used for defence, when one needs to raise the alarm but not attack. Raise porcupine energy when it's time to signal a warning. Like skunk, porcupine imparts respect for all living creatures without being intimidated by them.

If porcupine appears, this suggests that the individual needs some cheering up. Porcupine can indicate a time of fun, or a time to take a more playful attitude in work and at home. It could mean that the individual needs to defend himself, without taking the offensive, or it may symbolize the fact that the person is either about to walk into a prickly situation or getting a bit prickly him- or herself.

In a time of crisis, the porcupine individual will seem unconcerned. This person can wheedle his or her way out of most situations. Porcupine people usually have bad vision. Sometimes, individuals with porcupine medicine may appear stupid or slow, for they won't react until the problem is right in front of their face. Porcupine usually doesn't get rattled. When pressed, the porcupine person will have a barbed tongue, and the comments that he or she makes are not easily lived down. Porcupine medicine produces good mothers, although the porcupine fathers generally do not get involved in the process of childrearing.

# RABBIT

European rabbit: *Oryctolagus cuniculus*
Cottontail: *Sylvilagus foridanus*

## BIOLOGICAL INFORMATION

The pygmy rabbit is the smallest species, measuring about 25 cm (10 inches). The marsh rabbit comes next, ranging between about 35 and 45 cm (14 – 18 inches). The European rabbit is one of the largest, at a full 60 cm (2 ft). All rabbits have long ears and stubby tails. Often the ears will have black tips. The normal colouring is greyish brown above with a lighter undercoat. However, the European rabbit, which has been domesticated and bred, comes in a variety of colours. American cottontails are smaller than their European counterpart.

### HABITAT

Anywhere where there is enough vegetation, one finds rabbits. Some are specialized to live in a desert environment, while others have adapted to the Arctic tundra. The pygmy is one of the few in the US that digs its own burrow system. Rabbits cover the entire North American continent. Similarly, they are found across Europe into Asia and northern Africa. The symbol of the rabbit adorned Egyptian tombs.

### CHARACTERISTICS

Rabbits and hares are grazers. The does are usually larger than the bucks. The European lives in elaborate warrens. They prefer to roam about during the night. However, hungry does will often leave their children alone during the day. Thus, many people find these babies and think they are abandoned. If found, they should be left alone. Rabbits can have as many as five litters a year, numbering between two and five young each.

Rabbits are a prey species and their high reproductivity rate helps replace the numbers lost to predators. The rabbit thumps out an alarm call to others when it sees a predator. Rabbits freeze when threatened. If a rabbit chooses to run it often switches direction to confuse its enemy.

## LEGENDS AND TRADITIONS

Great communal drives for rabbit were held by the Paiute of California. These were combined with religious festivals and celebrations. Similarly, rabbit was associated with the Medicine Bow. It was believed that adorning the hunter's bow with rabbit fur lent speed to an arrow.

A Menominee legend credited rabbit with the creation of day and night. Before time began, rabbit represented daylight, owl night. Often they debated the merits of one over the other. Eventually, rabbit challenged owl to a test. They invited other animals to observe, so ensuring impartiality. Rabbit called upon daylight – *Wabon* – while owl screeched for night: *Unitipaqkot*. As the battle continued, owl slipped up and spoke the name for day. Rabbit won. However, rabbit revealed great wisdom. He decreed that half the day should be given over to darkness, for the creatures who loved night best.

Current beliefs tend to dismiss rabbit as fearful, even cowardly, and yet more tales have been written about rabbit than any other animal. These stories have been included elsewhere, and will not be repeated here. In Native American myth rabbit, was as wily as coyote, possibly more so, since the number of tales where rabbit outwits a mightier, faster creature exceeds similar stories about coyote. Rabbit breaks the flint bear, beats owl, even defeats alligator.

In Marie McLaughlin's *Myths and Legends of the Sioux*, rabbit features in seven different stories. Not even the sacred bear is credited with more than two – and rabbit appears alongside bear in both of these. In one, rabbit wins over bear. In the second, rabbit takes advantage of bear, getting him to do the dirty work while rabbit reaps the rewards.

The Lakota warriors of the Plains wore an armband of rabbit skin to capture its speed and agility. This medicine was particularly useful during long journeys and marches. Rabbit skin is often added to ceremonial objects in the belief that it will encourage rabbit's fruitfulness and swiftness.

In Egypt the rabbit/hare hieroglyph represented the phonetic *un* and was often seen in combination with the wavy-line glyph for 'pool' or 'water'. Interestingly enough, these symbols provided the root for words like 'wolf', 'dog' and 'wolfsbane'. It was also a part of such words as 'running' and 'speed'. When these glyphs were combined with that for the predator owl, they meant 'eat' or 'devour'.

Heraldry never admitted rabbit into its ranks, only hare. In European folklore the rabbit brings mainly good – unless one was about to go to sea, then its appearance suggested storms and disaster. Miners fared no better, for to see a pure white rabbit on the way to the mine portended calamity. However, snowy rabbit was not all bad. Saying the words 'white rabbit' three times on the first day of the month ensures good luck for the rest of the month.

The rabbit's foot, like hare's, has long been carried as a talisman against bad luck. It was valued because it was thought to provide:

- rabbit's primary source of long-distance communications
- the ability to summon rabbit's fleet foot and speed.

## MEDICINE AND POWER

| | |
|---|---|
| DIRECTIONS | West, North |
| ELEMENTS | Earth, Air |
| TRAITS | Community, abundance, quickness, vigilance, acute hearing |
| ASSOCIATIONS | Love, fertility, victory of wit over brawn, cowardice |

The Lakota considered the rabbit a symbol of love, and traditionally the Rabbit Dance was the only dance where men and women danced together.

In regional northwest America – Oregon, Washington state and British Columbia – the appearance of rabbit heralded a period of peace, and the moon was considered the eye of the rabbit.

Rabbit, like deer, is one of the most alert of all creatures. Both are prey species, and both have developed their large ears in order to hear distant danger that they cannot yet see. Both are grazers. Both 'herd' together – the deer in the winter months – for protection. Therefore, rabbit medicine is similar to deer medicine – storyteller, lover, creature of wit and guile.

Furthermore, this author would like to suggest that rabbit carries as much trickery as coyote. Rabbit teaches cunning. In order to survive it must out-think and outsmart all others who would like to make it. Therefore, rabbit carries the essence of strategy.

To some tribes the rabbit was disdained as a food source – especially by warriors – since it was believed that its timidity would be absorbed with consumption of the flesh. Other tribes, however, invoked its speed. This reputation for cowardice is the flip side of vigilance and alertness, because what else can rabbit do once it has spotted a predator, but run? It is said that rabbit's own fears can summon chaos.

Many emphasize rabbit's more positive qualities, and one of these is confidence in the act of procreation. Rabbit medicine also lends poise when dealing with changes or going through a busy period of life. The rabbit brings intelligence. It gives a strong sense of community. Rabbit can communicate over long distances. Rabbit is always attentive and able to assess a situation rapidly in order to devise an appropriate response.

If rabbit has appeared, it could presage a time of fertility; hence plenty. Likewise it could bring love. On the opposite extreme it may counsel caution. If already feeling frightened, it might be asking the individual to call upon rabbit's other qualities – wit, strategy and speed. Or it may be time to confront these fears and decide which ones are real.

The rabbit individual is jumpy and easily startled. They are also quicker than most other people. Like coyote people, rabbits are not above bending the truth a little bit when deemed necessary. Unlike coyote, rabbit rarely puts itself forward. These people stay in the background. They are home-loving, social individuals, albeit shy.

# RACCOON

*Procyon lotor*

## BIOLOGICAL INFORMATION

The raccoon varies a great deal in size. It measures 60 to 95 cm (24 to 37 inches) in length. Proportionately it has a long tail, between 19 and 40 cm (7 to 16 inches). It can weigh as little as 5.4 kg or as much as 21.6 kg (12 to 48 lb). The fur along its back is a reddish brown. The stomach is grey to black. Its tail has alternating rings of black, tan and grey, although these are incomplete or mottled, unlike the clearly defined rings of the related ring-tail.

The raccoon's most distinctive feature is its black 'mask', outlined in white, over its eyes.

### HABITAT

The raccoon usually lives close to water, along the shores of lakes, streams and ponds. It dens in hollow trees. The raccoon's range runs from the southern coast of Canada to Mexico. Only a few regions in the western US are free of the raccoon. Some naturalists believe that the adaptable and versatile raccoon might be a better national symbol for the US than the eagle.

### CHARACTERISTICS

Raccoons are intelligent, curious and determined. Few people have been able to guard their bins against this creature. They have great manual dexterity, with paws that resemble the human hand. They are able to grasp the most tightly bound rubbish bag and untie it.

The raccoon is nocturnal and solitary except when breeding or caring for its young. The raccoon will eat just about anything from grapes and nuts to crayfish and worms. They love water and are capable swimmers, and are known for washing their food before consuming it.

Overall, raccoons are lethargic, opportunistic animals, although males will travel miles in search of mates. Females mate with only one male per breeding season (February in the north, December in the south). Litters of between one and seven arrive in April or May. The young weigh 50 g (2 oz) at birth, and open their eyes at six weeks. They are weaned by the end of the summer. Some young will disperse in autumn; others spend the winter with their mother until they are driven away after the arrival of the next brood.

## LEGENDS AND TRADITIONS

A legend from the Menominee Nation spoke of raccoon medicine. The creature was walking one day when he came across two old blind men quibbling over dinner. Raccoon decided to play a trick on them, stealing their food out from under their noses. As they fought over who was eating more, they lost the rest of the night's provision to the raccoon. When the old men discovered their loss, they realized that they had been duped and promised not to fight again. Raccoon wandered away, confident that they had learned both patience and trust.

Another story told how raccoon got his markings. One night a spirit came to raccoon in a vision and told the creature to paint himself with black and white, and that is why raccoon looks the way he does today.

The Seneca credited its unusual colouring to quite another source. The Seneca thought of raccoon in much the same way that they viewed crow – as the stealer of corn. The tribe set about catching raccoon. The chief ordered him beaten. Raccoon's eyes were blackened and his body bruised, giving him its mottled hue.

Probably one of the best ways to describe the raccoon's place in Native American legend – its attributes and its medicine – is to list some of its many names. The concepts and the words illustrate a common origin for both the ideas and the terms.

- Abnaki and Natick: *asban*, 'one who picks things up'.
- Dialectic and tribal variation (of the word and the definition) include:
  The Ojibwe and Menominee: *aispun*, 'they handle things'
  Chippewa: *aasebun, assisbun*, 'they pick things up'
  Cree: *essebanes*, 'they pick things up'
  Delaware: *eespan*, 'one who picks up things'
  The Lenape use the same word, *eespan*, along with *hespan*, for 'they handle things'
  The Ojibwa word was *essepan*, also applauding the raccoon's ability to pick things up

- For linguistic reasons, some of the words differ, but the concept remains the same:
  Lenape: *nachenum*, 'they use hands as tools'
  Delaware: *wtakalinch*, 'one who is clever with his fingers'
  Aztec: *mapachitl*, 'they take everything in their hands'
  Ofo-Sioux: *at-cha*, 'one who touches things'
  Takelma: *swini*, 'picks things with hands'
  Shawnee: *shapata, ethepata*, 'grasper'

- Variously there are those names that reflect other aspects of raccoon's manual dexterity – such as:
  The Algonquin: *ah-rah-koon-em*, Atakapa *welkol, wilkol, wulkol*, 'they rub and scratch'
  The Chinook: *q'oala's*, 'they scratch'
  Tschimshean: *que-o-koo*, 'washes with hands'
  Yakima: *k'alas*, 'they scratch'

- Sometimes the words are similar even if the concept is not:
  Choctaw: *shauii*, 'graspers'
  Hopi: *shiuaa*, 'painted one'
  The Mohican appears phonetically analogous: *sha-we*, 'grasper'
  The Biloxi Sioux: *atuki*, 'they touch things'
  Creek: *wukti*, 'they rub and scratch'
  Seminole: *wood-ko*, Atakapa *wutko*, 'one who rubs'

- The other terms have more to do with the raccoon as a spiritual animal. These names often refer to specific markings that are supposed to give the animal its particular medicine:
  The Aztec name *sede-o-ahtlah-ma-kas-kay* meant 'she who talks to spirits'
  The Dakota Sioux called raccoon *weekah, tegalelga*, 'magic one with painted face'
  Huron-Iroquois: *attigbrow*, 'blackened face'; *gahado-goka-gogosa*, 'masked demon spirit'
  Mandan: *nashi*, 'blackened face and feet'
  Mexico and Nicaragua: *macheelee*, 'white bands on face'
  Omaha, Osage, Otoe: *mekah*, 'one with magic'
  The Lakota (Sioux) *maccan-n-e*, bears little resemblance to the Yankton Sioux: *wayatcha*, which also means 'one who makes magic'
  The Wyot also emphasized raccoon's mask – *chel'igacocih*, 'one with marked face'

## MEDICINE AND POWER

| | |
|---|---|
| DIRECTIONS | West, South |
| ELEMENTS | Earth, Water |
| TRAITS | Dexterity, guile, adaptability |
| ASSOCIATIONS | Mankind, cleverness, trickery, theft, ablutions |

The raccoon is similar to coyote, the trickster. Raccoon is the clown who teaches man lessons. Raccoon is sly and crafty, quick and agile. He is a worthy adversary who outwits his opponent.

Like fox in England, the raccoon is a survivor. This creature has been able to adapt to the urbanized environment of man and take advantage of it.

Raccoon supports one in uncovering and accepting hidden aspects of the self. Witty raccoon is not itself easily fooled. Therefore, its medicine may be used to unmask the truth. Raccoon medicine imparts flexibility and allows one to move with ease between life's many roles.

Raccoon, as the clown, is playful and confident in this guise, thus its gift is the ability to learn to enjoy the many aspects of the self, even the silly ones. Raccoon aids one when going through changes, enabling the individual to find delight in the transition from one level to the next.

The raccoon has the ability to 'handle' all things and situations with agility. Call upon raccoon medicine during tasks that require manual dexterity, or when the events of life are hectic and chores require juggling. Its capability to grasp means that raccoon energy can be called upon if and when things start slipping through one's fingers. Raccoon is the sorcerer who imparts sleight of hand. Raccoon could also put the individual on the alert for theft. Its magic can be used as preventative medicine.

Raccoon is attributed with the talent to speak with the spirits. It imparts this gift to others. It can be raised during meditation if one wishes to talk with the grandfathers. Therefore, it could be called the 'spiritual medium' of the animal kingdom.

Raccoon people are fun-loving. They may carry their sense of humour to an extreme and become practical jokers. These individuals have innate mechanical ability. They can appear grasping, but only to others who envy their dexterity. The raccoon person is flexible and adaptable – able to make the most of nearly any situation. He or she is opportunistic. If there's ever an individual able to find the easy way out, it is the person with raccoon medicine.

# RAM/SHEEP

Family: *Ovidae*
Big-horned sheep: *Ovis canadensis*
Old World: *Ovis platyra*

## BIOLOGICAL INFORMATION

The ram stands 100 to 115 cm (3 to 3½ ft) at the shoulder. The horns spread 75 cm (30 inches). It is about 1.65 to 1.8 m (5½ to 6 ft) long and weight 57 to 42 kg (127 – 316 lb). The ewe is smaller at 66 to 100 cm (about 2 to 3 ft) and a svelte 33.6 to 90 kg (74 – 200 lb).

All sheep descended from the *Artiodactyla* order of animals. The divisions between sheep, goats and cows occurred during the Miocene period.

The Rocky Mountain sheep have big muscular bodies. The colour varies from dark brown to tan. They shed their coats in June and July. Although there are other breeds of sheep in the Americas, such as the Barbary and the Dall, the Rocky Mountain big-horn is the most well known. The males have huge horns which cover the ears and curl over the cheeks. The breed have a spongy base to their hooves which allows them to cling to the most precarious perches.

### HABITAT

The mountainous regions of western America, including the Rockies, the Sierra Nevadas and the Cascades. Their range starts south in Mexico and stretches to British Columbia and Alberta in Canada.

### CHARACTERISTICS

Big-horn prefer places little visited by man. They are active by day, feeding in the morning, at midday and evening. The big-horn sheep is one of the few hoofed mammals that beds down in the same place every night.

The big-horns live in herds of 10 which include ewes, yearlings and lambs. Rams join the herd for winter and the rut. At this time the herds can number 100 or more. They migrate from the high slopes to the valleys during winter, retreating back up the mountain in summer. During the rut, rams charge each other at 32 kph (20 mph). The cracking noise they make can be heard over a mile away. The fights may last 20 hours. Mating occurs between August and January; lambing takes place in spring. The ewes give birth to one or two lambs.

## LEGENDS AND TRADITIONS

| | |
|---|---|
| GODDESSES | Lahar (Babylonian), Aphrodite (Greek) |
| GODS | Amun, Khenmu, the *Ba* (soul) of Osiris, Montu, Tatenen (Egyptian), Jupiter (Roman), Zeus (Greek) |

The Shoshone were the only Native American people who were associated with sheep or goats – their name, literally translated, means 'the eaters of sheep'.

Most of the legends having to do with ram, or sheep, though, come from the Old World, starting in Egypt. Like fish, sheep (ewes) were considered unclean and therefore royals and those in the priestly cast were not allowed to partake of them. Neither were they to be used as an offering to the dead. In Egyptian times, flocks of sheep were turned loose to tread the seeds into the ground after the annual flood, so even ewes found their usefulness.

Ram was treated far differently than the humble ewe. Ram, with his amorous tendencies, came to be associated with fertility, and ram gods were worshipped from the earliest times. There were Herishef of Herakleopis and the ram of Amun which was always shown prone. In the

*Book of That Which is the Underworld*, an ancient god of the earth, *Tatenen*, was depicted as four crowned rams. Later the ram was attributed to Osiris, and the ram of Mendes was called the *Ba* or soul of Osiris. Meanwhile, another breed of ram, the flat-horned, became associated with Khnemu, originally a river god of the First Cataract.

Ewes could not be given as offerings, but ram was sacrificed regularly to please individual gods. Pictures of mummified rams can be found as early as the First Dynasty. For many of the Egyptians, ram meant solar energy. Often only the ram's head was illustrated and linked to the solar disk. The hieroglyph of a young ram leaping meant 'thirst'. Ram coupled with the whip signified royal status.

Worship of the ram was emulated by other cultures, such as the Greek. Zeus was linked with the ram. In a separate tale, Athamas of Thessaly proposed to sacrifice his two children, Phirus and Helle. It was believed that sacrificing the king ensured the good of the people. However, in this story, the king's offspring were to be substituted for the ruling parent. Instead ram took the children's place in sacrifice, transporting them to a place of safety across the sea later named for them, Hellespont. Phirus carried with him the golden fleece, a gift of Hermes. When he returned home, the fleece was nailed up on an oak and later stolen by Jason.

The Romans linked the ram with Jupiter. Its chief strength was its horns or head. Therefore, the Romans would cut off the ram's head as an offering to Jupiter each year at a special festival. They would take its skin and cover the statue of the god. Ram's skull was also used in a sort of exorcism to scare away demons.

The early Semites of western Asia also practised infanticide, or child sacrifice – but, like the Greeks, they later replaced the children with a sacrificial ram.

According to Heraldry, the ram was well-armed and capable of fighting. It was a symbol of great strength and force.

Ram represents the first sign of the Zodiac, Aries. Thus, it is linked with spring's renewal and fertility. It foretells of the coming fruits of summer. The sign retains many of ram's characteristics – running into things head-on, masculinity and virility.

## MEDICINE AND POWER

| | |
|---|---|
| DIRECTION | East |
| ELEMENTS | Fire, Sun |
| TRAITS | Lust, fertility, lack of forethought |
| ASSOCIATIONS | Strength, combat, creativity, vigour, spring, youthful zeal |

Ram speaks of strength to the Shoshone of northwestern American, as it did to both European and Middle Eastern cultures. Ewe, as the sower of seeds, symbolized spring, fertility and creation. Ram was linked with many of the creator gods of Egypt.

Ram later replaced the king in sacrifices for the renewal of a failing kingdom, which followed the bedding of the goddess or her representative on earth, the priestess. Therefore, despite all the masculine connotations associated with the ram, it originated with goddess worship.

Like the king, the ram (symbol of male virility) was sacrificed to ensure the return of spring. Ram was also held sacred in Tibet, where it supported and provided transport for the Goddess Khon-ma. She would be comparable to the Roman goddess Mania, holding the strength of ram demons at bay.

Ram is also connected with Mars. Thus it should be called upon when martial strength is needed. Its appearance could portend an upcoming skirmish; it declares the need to remain in a state of battle-readiness.

Similarly, ram is linked with solar power and all its implications of light, illumination and healing. Ram can be invoked when an individual's energy level is low, or when someone is feeling depressed. Ram imparts fortitude and vigour.

Ram power is a good one to raise at the beginning of any project, although it should probably be replaced with bull once the project is in progress. Ram does not give sustained energy. It is procreator; thus, ram provides the initial impetus, but not much follow-through.

In the latter category, the virility of ram has been summoned for sexual magic. It should be raised for any act of creation. Ram is more physical than metaphysical, but can mark the beginning of an extremely creative period in an individual's life. It comes bringing with it the sun's warmth and the promise of spring. It can be a sign of good luck.

On the other hand, ram also imparts martial qualities, which suggests war. Ram must work for what he or she achieves. Ram's style is to face conflict head-on. This is good medicine to have when under attack, but not always the most appropriate in times of peace.

The ram individual is the type of person who leaps first and asks questions later. Ram gives courage, but doesn't instill caution, insight or foresight. If one wants to develop intuition, ram is not the animal to summon.

The ram person is a go-getter. Ram provides illumination by example. Ram's lesson is action. Therefore, the individual with ram medicine will act. He or she will lead. This person pushes him- or herself to the front of any enterprise and generally doesn't tolerate being second best. The ram may appear deliberately combative, but this is because tact is not a ram trait. This person is blunt and frank. The ram often offends without trying and, more often, without realizing it.

# SALAMANDER

European fire salamander: *Salamandra Salamandra*
Hellbender: *Cryrptobranchus megalobatrachus*

## BIOLOGICAL INFORMATION

Salamander is another broad group. In terms of length, the salamanders of England stay within a range of 7 to 15 cm (3 to 6 inches). Many of the salamanders native to the US are of comparable size. However, the Hellbender is a giant, measuring up to 64 cm (2 ft) in length. Colour and markings vary. Globally, the colouring encompasses yellow to bright red, greenish grey or brown or black. They may be spotted or sport stripes.

### HABITAT

Salamanders, like all amphibians, need water in order to survive. They live in or near rivers, streams, marshy areas, stagnant pools and ponds.

### CHARACTERISTICS

The salamander is carnivorous. It preys upon insects at all stages of their development. The salamander is an egg-layer. The time of year varies on the location. Like tadpole, the infant is born with gills. All must keep their skin moist.

The North American Hellbender represents the extreme. In many ways, though, it is quite typical of all salamanders. It will eat anything. When small, the infants swallows worms and larvae. Later Hellbender feasts on crayfish and fish. It breeds in August. The female produces 300 to 400 eggs. The babies are 2.5 cm (1 inch) long when they hatch. It takes a full five years for the Hellbender salamander to reach sexual maturity. Its total life expectancy is 30 years.

## LEGENDS AND TRADITIONS

Despite the fact that salamander goes through a similar metamorphosis to both frog and toad, the salamander was the Egyptian hieroglyph for 'constancy', which seems to suggest that the Egyptians noted that salamander's transformation was not quite as profound as either frog's or toad's. In other words, the young of the completely aquatic stage resemble the adults of the terrestrial phase. Because salamanders were so prolific, the hieroglyph also meant 'multitude' or 'throng'.

Many of the traditions related here were also applied to lizard (*see page 214*). Ancient and medieval man did not separate the reptilian lizard from the amphibious salamander. Thus, many of the myths are the same. For example: it was believed that salamanders lived in flames, a trait which was also attributed to lizard. The connection between salamander and fire is strong, possibly because the gill structure of the immature salamander appears as flame-like projections around the neck. Comparisons were made to a lion's mane with all its solar associations. Alchemists believed salamander was born of flames. It was a symbol of fermentation and separation – i.e., transformation. Both processes required the application of heat or fire.

According to the allegories of the time, the eagle of spirit fights the lion of physicality on the back of a dragon, or salamander. Fire was equated with chemical sulphur and with dryness and heat, hence the mistake between dry-skinned, heat-loving lizard and salamander.

Finally, in Victorian England, this theory was contested when someone chose to experiment by putting a living salamander into a fire. Needless to say, the salamander died.

## MEDICINE AND POWER

| | |
|---|---|
| DIRECTION | South |
| ELEMENTS | Fire, Water (sun) |
| TRAITS | Cold-bloodedness, water-loving, amphibian |
| ASSOCIATIONS | Transformation, metamorphosis, masses, sulphur and fire |

Despite the fact that salamander proved itself not to be 'flame-retardant', it is still associated with fire. It would seem some symbolic bonds are too strong to break. Because it is cold-blooded, it has to sun itself in order to warm up its circulatory system, so perhaps it deserves its reputation as heat-loving. Certainly salamander speaks of the balancing of opposites or opposing energies (water and fire).

If salamander means transformation, then it is a gentler form of transformation than found in the frog, or less obvious to the outside observer. Many salamanders don't change all that much; the young and the adult retain the same shape.

Salamander represents the metamorphosis of fermentation. It can represent total separation, depending on the breed or species. The medicine of the Hellbender would be warrior energy. This was an animal to be respected; therefore, always check the specific type of salamander rather than thinking in vague generalities.

Salamander medicine should be called upon when going through a change. It should provide, in the classic definition of the animal, vim, vigour and the energy of fire. Also salamander brings illumination, unless one moves in too close, when one can become burned or consumed.

Salamander's second gift is water medicine. It is perfectly adapted to an aquatic environment. Indeed, if its skin dries out, salamander dies. Yet it can move about on land. Thus, its medicine includes working with emotions and grounding.

Because this energy is so slippery it is a difficult one to master. Yet, once mastered, it bestows balance. It can bring light to the murky dark waters of feelings. Likewise, salamander medicine can ground one who has been overwhelmed by emotion. Its energy can be used to smooth transitions. But this same power run awry can burn, consume, inundate. Like snake, salamander should be handled with care.

The salamander individual will appear cold. This person may have flourish or dash, a fiery mane, but this medicine also repels. This person may be described as 'slick', unfeeling or aloof. The salamander is the knower of wisdom, but it rarely confides in others. People with this trait would prefer to sit on the sidelines rather than share their gift with others.

# SALMON

*Salmo Salor*

## BIOLOGICAL INFORMATION

Salmon can grow up to 1 metre (about 3 feet) in length and weigh well over 10 kg (22 lb). They are silver in colour, although the sockeye salmon turns a dramatic red just prior to mating. The salmon in the Pacific northwest fall into four different categories, usually (though not always) named according to the river of origin. They include the Chinook, Coho, Sockeye and pink.

In England the salmon is not distinguished according to its hatching ground. Many are now farmed, being bred in tanks and moved to salt water once they've reached a certain age.

### HABITAT

All salmon live most of their adult lives in salt water, either oceans or bays. The American salmon spend four years in the Pacific and travel some 9,600 km (6,000 miles) before they embark on their 640-km (400-mile) journey upriver to spawn, for which they prefer freshwater. Their eggs would be destroyed by salt water, which means they must return to their original freshwater hatching grounds. They are found in the North Pacific rim up to the Aleutians.

European salmon live in the waters around Scotland and Norway. Their voyage upriver to breed is not as long. Therefore, they usually survive to breed again. The Atlantic salmon can breed as many as 13 times in their lives.

## CHARACTERISTICS

The Pacific salmon eats a diet of squid and herring. In the course of their lives, they travel some 11,200 km (7,000 miles). Only 10 adults per 1,000 hatchlings return to their breeding grounds. The salmon steers by the stars, magnetic fields and by smell. The rains that fall on their forest home acquire a certain chemical scent which leads them back to their hatching grounds. Two million salmon will spawn along a single stretch of river. Each female carries about 4,000 eggs. The males establish their breeding rank during the trip upstream; the females must fight to maintain their nesting territory once they've reached their final destination. They bury their fertilized eggs under sand and loose scree to keep them from floating away.

The annual migration begins in the spring, when the salmon first arrive at a freshwater coast. To make it this far they've had to run the gauntlet of killer whales, seal, sea lions, and salmon's biggest predator, man. Fisheries take some 3/4 of the fish before the salmon arrive at the river. By mid-summer those who have succeeded have made half their trip upriver, a journey of around 320 km (200 miles). At this point the predators change, as grizzly bears and black bears line the banks of the river for this annual feast. Eagles, golden and bald, also lie in wait, together with foxes, gulls, ravens, and the ever-present predator man, in the form of sports fishermen.

During the 640-km (400-mile) journey upstream the salmon can't eat, and their skin, acclimated to salt water, begins to dissolve. The final destination is achieved by the survivors at the beginning of autumn. They spawn only to die. Their decaying corpses dump some 150 tons of phosphorous into the river. The original location of trees can actually be determined by chemical analysis which includes the amount and type of phosphorous they retain. In the area around the Russian River in northern California, all waste from the catch must be returned to the water by law, for it has been discovered that, in those places where this is not done, the river turns barren and lifeless, and salmon cease to spawn. So the adults nourish the river and their young, even in death.

Not all salmon participate in this drama. Since it takes up to four years to reach sexual maturity a certain percentage remain in the saltwater seas until their biological clock tells them that they are ready.

The Atlantic salmon follow a similar cycle and migration. They feed on herring. However, they survive the change from fresh to salt water through diffusion and osmosis, absorbing either water or salt through the skin to keep their salinity level constant, and once they have reproduced they return to the sea.

## LEGENDS AND TRADITIONS

The peoples of the Pacific Northwest believed that there were people, just like themselves, who lived in the sea. The denizens of the deep were sleek and healthy because the water was so much richer than the impoverished land. Once a year, though, the sea people took pity on their land-bound brethren, turned themselves into salmon and came to man to nourish him with salmon's bounty. The Native Americans of the Pacific were able to dry enough fish during the annual migration to feed the tribe for the entire winter.

In the Kwakiutl country of British Columbia, salmon was sacred. The spawning run, with fish returning year after year, seemed symbolic of the way the dead travel back to life. It was the complementary ceremony to the deer dance, the salmon ceremony celebrating the main other turning-point of the year. For the Kwakiutl as much as for the bear, the return of the salmon was the final bounty before winter's cold hard sleep.

Other peoples of the Pacific coast as far south as California celebrated the salmon. The Yurok, Hupa, Haida and Karok groups of northern California also held these two world-renewal rites – the deer and the salmon, which was something of a New Year's celebration. This included eating the first fish of the season.

Once the feast was over, the bones, head, tail and fins were returned to the Great Provider, the river, as a thanks for the sacrifice that had been made. This also was meant to ensure the return of the salmon next year.

This link between the body of the fish and the richness of the river is a fact that has only recently been acknowledged by science. As mentioned, in death the salmon fertilize the river. Thus the Native Americans knew instinctively what 200 centuries of study led the white man to 'discover'.

For the Native Americans of the northwest, salmon was bringer of plenty. It was both figuratively and literally the symbol of rebirth and renewal, hence survival.

In the Atlantic, the salmon return many times so likewise were associated with the spirits of the dead. In Britain and northern Europe the salmon was regarded as the king of fishes. In Scandinavia and Germany, this belief stretches back to ancient times. Salmon's navigational skills were recognized. Thus, it was said that salmon swam in waters of inspiration and foreknowledge from which it gained wisdom and strength of purpose.

Salmon was equally important to the Celts. It was a symbol of intelligence. In stories of old it was said that the child Taliesin, the mage, was found in a fish weir. In another legend, Gwhryr questioned all the animals to see which one was smartest. He decided that the salmon of Llyn Llyw was not only the oldest, but the wisest. Salmon lead Gwhryr to Mabon and ultimately to wisdom and rebirth. In another tale, Cuchulainn used a salmon's leap to get across the Pupils' Bridge in order to gain Scathach's knowledge. Each leap brought Cuchulainn more wisdom. Meanwhile Cormac, the Irish Wolf King, found five salmon in a well. A hazel nut tree (also associated with wisdom) stood over this spring. The nuts were unseated by the fish, which Cormac and the salmon ate, thus acquiring knowledge. Some of the nuts drifted downstream, and those poets and any others who drank of this water found inspiration.

The European people of the Middle Ages retained these beliefs, including the conception that salmon's wisdom could be assimilated by eating the fish.

## MEDICINE AND POWER

| | |
|---|---|
| DIRECTION | West (autumn) |
| ELEMENT | Water |
| TRAITS | Endurance, strength, determination |
| ASSOCIATIONS | Plenty, bounty, rebirth, renewal and death, knowledge, spirit |

Salmon medicine is that of continuity of the species. Each year, the fish fight their way upstream in order to spawn. Therefore salmon represents the cycle of life and death. Its procreation can mean its demise; yet its young remain. The parent dies so that the child can live, and the parent is made flesh. Therefore, salmon also means sacrifice, resurrection and regeneration, for each year the fish are reborn.

And what else can be gained in the process of birth, life, death and renewal, but learning? Learning, retained long enough, must inevitably become wisdom. Thus it is easy to see how the Celtic people saw the salmon's cycle and drew their own conclusions. Neither is it a great leap to associate salmon and fish with the resurrection of Christ.

Salmon's navigational skills can be called upon in order to find one's way. Its intelligence can be invoked as an aid to any kind of in-depth study. If ram sparks the fire of initiation, then salmon provides the endurance required to continue with a project, and the determination to complete it.

Salmon medicine teaches awareness of life's journey. It can help one find meaning and purpose. Its medicine reveals one's spiritual path. On the physical level, salmon's magic is progression with perseverance towards one's goal, or one's destiny. It is trusting in the unknown and surrendering to the mystery of life.

Salmon doesn't divulge its secrets easily. Often the waters of inspiration and foreknowledge must be plumbed in the depths of the emotions. Salmon deals with the unconscious, the place from which all elemental magic and instinctive wisdom comes.

Salmon's appearance signals a time of plenty. It suggests stocking up for winter. It can mean a symbolic 'death' followed by rebirth and renewal. If salmon foretells a passing – such as the end of a relationship, a move resulting in the loss of friends – it also carries within it the promise of a new beginning, a birth. The salmon gives up its life after the eggs are laid, the deed accomplished, the goal attained. The Atlantic salmon live to spawn another day.

Salmon endows intelligence. So, the person with salmon medicine is a 'wise man', the true meaning of shaman and holy man or magician. Like the salamander, the salmon appears cold. This person may seem a bit odd (a fish out of water), yet is someone whose intelligence is profound, and upon whom one can rely for sound advice. This is the sort of annoying person who always knows where he or she is going, and even more irritatingly, always gets there.

# SEAL/ SEA LION

Eared seals: *Otariidae*
Hair seals: *Phocadae*

## BIOLOGICAL INFORMATION

The eared seal group includes sea lions and fur seals. The hind flippers rotate to steer in the water, and the animals can 'gallop' across land. The flippers are thick and hairless with a well-developed nail on the third digit. The colour varies, but none of the species displays any distinctive stripes or spots. They can weigh from 38 kg (84 lb) for a small fur seal female to an excess of tonnes (tons) in the case of the walrus or elephant seal.

The earless seals have their hind flippers turned completely back and locked into position. On land, the top speed they can reach is 1.6 km (1 mile) per hour. They can also be found in fresh water. Most species are gregarious, gathering together into groups where food sources will sustain them.

### HABITAT

Salt water, oceans, bays and seas. They must breed on land. Some sort of seal or sea lion can be found from the north polar regions to the South Pole. They prefer colder water and kelp forests.

### CHARACTERISTICS

Graceful in water, but clumsy on land, these animals can stay submerged for periods of up to 45 minutes. They can dive to depths in excess of 850 metres (about 2,500 ft). When diving their heartbeat slows to seven beats per minute to conserve oxygen, and most of their blood is directed towards the brain. This animal is strictly a carnivore, and actually one of the sea's top predators – only exceeded by the shark and porpoise. The latter two often prey on seal and sea lion.

The sea lion is the smaller of the two. It is more agile on land because its flippers are not fixed. It is the sea lion we see most often in circuses, sea parks or aquaria. Therefore, people confuse the animals, often referring to the sea lion as a seal. The most distinguishing characteristic between sea lions and seals is that the latter have no external pinna to mark their ear canals.

Both form herds to breed, the time of year dependent on the hemisphere. Sea lion bulls maintain a harem of several cows. The offspring begin swimming at two weeks of age. They are weaned at four to six weeks after birth. There is usually a single pup. Twins are uncommon, but not unknown.

The *phocids* or haired seal are monogamous, pairing up for the breeding season. The young of the eared seal are born with fur, while the earless seal has extended hairs so that it presents a fuzzier appearance.

## LEGENDS AND TRADITIONS

The Haida, a seafaring tribe of the American northwest whose land stretched from the Queen Charlotte Islands of British Columbia up to Alaska, depended upon fish, seal and sea otter for sustenance. In the teachings of Totemic America, an artform similar to heraldry, a person might be part of a seal 'sib' or clan. If someone dreamed of a particular animal, such as a seal, they would be able to exhibit the animal's totems (signs) to proclaim their magic or power.

The Inuit were almost totally dependent upon the seal for food, fuel and fur. According to Inuit legend, the first woman turned herself into a bear, and from her all sea mammals, including the seal and sea lion, emerged.

The Aleut, from which the Aleutian Islands along the Bering Strait derive their name, used the skins of walruses and seals to make their shelters. They created *baidarka*, the Aleutian kayak, also from the skins of sea lions. Therefore, the sea lion/seal were sacred and certain rituals had to be performed in order to appease their spirits before a hunt.

Some of the Arctic tribes believed that the bladders and bones of the seal contained the spirit of the animal, which if returned to the sea would be reborn in the flesh, thus repopulating the oceans and maintaining the food supply. After every hunt these parts were removed very carefully and, at an annual festival, were honoured with dances and food, after which the remains were taken and thrust back through the ice into the sea.

The selkies of the Shetland and Orkney islands and Iceland were associated with the grey seal. The seal was thought to shed its coat at night and then take human form to seduce young men and women. Myth has it that if a barren woman shed seven tears for a male selkie, she would be rewarded with a child. The Breton believed the seal skin remained in tune with the ebb and flow of the tides and that, even after being parted from the animal's body, the fur could be seen ruffling when the tides changed.

## MEDICINE AND POWER

| | |
|---|---|
| DIRECTION | Depends on location |
| ELEMENT | Water |
| TRAITS | Community, successful adaptation, play |
| ASSOCIATIONS | Wealth and plenty, joy and play, grace, sea rhythms and dance |

Seal and sea lion contain some of the same elements of otter, particularly in the case of the *Phocadae* family of hair (earless) seals. It is believed that they descended from the family *Mustilid* (otters). All have conquered water, which symbolically deals with the emotions and creativity.

Seals and sea lions are associated with the shoreline, which in times past was considered a 'between' place and attributed to the faeries. In English-speaking lands, tales of the seductive power of the selkie are still told.

The tears of the creature are significant. This is how it clears its vision underwater; thus, we have the notion of the cleansing power of tears. This suggests vision through emotion or the ability to gain access to subconscious wisdom by getting in touch with one's feelings.

In spite of all the feminine implications, the furred seal populations are male-dominated systems. Thus, the seal/sea lion speaks of masculine energy contained within the feminine. To the human eye, the breeding sites appear chaotic and disordered, yet the females and their young live within a well-defined territory.

Seal/sea lion should be invoked when one wants to get in touch with the water element and the rhythm of the ocean tides. On a purely practical level, their energy can provide insulation from the cold, both metaphorically and physically. The seal, especially the bull, provides strength and more 'war-like' characteristics. Sea lion, like otter, teaches joy. From both one can learn to dance upon the waves of life, skating on the surface of feelings. Conversely, they can act as helpers and guides when it is time to dive deep into the shifting world of emotions.

A creature of the cold climates, seal brings wealth, nourishment and sustenance despite the prolonged Arctic winters. Thus the seal, like the salmon, contains the promise of plenty. It feeds the human population through the sacrifice of its life. The seal and sea lion had all the same symbolic implications for the Inuit and the Aleuts that buffalo had for the people of the Plains and which deer brought to the tribes of the west coast.

The appearance of seal/sea lion promises fertility, nourishment and sustenance. If its arrival coincides with a time of want or when life has become ice-locked, both seal and sea lion can help the individual dig a way to freedom. Only seal/sea lion knows the secret of maintaining openings in frozen sea. Other animals take advantage of these holes, including polar bear and man. Thus, seal helps more than just himself.

Sea lion and seal people tend to be possessive of their territory, their partners and their young. They are highly protective. Seal men may bluff and bluster, but usually they save these displays of bravado for other men. The sea lion male is more domesticated. Seal and sea lion people are graceful in the water. Those with seal medicine tend to be more clumsy on land. They have the ability to dig underneath the surface, the facade or masque one presents to the world, and intuitively understand the emotions of others.

# SKUNK

Striped skunk: *Mephistis mephitis*
Hooded skunk: *Mephistis macrura*
Spotted skunk: *Spilogale putorius/gracilis*

## BIOLOGICAL INFORMATION

The striped skunk is the most common species. It measures 52 to 80 cm (20 to 31 inches) in length. Its tail is 18 to 39 cm (8 to 16 inches). It weighs 2.7 to 6.7 kg (6 to 14 lb).

Like most members of the *Mustelidae* (weasel) family, skunks have short legs, rounded ears and a pointed snout. All the breeds are black and white, but none has the single white stripe often portrayed. The striped skunk actually has two stripes which meet to form a cap on top of its head.

The eastern spotted skunk has both mottled spots and stripes running along its sides. It is the smallest and most agile of all the species. Meanwhile, the hooded skunk's stripes adorn its flanks rather than its back.

### HABITAT

The skunk has adjusted to many diverse environments, including deserts, woodland, grassy plains, suburbs, farmland, scrub and rocky beds.

Generally it prefers to live where there is cover. Between the three kinds of skunk, the entire continental US is covered. The most well known, the striped skunk, inhabits each one of the 48 continental States. Its range extends into the lower half of Canada. The spotted skunk is found mainly along the Mississippi River basin. The hooded and hog-nosed skunks have taken up residence in a small stretch of land in the American southwest, along the Rio Grande (Arizona, New Mexico and Texas).

## CHARACTERISTICS

The skunk is solitary and primarily nocturnal. Skunk usually live in the abandoned dens of other animals. Rarely will they dig their own burrows. Omnivorous, they root around for insects, grubs and seeds. They also eat berries and fruit. Skunk's only predator is the great horned owl, which has no sense of smell.

Skunk sprays musk. It is produced by two glands about 3/4 inch in diameter located at the base of its tail. It sprays only as a defensive measure and gives three warnings – a stamp of the feet, a change in position so that the back is facing the target, and a lift of its tail. If the opponent backs away during the first two warnings, the skunk will usually lose interest. However, once the tail is raised, it is too late.

The skunk can spray up to 15 feet. The musk consists of seven different chemicals – one that is found nowhere else in nature, one that has never been observed previously, and several that still cannot be reproduced in a lab. If the spray gets in the eyes, it burns and there may be a period of temporary blindness.

In their reproductive cycle, skunks delay implantation (in the case of the spotted skunk, for up to 200 days). This allows the animals to mate in summer or autumn and not bear young until the following spring. The mother is protective – seeing a mother skunk waddling along as she leads a line of several young is not uncommon.

## LEGENDS AND TRADITIONS

Among the Hidatsa and Mandan of the Kansas/Nebraska/Dakota area, the women's Skunk and Enemy Societies were concerned exclusively with war. It was their duty to meet their men after battle and carry their trophies, scalps. They paraded through town and performed victory dances for the warriors.

The Santa Clara Corn Dance of the Tewa Pueblo tribes dealt with fertility and renewal. The dancer wore skunk fur tied around his ankles, suggesting that skunk was associated with the fruitfulness and productivity of the earth.

For many tribes skunk was a symbol of strength and courage, especially in warfare. Feisty skunk never fled, no matter how big or impressive its adversary. Skunk proved its valour every time it turned its back upon an enemy, for only the mightiest warrior could afford to take such a risk. It was for this reason that young Dakota and Lakota braves placed skunk fur upon the heels of their moccasins before going into battle. By doing so the warrior invoked the power and bravery of skunk. This custom seems to be a later import, for in Mary Henderson Eastman's *Dahcotah, Life and Legends of the Sioux*, first published in 1849, one elder complained of this new 'fad' among the dandified young men of his tribe. The Oglala tribe of the Plains Lakota linked skunk with earth powers similar to those of the badger.

Perhaps both the fashion for wearing skunk fur on their moccasins and the association with badger were adopted from the Dakota's traditional enemies, the Ojibwe. Skunk featured in one Ojibwe story about creation.[11] When time began, skunk was bigger. For some reason, he started to shrink. Skunk knew that if he grew too small he couldn't hunt unless he made some powerful medicine. Skunk was wise, and he made a special powder of roots and herbs. He mixed this powder with water and drank it. He tried his medicine upon a mighty oak. The tree withered and died. So clever skunk has created his own protection.

Skunk was also a primary character in the naming of the United States' 'second city', Chicago. In this story, however, skunk didn't fare as well. Once a hunter of the Ottawa tribe was trapping on the shores of Lake Michigan. He and his wife quarrelled and she decided to leave. The hunter was angry, and he tracked her. But as he followed, the footprints began to change. Eventually he reached a marshy area where wild onions (skunk grass) grew. He did not find his wife, but a huge skunk in her stead, so he named the marsh *Chicago*, which in the Ottawa language meant 'the place of the Skunk', and that's how the city now standing on this site got its name.

Skunk revealed a certain lack of insight in the southwestern tale of the jaguar and the skunk. Jaguar adopted skunk and took him out to teach him how to hunt. Their first time out, jaguar killed a huge deer with a single swipe. When the meat ran out, skunk decided to try his luck. He did as jaguar did, but the stag impaled the skunk, who then died. This story contained several lesson for the children of the tribe. The first was to listen to their elders. It also warned of overconfidence and reflected the old adage: a little bit of knowledge is a dangerous thing. It also cautioned the young hunter to know his limitations while it admonished the teacher to be clear in his instruction.

In another legend, skunk proved itself even trickier than coyote. The two joined forces to hunt prairie dog. Coyote told skunk to lay down and pretend to be dead. Coyote then began to dance around the skunk's body, calling, 'Come look, see.' Ever curious, the prairie dogs came over and coyote asked them to join his dance. He told the prairie dogs to close their eyes, adding the sinister note that anyone who opened their eyes would by struck dead by the Great Spirit. The prairie dogs obediently closed their eyes, and coyote killed one. After a while he called a break, and the prairie dogs opened their eyes to discover one of their number dead. Coyote snarled that this one must have disobeyed the injunction. And so it went: they'd dance and rest, and each time they rested they found another prairie dog dead – until there were none but coyote and skunk left.

Skunk rose from his faint and the two started to argue over who would get the fattest prairie dogs. Coyote proposed a race. Skunk protested that he was small and could not run as fast. Charitably, coyote gave skunk a head start. The skunk darted away and, as soon as he was out of sight of the coyote, skunk dived into a cave and waited until coyote galloped past, then returned to the prairie dogs. By the time coyote returned he found a very satisfied skunk and just two scraggly prairie dogs left.

## MEDICINE AND POWER

| | |
|---|---|
| DIRECTION | East |
| ELEMENT | Earth |
| TRAITS | Courage, standing one's ground; defence, making a stink |
| ASSOCIATIONS | Playfulness, nonchalance, musk and sexual energy; herb lore |

European impressions of skunk have been shaped by two characters – the Warner Brothers cartoon character Pepe le Pu, who reflects skunk's amorous tendencies and thereby, ironically, its association with sexual energy. Then there's the character named Flower in the Disney cartoon film *Bambi*, who reflects something of skunk's sense of humour and playfulness. Unfortunately, these characterizations have left most people with the impression that skunk is laughable. During lectures and guided meditations, if an individual comes up with skunk as a power animal he or she appears a bit sheepish and, when announced, this admission usually elicits a chuckle from the rest of the group.

Nothing could be further from the truth. In the US skunk is respected, and any person or animal who has ever had a confrontation with a skunk understands why. Fun-loving, relaxed skunk combines the best of otter: playfulness without the ferocity; the best of porcupine: protective capabilities but with an even more effective and long-range defence mechanism; and the best of badger: sharing its knowledge of herbs without badger's so-called aggressive tendencies. Its weapon is more gentle than porcupine's, causing less permanent damage, although skunk's spray is painful and can blind temporarily. Skunk assails the senses, not the body. The spines of the porcupine are barbed. They work their way into the flesh and can cause great damage. Left alone, a single spine can result in infection, septicaemia, even death. Nevertheless, skunk (unlike porcupine) can take on a bear at a few paces and *win*, using little more than insulting body language and a flick of its tail. Porcupine is at a greater risk, since the predator must touch the creature in order for its defence to be activated. Few get that close to skunk. Once touched, porcupine can be flipped over, exposing the soft flesh of its stomach, but skunk is prey of only one: the owl, which has no sense of smell.

The connection of skunk with herb lore, medicinal plants and roots is rarely discussed, much less explored, yet skunk has the same knowledge as badger. If the fables are correct, skunk medicine is possibly greater than badger's in that skunk was able to create his own medicine. Skunk is self-taught and self-contained. The rites of badger medicine rely as much on its powerful claws as on plants and roots. Thus, badger digs out a complaint. Skunk techniques are verbal. They do not rely on 'ritual' surgery, as when the shaman draws the claws of the badger across the affected part.

Skunk is courage without aggression. It imparts constancy and faith. The skunk as a power animal is a steadfast and staunch supporter. Skunk imparts nonchalance along with bravery, for skunk never runs from an enemy. The ability to intimidate without actual threat should not be taken lightly. It suggests balance and a respect for the rights of other creatures based on self-respect. This respect for the self and others embodies the ideal of 'all our relations', and engenders in the recipient a similar respect for others.

Skunk is playful and endows the individual with a sense of fun. Skunk's arrival can indicate that the individual is taking him- or herself too seriously. Skunk appears when the person is confronting issues of self-respect and self-esteem. It could be that the person needs to give a warning stamp to another who is trying to take advantage. It can signal a time to stand up for one's rights, as skunk did with coyote.

If one calls upon skunk, it will impart not only the courage to confront, but the balance to do this without getting flustered or causing harm to another. Skunk can be invoked for protection, but steadfastness and equilibrium are skunk's greatest gifts.[2]

People with skunk medicine will exhibit a curiosity about herb lore and alternative therapies, such as aromatherapy. Independent, the skunk person will never accept facts from another authority. This individual will prefer to explore the possibilities for him- or herself. Skunk people exude confidence, but not cockiness. Skunk has nothing to prove. They also exude sexual energy; therefore they have an ability to attract rather than repel. If Pepe le Pu lived in fact, the object of its attentions probably wouldn't run away. Skunks are very charismatic and surprisingly co-operative.

# SNAKE

*Typhlopgidae*
*Leptothyphlopidae*
Viper: *Viperadae*
Pit Viper: *Crotalidae*

## BIOLOGICAL INFORMATION

Snake is a group that encompasses some four different families. Snakes can vary in size, from 31 cm (1 ft) to an excess of 10 metres (33 ft). Some of the most deadly snakes actually appear innocuous. The highly venomous tree snake is not much larger in diameter than the average drinking straw. It grows to about 45 cm (18 inches), but its bite can cause death to a full-grown man within seconds. The garter snake can be as large as 1 to 2 m (approximately 3 – 6 feet) and several times the size of the tree snake in diameter, yet it is nonpoisonous and a relatively timid creature. The anaconda, meanwhile, grows to 11.7 m (39 ft). It is as thick as a man's thigh. The python is longer, but not as stout.

Fossils of snakes have been located in the late Eocene crustacean deposits. These reveal that snakes had already evolved the elongated bodies, fused eyelids and suppressed limbs which mark the group. Snakes have relatively poor sight. Their eyes are susceptible to the infra-red end of the spectrum, so they detect heat rather than possess what we would consider visual acuity. Snakes have an exceptional sense of smell with two olfactory organs – the nose and Jacobsen's orb in the mouth. Thus, by extending its flicking tongue the snake collects tastes and smells. This ability is so highly developed that a snake can decipher the type of prey by tasting the air several yards away from it.

Most poisonous snakes deliver their venom by biting. However, the cobra spits its venom, its aim being to blind. Like the skunk, it assaults the senses. This does not mean that cobras don't bite. Some authorities believe that it was a cobra that bit Cleopatra, since it is a species native to Egypt while the asp is not.

## HABITAT

There are snakes who swim in water – oceans, rivers and lakes. Snakes also live on land and have adapted to the trees. Snakes may make their homes in woodland and on the forest floor. The two largest species, the boa constrictor and the anaconda, come from the tropics. Garter snakes live as far north as Hudson Bay in Canada where they hibernate throughout a large portion of the year. Sidewinders (the name describes their movement) are habituated to desert environments. Their sideways slide works well in rough sand and keeps the majority of its body off the hot sand most of the time.

The sandswimmer of Arizona has come up with a different solution to the same problem: its head is streamlined and tapered to provide as little resistance as possible. Its eyes are covered with scratch-resistant lenses; it plunges into the loose sand and propels itself along using its scales. The sandswimmer does not tunnel as much as it dives and thrusts itself through the surface. Beneath the sand, the sandswimmer is virtually blind, so it hunts by vibration.

## CHARACTERISTICS

Snakes are differentiated according to whether they are venomous or not, and through their tooth structure and locomotion. The poisonous variety encompasses three of the four groups. The viper is differentiated from the merely venomous by its tooth structure. The viper's elongated fangs fold back when not in use, with the pit viper further distinguished by the characteristic pits, an additional sense organ, located below the eyes on either side of the nostrils.

Scales are the secret of snake's success. It is able to grow because it can shed its skin, and it can move despite the fact that it has no legs because the textured scales provide both impetus and resistance.

Means of reproduction also vary. Snakes may be egg-layers, like the rattler, or give birth to live young like the garter snake. The mating patterns of the garter are frightening to behold. The males wake up first and move out to warm in the sun. As single females (the larger of the two genders) emerge, still groggy from sleep, they are covered by hundreds of squirming males until they are completely engulfed. Some snakes have retained a single adapted leg to hold the female in place when they mate.

With egg-layers, the intensity of the heat – or the heat at which their eggs are kept – during incubation decides the gender of the members of the clutch.

## LEGENDS AND TRADITIONS

| | |
|---|---|
| GODDESSES | Ua Zit (Neolithic), Ishtar, Tiamat (Babylonian), Nebkhet, Wadjet (Egyptian), Nina, Nidaba, Ninlil, Inanna (Sumerian), Gaeas (Greek), Venus (Roman) |
| GODS | Set, Apep (Egyptian), Typhon (Greek), Mercury (Roman), Quezalcoatl (pre-Columbian Mexico), the Horned Serpent by any name (Native American) |

The spiral carved on the Pampas Colorado by the Nasca of southern Peru is believed to represent a snake. Many have questioned whether the South Americans of 10,000 years ago (8,000 BC) had the capacity to create these monumental figures with such precision and accuracy, which seems an insult to the ingenuity of the native peoples of South America. Recent studies confirm that the Nasca had not only the tools, but the skills to complete these magnificent drawings, for they have been replicated using only those materials and implements which, according to archaeology, would have been available at the time.

The serpent, along with jaguar and deer, was the most frequently portrayed symbol in Mayan art. Curiously, the snake itself rarely appears without embellishments. Yet the presence of its parts are immediately recognizable when viewing Mayan temples and stelae. The snake was assimilated in the divine images of Quezalcoatl (the feathered serpent), the Serpent bird, and the two-headed dragon. The serpent often adorned other statuary or reliefs. Snake appeared with a human head or as a tongue spewing from the mouth of other beings – bird or human. The serpent decorated columns and altars. Its repetitive undulations made good border designs. Experts agree that the snake pictured by the Mayan was the rattler, for an unmistakable and stylized bobble is always represented on the end of the tail.

The symbol of the feathered serpent was common to both the Mayan and Nahua, and was later adopted by the Zapotec, Toltec and Aztec. It reached as far south as Argentina, for the snake figures largely in Calchaqui art. The snake was one of many animals which featured in Inca mythology. When the feathered serpent was embraced by the Aztecs it became a secondary divinity – the positive (daylight) opposite of the smoking mirror, Texcatlipoca.

The power associated with the feathered serpent remained relatively consistent and benign, even the name remaining the unchanged. Quezalcoatl (the feathered serpent) represented rain, which in the Yucatan peninsula, with its predominantly lime soil, would have been a vital commodity. The surrounding jungle is dwarfed in comparison to the jungle areas of the Amazon. The porous sand of the Yucatan literally draws water away from the surface and flushes it back out to sea. Therefore, water would have been collected and stored in order to maintain any kind of consistent agriculture, although studies suggest that the soil then was not so poor as it is now.

Water would also have been a vital resource to the desert-like climates of the Mexican plateau, the arid Pampas Colorado of the Nasca, and the mountain-based Incas.

Rattlers can swim if necessary, although most species are land-loving and prefer dry, desert climes. Some are found in forests, yet the link with rain seems tenuous. The water-loving anaconda has long been worshipped by the peoples of Central and South America. Perhaps the two species were merged, just as the image of bird and serpent was united to form the Feathered Serpent. Could the two-headed dragon be another merging of these two species?

The snake symbol was often linked with the horned serpent of North America. The horned serpent was worshipped in the US from the Pueblo tribes (often thought to be those first affected by the dissolution and migration of the Aztecs) including the Zuni, Hopi and Tewa, to the far northwest. The belief in the horned serpent was held by the Iroquois of the northeast and Algonquin of the north and northwest. The Plains and Great Lakes tribes of the Lakota and Dakota, Menominee and Blackfoot believed in a horned serpent, so its influence spread from sea to sea. The horned serpent was the avid enemy of the thunderbeings or thunderbirds. Indeed, the golden eagle is a snake eagle.

Snake was revered by the mound peoples of the Ohio and Mississippi basin. Many of these earthworks were burial mounds which, when excavated, revealed up to 1,000 bodies (along with their grave goods) in a single structure. One of the most famous of these earthworks is the serpent mound located in Adams County, Ohio. It is .93 m (3 ft) high and 405 m (1,350 feet) long, and was built by the Aedna people in around 2000 BC. These people, like the Maya of the extreme west, bound their skulls to flatten them. The later mound builders of the Ohio Valley, the 'Hopewell' Indians, maintained the custom of binding.

Little is known about the tribes of the southeast, except for the fact that their society was highly structured, with a noble class and a commoner class. These were further subdivided into clans represented by an animal spirit. Some tribes were more egalitarian than others. In one, the Calusa, a nobleman or noblewoman could only marry a commoner, so each successive generation became less 'noble' than the last until after five generations they were considered commoners. The concept of nobility was so ingrained in the Natchez people that the king wed his sister to prevent such thinning of the royal bloodline. The nobles were categorised into Suns, Nobility and Honoured People. In 1750 the great Natchez War Chief Tattooed Serpent died. The name itself, attributed to one of the nobles of the Great Suns, suggests that the snake was significant for the Natchez.

The Seminole, who were later imports, fleeing to the inhospitable Florida Everglades to escape the white man, also had stories of a horned serpent. The Cree, who originated in Florida, likewise relayed legends of a horned serpent. There is no reason to presume that earlier tribes did not share these legends.

How does one explain the universality of these snake stories and symbols? The most logical, albeit unproven, explanation involves commerce. Yet many present-day scientists continue to deny the likelihood of trade between Native American cultures, preferring to believe that 'primitives' could not develop such a sophisticated or far-reaching system of barter and exchange. The fact that Ai of the Florida Keys went immediately to war when the Spanish first arrived in 1600 indicates prior knowledge of the *conquistadors*, their methods and their goals, which could only have come from an outside source. This suggests a commerce between the native cultures of the Gulf that would have included the Maya in the extreme west and the seafaring Ais of the east.

The Mandan of Nebraska/South and North Dakota were primarily farmer-traders whose goods were found as far west as the Sierra Nevada Mountains of California and the Cascades of Oregon, east beyond the Mississippi to the Great Lakes, and far into Canada. This system, which was 'discovered' in the late 18th century, had been long established. The fact that trade with or through the Mandan tribe had reached the coastal areas is evidenced by the presence of shells as decorations in tribal dress.

Other so-called experts contend that any culture which relied on oral tradition to relay its history could not have retained a societal memory from 8000 BC through AD 1600, nor disseminate the information from Argentina to Canada, the Pacific coast to the Atlantic. One might argue that if tribes were able to preserve their ceremonies despite a century of government suppression, religious repression and outright persecution, then oral transmission would more than meet this objective.

Another theory has to do with the 'ripple effect' resulting from the fall of the Aztecs. Archaeological discoveries reveal Aztec artefacts at Anasasi settlements in New Mexico. The religion of Central America has been revealed in the Skidi Pawnee, who migrated from Mexico to Oklahoma and Kansas.

The timing of these events – the Nasca carvings of 8000 BC, the snake mounds built in 2000 BC, the Mayan temples of AD 800 to 1100, and the Aztec artefacts of AD 1500 – gives us no real clue. However, recent revelations in the Middle East have forced many archaeologists to review their limited ideas about primitive man and trade. New finds indicate that commerce existed long before previously believed. To expect any less of the Native American would be condescending to the extreme.

Even if no real conclusion can be drawn, it is safe to say that the horned serpent was well established before the arrival of the Europeans, and that belief in it was pervasive.

Snake has always been either revered or reviled. The Cree, who have remained in the Carolinas, do not disturb snakes when they come across them. In fact they will move to the other side of the path to avoid one, for they believe if the snake is harmed it will wreak vengeance upon the guilty party and their family. Native peoples from such diverse places as the Seminoles in Florida and the Cherokee, now located in Oklahoma, share these beliefs. If a Cherokee kills a rattlesnake, he apologizes. Reparation must be made to the snake's spirit, often through an intermediary such as a holy man.

A tale from the time when the Cherokee still lived in the south, before the Trail of Tears, describes snake as hypnotic and enticing. To see a two-horned snake meant bad luck. Once the tribe caught a Shawnee boy and promised him his freedom if he would go out and kill the two-horned snake. The Shawnee boy survived by hiding behind fire from the snake's poisonous venom. The Cherokee went down to the spot where snake had died and tied up his skin and his bones and made them into a medicine bundle, which they believed would bring good fortune to the tribe. On that spot a black lake sprung where the women dyed reeds for their baskets.

The peoples of the southwest had probably the most positive image of snake. It was associated with the sun, rebirth and sexuality. However, its venomous qualities were not forgotten. To be adopted by snake as a power animal meant trial by ordeal. The person would have to handle poisonous snakes. He or she might be bitten – not all handlers were – and if he or she rejected the poison and survived, snake's medicine was ensured. The Native Americans observed that snake was slow to anger, so for some, it was considered symbolic of tolerance.

In the north and in the southeast, snake was an animal not to be trusted. The Sioux received their name from the French, which was an abbreviated version of the Algonquin words *Nadowa sioux* ('snake little'). The Chippewa adopted the Algonquin term *Nadowasioux*, but gave it a new context and a new meaning – variously 'lying adders' or 'lying snake'.

For the Lakota and Dakota who received this appellation, *Zuzeca* ('snake') had dominion over the ability to do things slyly. It was able to move unseen and unnoticed: commendable traits for the scout and warrior, but not for the peace-maker. *Zuzeca*, therefore, also meant 'liar'. The term 'forked tongue' comes from this, though there are suggestions that it comes from the Lakota word for 'two-faced woman' – literally, someone who speaks out of both sides of her face. So the Lakota and Dakota view was mixed.

If an Oglala warrior saw a snake on his path, he viewed its appearance with foreboding.

Snakes were worshipped in the Old World from the earliest times. The primary divinities of Sumeria were snake goddesses, *Nidaba*, scribes of Sumerian heaven. Ninlil, who brought the gift of agriculture, had the tail of the serpent. Stephen Langdon, the archaeologist who led some of the earliest excavations in Sumeria, asserted that Inanna (or Ininni) was connected with snake worship. He wrote of a Nina, an earlier version of Inanna, the serpent goddess which dated back to the earliest periods. The serpent was the interpreter of dreams. The people of Elam also worshipped snakes.

Ishtar of Babylonia was associated with the planet Venus. Both Ishtar and the Roman goddess Venus have been linked with snakes. The other name for the planet Venus was *Masat*, translated as 'Prophetess'. Ishtar bore the staff, entwined with serpents, which would later be adopted by Mercury. The Babylonian-Kassite serpent-dragon, Tiamat, was the creator of the universe.

Evidence of snake worship in one form or another has been found all over Crete. Statuary show priestesses who hold snakes in their hands or have them coiling around their arms and waists. Pottery, temple walls and other artefacts depicted snakes. In Knossos, certain clay pipes were described as 'snake tubes'.

The Egyptian Set, god of destruction, often took the shape of the great serpent Apep, and as such held dominion over all reptiles. In one story, Set slew Horus while in this guise, biting off his head after battle. In another version of this tale, Horus decapitated Set who was then transformed into the great serpent which guards the underworld. Phonetically, the hieroglyph for serpent represented the sound *tch*.

The Egyptian cobra was a symbol of royalty. Coupled with the vulture, it was worn on a diadem of the combined Upper and Lower Kingdoms. The vulture represented the goddess Nebkhet and the cobra Wadjet of Buto. This goddess was the Greek Edjo. Her name meant she-of-the-papyrus. In an earlier age the cobra was worshipped under the name Renenutet, the provider of nourishment, and later in the 20th dynasty as Meretseger, the lover of silence.

The cobra was often depicted with the disk of the sun. The symbol represented Re (Ra) and was associated with the person of the king. In a funerary context, the cobra guarded each of the underworld gates which had to be passed on the way to the Field of Reeds.

Serpent in the form of snake or dragon figures largely in many of the creation myths. One such was Gaeas, mother of the Titans. The ungrateful children cleaved her in twain, and from one half they created the firmament and the other the earth. Snake/dragon in the form of a goddess created man according to one Chinese legend, moulding him from clay. Serpent also flew as Typhon, who also had a place in the creation of the world through his mother Gaeas in the creation of the universe. He later was transformed into the volcano of the same name. Snake was chaos, she was void – life *en potentia*, before form and matter rushed in to fill the emptiness.

Thus, snake was acknowledged by Romans and Greeks. The chariots of Demeter were drawn by a winged serpent. Greek associations with the serpent goddess are best illustrated in Delphi where the oracle of divine wisdom was known as *Pythia*. In later Greek writing this oracle is referred to as male, but earliest transcripts state that the original Pythia was female. Indeed, Delphi itself was once called Pytho. The first temple was built by women, and the shrine was dedicated to the primeval prophetess. Only later was the temple linked to Apollo and Zeus. Again, the snake's association with divination is clear.

For Christianity, of course, Satan first appeared to man in the form of a serpent, tempting Eve into partaking of fruit from the tree of knowledge. This link between the devil, snake, woman and knowledge is another example of the Catholic faith appropriating earlier myths and changing them for their own purposes. Snake and woman did not lose their divinity, nor their place in the creation, they were simply demoted. Serpent was no longer the bringer of good but of temptation and evil. The former paganism exalted women and sexuality. Pagans took the words of the divine and credited them to a snake.

Further north, serpents and dragons meant trouble to the Vikings and the Celts even before their introduction to Christianity. The Vikings told of a great snake, Nidhoggre, coiled at the base of the universal tree Jorgmundr. If ever the serpent broke free, it would spell the end of the universe. Their appearance portended sterility and doom for the Celts. Arthur dreamed of serpents at the time of Mordred's conception. Thus, the serpent is a warning or bad omen. This theme recurs when Arthur is devoured by a snake in a dream the night before his battle with his ill-fated offspring. A serpent even prompts the fight.

Alchemists believed that the shape of a vessel influenced the kind of transformation that took place therein. They developed a 'winding pipe', called the mercurial serpent, which was used in the distillation of aqua vitae.

The two-headed serpent represented the triune aspect of the earth-god-Mercury (animal, vegetable and mineral). The mercurial serpent spews forth the fumes of *prima materia*. It was associated with cleaving the lunar egg (fertilization) and putrefaction. Thus, it was birth, death and rebirth.

Other cultures, notably the later Gnostic, viewed the Ourboros (an image of the snake biting its tail) as symbolic of time and its continuity – hence infinity. It was also considered an emblem of self-fecundation and self-sufficiency. Heraldry credits the origin of the sign to the Egyptians, where it was used to symbolize gold.

Mithraic cults, Buddhism and Hinduism all have their legends relating to serpent, or to gods/goddess in the guise of a snake. In Hinduism the god Shiva was blessed when a coiled snake turned into a garland of flowers and covered the God in beauty. The number of divinities or stories about divinities that have some kind of connection to serpent is too long to detail here. Besides those mentioned above, these include: Medusa the Gorgon, Hercules, Jason, Artemis, Hecate, Lilith, Persephone, Isis, the Iliad, and the Caduceus.

In Grimm's fairy tale the White Snake, partaking of the flesh of this kind of serpent granted wisdom and the ability to understand the speech of all animals. So the association with magic remains, and superstitions about snakes abound. To kill the first adder one saw in the spring was supposed to ensure good luck throughout the year and triumph over one's enemies. An old English belief was that if a person saw an adder by the door this would portend a death.

## MEDICINE AND POWER

| | |
|---|---|
| DIRECTION | South |
| ELEMENTS | Fire, Sun |
| TRAITS | Shedding of the old, hence transformation and growth |
| ASSOCIATIONS | Rebirth, creativity, sexuality, magic and prediction, alchemy, reproduction |

The reverence of serpent is universal. No culture remains untouched. The reaction of fear and fascination also appears to be widespread, while the current trend seems to be to sanitize and anaesthetize previous pagan faiths. What can be made of such rich, albeit diverse, perspectives?

Snake was birth; snake was death. Snake represented the forces of creation ... and destruction. Serpent was equated with the sun; it was guardian of the night gates of the underworld. According to Freud, snake was a masculine symbol – the penis. For Jung, snake was the champion of the collective unconscious which assimilates symbols of the past into the present.

Which interpretations are correct? Quite simply, all of them. The serpent represents the totality of the life cycle, both the good and the bad. There cannot be one without the other. This is the proverbial coin that has two sides which cannot be separated. In this world there can be no birth without death. The predator-prey cycle and sacrifice of one for another are necessary parts of existence. White man has discovered this concept almost too late, after he has killed all the animals he has deemed bad and then found himself overrun with foraging deer and elk, who soon stripped the forest and then began to starve without the balancing influence of predatory wolf and bear.

The snake is not good or bad, or even both, it is the cycle itself: change and transformation. The Ourboros is a logical extension of this idea. Snake sheds its skin, leaving the dead behind and beginning anew. Only after it has shed its skin in a mini-death can there be growth. Thus, snake contains the essence of transmutation.

Snake is the good experiences (or luck) and bad which must inevitably hit us all. It embodies change, necessary change and yes, the pain that accompanies it. It bestows the power to transmute poison. This is the basis of the shamanistic rites developed by southwestern Native Americans. The initiate had to be able to assimilate toxins and shed them. Snake was also the protector of hallucinatory plants. With the ingestion of peyote, the snake turns into a flying serpent. The Greek Caduceus, twin snakes twining around a sword, has come to represents the medical profession, hence healing.

In Egypt, snake was associated with writing. Archaeological evidence seems to indicate that the cuneiform script was invented by the Priestess-goddess of Sumeria and Babylonia. In the male-oriented world of the Greek, the god of communication, Hermes, carried the Caduceus. Snake was the protector of the ancient mystery schools, guarding access to knowledge and wisdom.

Thus, snake medicine is probably one of the most powerful to have. It is the medicine of sexuality and creativity. It is the Kundalini, pure energy which provides the spark of life. This energy can be used for healing. Likewise, snake medicine can be employed to turn bad experiences to positive advantage.

When snake appears it suggests an initiation of sorts, a time of transition. It suggests getting in touch with the universal creativity. As guardian of mysteries, snake implies the workings of divine energy through one's life, as an introduction to sacred knowledge. Snake supplies support for transformation at the deepest levels.

Remember, though, this process is probably best represented by the double-edged sword, for snake also suggests lying and deceit. Its energy is destructive as well as fruitful. The slippery nature of snake energy requires cautious handling, for it can be used for good as well as ill. The most positive application of snake energy is to deepen one's understanding.

The snake individual falls into almost as many categories as the snake itself. This person can be inoffensive to the point of being invisible, or this person can be venomous. This person can be truly inspired, or show the more destructive side of the snake's nature. He or she may contain elements of both which, after a particularly poisonous statement leads to sugared apology, can leave the recipient stunned and bemused. Snake can wrap one up with support, or it can strangle and suffocate. Those with snake as a power animal may be able to help others addicted to alcohol or drugs. Yet on the opposite extreme they are most likely to suffer from addictions themselves.[1]

# SPIDER

*Arachnidae*

## BIOLOGICAL INFORMATION

Spiders range in size from those as small as the head of a pin to those as large as a man's hand. The Italian tarantula is one of the most well known. It grows to be about 10 to 12.5 cm (4 – 5 inches) across. The largest can kill and consume a mouse. The Banana spider of Central and South America is actually larger than the tarantula, but its legs are more delicate. Its body is iridescent and smooth and it is specifically adapted to only one environment, banana trees; therefore it has never attained the same notoriety as the tarantula.

Despite their diversity, all spiders share certain characteristics. All have the same the fragile legs – eight, to be precise. Spiders' bodies are split into two sections, unlike insects which are segmented in three. Most but not all are weavers, able to create a type of silk in a gland in their back legs.

### HABITAT

Spider inhabits a wide range of environments. They can live in dens underground; there are certain breeds that weave tiny parachutes and drift high over the tops of the Himalayas. One spider creates an air pocket and spends most of its life under water. Spiders are happy to live in trees or on the ground, and make themselves at home inside the average dwelling. In other words, spiders can be found just about anywhere. They have adapted to every environment and to three of the four elements.

## CHARACTERISTICS

It is difficult to generalize about spider's characteristics. All spiders are predatory. Many, like the tarantula, are venomous; they paralyse their prey. Even some of the smallest spiders produce some sort of chemical which not only stuns, but eventually kills and pre-digests the victim. The brown recluse spider of Mexico and the southwestern US leaves a permanently open wound on a human. The wolf spider hunts or stalks its victims and does not create a web. Most, though, weave a deadly trap in the form of a web. Indeed, the spider is the only species on the planet, besides the human, that builds a snare to trap its victims.

Not all webs are circular in design. The ladder spider constructs a rectangular and vertical web. It is specifically designed to catch larger flying insects such as moths and butterflies, who usually manage to evade the standard spiral webs by sheer weight and mass. When a moth hits a ladder web it gets tangled, as it does in the ordinary web. However, when it frees itself it falls onto the next 'rung' and the next, until finally it exhausts itself – making a nice compliant snack for the spider.

The female is usually larger than the male; for some species the act of procreation is the dance of death, with the female eating the male after impregnation, but an ingenious wily male can occasionally escape to breed another day. Spiders are good mothers, staying with their eggs and protecting them until they hatch – although in the less temperate regions the female may not survive the winter to see the birth of her young. Some actually carry the eggs on their bodies until they hatch. One common spider found in English gardens makes the ultimate sacrifice: this mother lets her young prey upon her body.

Like most shelled creatures, spider must shed its skin in order to grow, emphasizing the link between spider and snake – another thing these two have in common is people's instinctive (negative) reaction to them.

# LEGENDS AND TRADITIONS

Iktomi or Unktomi (Lakota)

One of the most famous and the most photographed of the Nasca figures is spider. It is most likely the complexity of this figure and the inability to see its totality from the ground that presented some of the first doubts to scientists about whether the native farmers of southern Peru had the engineering skills to accomplish such a work. However, the Nasca were excellent weavers whose cloth was much finer than anything made today, more compact with more strands per square inch. In an experiment done in November 1975, Bill Spohrer was able to construct a hot air balloon with a woven reed basket and cloth of the same quality as that of Nasca manufacture. The balloon flew successfully, which would seem to corroborate previous experiments where certain Nasca images were duplicated using surveying technology that would have been in place 12,000 years ago. Evidence of what appears to be large balloons can be found depicted in pottery, yet despite the experiment there still is no proof that the Nasca ever built or rode in such vehicles.

The species of spider illustrated among the Nasca figures was *ricinlei*. This is one of the rarest spiders in the world and found in the far north of the Amazon region. This not only verifies the path of the tribes' migration (the actual carvings date to 10,000 BC), but indicates that the animism as representative of a family or clan was established long before the Nasca arrived in Peru. The spider is shown with one leg extended. What is pictured is a unique reproductive organ which can only be seen under a microscope.

The symbol of spider and spider's web was often used in Dakota and Lakota decoration, for it was believed that any warrior so adorned would become invincible to arrows. When guns became available bullets were added to the list. It was believed that the projectile would pass through the brave and leave him unharmed, just as an arrow or bullet could pass through a spider's web, leaving it relatively intact. Because spiders' webs are difficult to see unless wet, the symbol also endowed the wearer with a type of invisibility. Spider was associated with the thunderbeings. So a spider web, like cocoon power, could be projected against the enemy to cause consternation and confusion.

The mythology of the Lakota is most complex, reflecting both fear and reverence for spider. The god, or more appropriately 'mystery' Iktomi (Unktomi) appeared in the form of the spider. On one side there is spider, symbol of fear, trickster, transformed from the one-time god of wisdom who abused this trust. On the other hand, Iktomi is credited not only with giving all animals their names – hence their shapes, personality and identity – but also with leading man from the darkness of the caves onto the surface of the earth and teaching him the rules of social etiquette. As a result of the process of naming, Iktomi eventually ran out of words before he remembered to name himself – so he ended up as spider, a thrashing miscellany of parts with innumerable manifestations.

Probably the best way to illustrate spider's wide range of powers is to list the many Lakota names for the divine spider:

*Iktomi Kinyan*, 'flying spider'
*Iktomi Luzahan*, 'fast spider'
*Iktomi Wakagisni*, 'daring spider'
*Iktomi Hunkesni*, 'weak spider'
*Iktomi sabic'iya*, 'spider who paints himself black'
*Iktomi ognaya sica*, 'spider who is hard to fool'
*Iktomi mniakinyan*, 'spider who flies over water'
*Iktomi ektasniyetunwan*, 'spider who does not look there'
*Iktomi takuni oholasni*, 'spider who respects nothing'
*Iktomi Maka mahel mani*, 'spider who walks underground'.

Because of spider's divine status, to this day if a Teton kills a spider, he says: 'Wakinyan killed you', for only the thunderbeings have the right to kill Iktomi.

For some, spider's legs represented the four winds of change and the four directions on the medicine wheel, while other tribes credited the gift of fire not to coyote, squirrel, fox or raven, but to spider.

In southwestern America, where weaving was an honoured art, spider was the creator goddess. For the Navajo and Hopi, spider was not only the great weaver, she was creatrix. The Spider Woman cast out a thread east and west to make the horizon, and north and south. She sang her song in the centre of the web of the universe, and gave life to Ut Set and Na Ut Zet. These twin goddesses created the sun and the moon. Then spider created twin sons, the north and south poles who, in turn, made the seasonal cycles. Then Spider Woman spun the earth, trees, bushes, plants and flowers, and moulded animals from the same stuff. Her many names among the tribes include: Hatai Wugti, Awitelin Tsita, Hurung Wuuti, Sussistanako (thought woman), Kokyangwuti and Tsitsicinako.

It seems that the desert tribes were much more tolerant in their view of animals. Perhaps because life in the desert is a precious and rare thing, even the spiders, snakes and lizards were seen as valuable. Spider was credited with giving humanity the first alphabet, so yet again writing was equated with feminine wisdom.

The benevolent nature of spider is conveyed in the following story (origin unknown): Spider was sent by the moon to bring words of comfort to man. She ran into hare, who asked spider what she was doing. She told hare of her message and hare agreed to take it to man, but hare did not wait to get the full message and the comfort it was intended to provide. By the time spider arrived, man had heard only half the tale – that he must die – to this day spider weaves the moon's full message of comfort into her web, but no one pays any heed of her work.

Spider Woman gave the gift of life to two Hopi children, when Muiyinwuh (god of all growing things) forgot to tend the land. The boy made a toy for his sister, a tiny hummingbird, to take her mind off her hunger, and Spider Woman instilled it with flight. The hummingbird found food for the children, and finally located Muiyinwuh himself. The hummingbird scolded the god for his neglect. Then the bird flew off to find the children's parents. The god considered what the bird had said and relented. Thanks to the gift of life Spider Woman provided, the rains fell; plants returned to the land; and the children were fed and eventually reunited with their parents.

The Victorians had a more pragmatic view, seeing the fly-eating spider as 'a surprising part of the animal economy'.[1] Thus, the first echoes of modern ecology are found in the book of heraldry.

Spider sitting in its web watching with assiduity till its prey is entangled was equated with the Hindu concept of *Maya*, being caught or trapped in the illusion of the physical or material world. This is not too different from the Greek concept of the three sisters of fate who weave the destiny of each individual, or from the Norse wyrd sisters.

Spider was blessed in Russian legend. It called a knight to come and relieve mankind of plagues of mosquitoes. Through trickery and guile, the knight drove the insects into spider's web and humanity was saved. Spider or its parts were often used as an ingredient in many home remedies including cures for gout, ague, whooping cough and asthma.

If a spider drops from the ceiling onto someone's face, then good luck and money will follow. Elsewhere it was believed that to see a spider spinning its web indicated that the individual would soon receive new clothes.

## MEDICINE AND POWER

| | |
|---|---|
| DIRECTION | North |
| ELEMENTS | Earth, Air, Water, Fire |
| TRAITS | Weaver, spinster, predator, snare |
| ASSOCIATIONS | Fate, magic, illusion, written language and communication, creation and destruction, sex and death, entrapment, fear and phobias |

Spider, like snake, elicits both aversion and allure. Indeed, if it weren't for the fact that the names of the deities associated with spider are different from those associated with snake, one could probably lift everything that was said about snake and drop it down here.

Spider is creatrix; she is death. With her lunar qualities she's equated with the unconscious; sex with her can be equivalent to extinction. Thus, on a Freudian level spider embodies woman. Spider is the creative force, weaving the designs of life and fate. Spider wove the web that brought humans the first alphabet. The letters were inherent in the angles of her web.

Even in its more negative manifestation, Iktomi, who named all the plants and animals, is associated with words and communication. Iktomi lead man from the caves. Spider was a friend of Wazi the Wizard who was equated with wisdom. Yet Wazi, who lived in the north (winter/death), was forever battling against the giant of the south (summer/youth and life). Iktomi was the presiding genius of pranks and practical jokes. Spider, like coyote, is linked with *Heyoka*, where doing something the wrong-way-round provided satirical lessons for other members of the tribe.

Spider endows the power to work magic over persons and things. With its weaving, it gains a certain element of control; once the prey is wrapped up, this control is complete. Spider energy is sometimes equated with that of scorpion.

Some people find the shape of the spider's body, in the form of an eight, and the number of legs, also eight, significant. They call upon numerology and equate spider with the symbol for infinity. So spider, like snake, is the totality of the life cycle. It is the beginning and the end, birth and death, sexuality and betrayal – hence fate. Its medicine should be called upon when one feels trapped. If a web is destroyed, spider can recycle it and weave it anew. So spider allows the individual to assimilate negative experiences and use them for gain.

Spider as Maya refers to being caught in the illusion of physical existence, without recourse to alternative solutions. In this context the web can be equated with the tarot card Wheel of Life. Thus spider's appearance can mean a trap in the making; it can also be a symbol of one's fear. When spider arrives, it is time to confront one's phobias. If this is not done, then they are sure to surface later no matter how hard someone tries to suppress them.

Spider can facilitate inner connection and integration. It allows one to contact one's deepest wisdom. The web, as the vehicle of interconnectedness, supports one in tying together loose ideas into a tidy package. Spider nurtures a sense of connection and integration at all levels.

The spider person seems to have two speeds: motionless and the lightning strike. The spider woman is independent and doesn't necessarily see any point in keeping a man around once the process of fertilization is completed. This individual can have a stinging bite when angered. The negative side of the spider personality is deceit. Spider medicine can weave a web of rumours, gossip and lies, and this destructive tendency will have to be watched. The person with spider energy may be ruthless and, once aroused enough to attack, his or her punishment is decisive and lethal.

# SQUIRREL

Red squirrel: *Sciurus vulgaris*
Grey squirrel: *Sciurus carolinensis*

## BIOLOGICAL INFORMATION

The family of *Sciurdae* (squirrel) is large and diverse. The genus name means 'shade tail' in Latin. There are nine genera and 63 species. This section will cover the two most familiar, the red and the grey. They range in size from 15 to 38 cm (6 to 15 inches). The fur of the grey combines grey, brown and black, with a yellowish underbelly. Not all greys are grey, though; groups of pure white and dark black exist in the US. The red squirrel is smaller than the grey and has russet-coloured fur and ear tufts.

### HABITAT

Both grey and red prefer woodland habitats, often competing for the same food and land. The grey is the much more adaptable of the two. Therefore, in England it has been much more successful than the native red and has pushed the smaller red further and further north. The same is true in the US, where one or other of the two species usually predominates; it's rare to find places where their territories overlap. Still, they managed to find a balance long before white man arrived on American shores, a balance that exists to this day. Perhaps in England an equilibrium will also be reached eventually. In both countries, the US and the

UK, it's impossible to find an area without one of these two kinds of squirrel.

### CHARACTERISTICS

Most squirrels are diurnal. Of all the breeds in the United States, only the flying squirrel is nocturnal. Many hibernate, some even in summer. Many burrow, digging dens in the ground. Others make their nests in trees, either in round, ball-like collections of leaves and twigs or in the hollows of trunks. Both the red and the grey squirrel are arboreal.

Of the two types, the red squirrel is the more aggressive. The reason why the grey squirrel has prevailed is not because it is the more assertive of the two. In a stand-off it is the grey squirrel who will run while the red will stand its ground or even attack. Grey squirrels predominate because, as a group, they are willing to accept the proximity of man and are able to make better use of the environment.

In the UK the grey squirrel has met with hostility from the public, is seen as an interloper and predator of the red. It is silly to call grey squirrel vermin or pests and to blame it for the plight of the red. The grey squirrel did not hop aboard a ship to see Buckingham Palace. It was brought unwillingly during Victorian times. The grey's only crime is that it fills the same ecological niche more efficiently than the red squirrel. The grey squirrel and the red coexist quite happily in the US. The red dwells in the woodlands while the more flexible grey resides in regions inhabited by humans. Could it be that overpopulation in southern England is responsible for the red squirrel's retreat to the north, rather than being caused by some kind of 'invasion' by the 'alien' grey?

## LEGENDS AND TRADITIONS

Squirrel appears on frescos discovered in the Mayan ruins of Acanceh. Most Mayan temples were constructed in layers, with succeeding generations of priest-kings building another monument atop the old, perhaps with an intent similar to that of the Pharaohs – to show not only their dedication to the ancestors and previous god-priest-kings, but affirming their descent by honouring the burial ground of previous monarchs. Additionally, the increasing grandiosity and size of the temple would indicate the enhanced might of a priest-king over his forebears. His power was built upon the foundations laid by ancestors in their temple tombs (on their bones, as it were). In this context, it comes as a great surprise to find a representation of a squirrel at the base of these tomb frescos.

Squirrel has been found nowhere else in Mayan art. It has been suggested that this was an import from the northern Nahua people. The fact that squirrel was found in the very first simple square base structure could be indicative of early contact between the two cultures. From this one might infer that the priest-kings of the Mayan had similar responsibilities to the Egyptian Pharaohs, whose duties included keeping the people fed; therefore they were required, like squirrel, to keep stores. Many were remembered as much for their ability to nourish the people as for any capabilities in war.

According to a Karok[1] legend, Squirrel was touched by fire spirits when coyote stole a coal to bring back to earth. So it was that squirrel's tail curled over his head to create the fine umbrella under which it hides today.

Squirrel shows its mettle in the Blackfoot story of the Old Man and the Roasted Squirrels. Some squirrels were playing in hot ashes one day when an old man begged to join their game. They explained that the game entailed leaping into the hot ash to be buried. The squirrel who lasted longest before being pulled out was the most brave. The man asked to be buried first to prove how brave he was, but the squirrels deferred, stating that he did not understand the game and might be burned. They preferred to demonstrate. The old man buried them all at once, except a pregnant mother squirrel who pleaded to be left alone. The old man waited until the squirrels began to squeak and cry: 'Pull us out!' Then he heaped more ashes on the fire and roasted them alive. The old man did not go unpunished for his duplicity, for lynx stole the roast squirrels from the old man; but poor lynx had his face bashed in, his legs stretched and his tail torn off for his trouble.

At first glance one might think that squirrel was foolish to play such a game, much less to trust the old man. However, the boys of most tribes were trained from an early age for a harsh environment. In the culture of the time, squirrel revealed itself to be not only brave – the game a proof of squirrel's courage – but honourable – unlike the man. They did not risk the man's safety, preferring to demonstrate the game for him first. In their integrity, they did not even consider that the old man might deceive them.

Much of squirrel's 'cute', apparently playful behaviour – chasing, capering and carrying on – is in fact territorial combat. Squirrel usually lives alone, and squirrel is vigilant. Squirrel acts as guard not only for himself, but for others. Squirrel's chattering alerts many to the unwelcome arrival of predators.

The squirrel's ability to run upside down on a branch or a wire, its delight in racing in a complete circle around a bough, is confusing to the landbound. Thus, some species of squirrel came to be equated with distraction, and thus squirrel was not treated with a great deal of respect, despite its attentiveness. While squirrel probably provided a limited amount of protection to the women and small children of a village when the men left for the hunt – warning the village of danger and raising the alarm when necessary – its chattering would probably have been regarded as a mixed blessing.

Squirrel was not credited with the wiliness of rabbit, fox or coyote, for it preferred direct confrontation, announcing its attendance despite the size of the invader, and then if this did not work, running like crazy. Their erratic behaviour led squirrels to be associated with distraction, scattered energy and confusion – yet these represent powerful medicine to be thrown at an enemy.

One of squirrel's perceived traits was selfishness, for it hoards food. Similarly, squirrel coupled stupidity with waste (a cardinal sin in Native American culture), as the silly creature often forgot the location of its cache. Not that native peoples were above raiding a squirrel's hoard. Most women were trained to look for signs of mouse and squirrel stores of seeds.

An old Bible story claims that, of all the animals, squirrel was so shocked to see Adam and Eve eat of the tree of knowledge that he drew his tail across his eyes. For this sensitivity and insight squirrel was rewarded with a fine bushy tail. Therefore, the European view is slightly more favourable. The squirrel is associated to a limited extent with the divine. It understands the concepts of right and wrong; therefore, it confronts problems head-on, a laudable quality. One superstition suggested that if a hunter killed either a red or grey squirrel, he was courting disaster.

Heraldry made a comparison between squirrel and fox, but explains that squirrel is strictly vegetarian. At Brunholdt in Germany it was a custom to burn a squirrel on the Easter bonfire, with the intent of ridding the field of vermin. In some towns this was replaced by the more civilized custom of charring a piece of wood that would then be carried from the fire and placed within the garden or home as a preventative against pests. In some places, a cat, fox or serpent, even a man, replaced the squirrel in this burning ritual. The Celts of old burned condemned criminals within their straw mannequins. The more 'humane' Christian celebration substituted animals, mainly cats though also at times foxes or snakes – all of the animals people associated with witchcraft and the devil. Therefore, it could be inferred that the Germans made a connection between Satan and squirrel. Squirrel was a hoarder and materialist – qualities not very admirable to a church that wanted men to tithe 10 per cent of their income and pay for special dispensations and indulgences. If all humanity had chosen to emulate squirrel, where would Rome be?

## MEDICINE AND POWER

| | |
|---|---|
| DIRECTIONS | Red squirrel: West (US), North (UK); Grey squirrel: North (US), South (UK) |
| ELEMENTS | Red squirrel: Fire; Grey squirrel: Earth; Flying squirrel: Air |
| TRAITS | Guardian, sentinel, preparedness, forthrightness |
| ASSOCIATIONS | Distraction and confusion of one's enemy, courage and cowardice, alarm, waste |

Squirrel stands for honesty; it does not speak with 'forked tongue' but states its presence to any who would encroach upon its space. The grey squirrel does not stand up well under scrutiny, though, preferring to live and fight another day. Where squirrel medicine was revered, it was generally in an area inhabited by the red squirrel rather than the grey.

Still, warriors were not above using squirrel medicine to baffle the enemy. Surprised, squirrel would remain frozen in the trees, blending in with the red or grey of the bark. So, squirrel provided a form of invisibility. One tribe would throw a squirrel fur or tail upon the path of an attacking enemy. Squirrel medicine was supposed to send the enemy in the wrong direction. The idea was they would follow the wandering, skittish course of the squirrel and never reach their destination.

Another important meaning of squirrel is preparedness. Squirrel plans ahead for the lean months of winter. It is wise enough to store; it is not always smart enough to remember where. Thus, squirrel provides growth and reforestation, for as often as not it forgets where it has stored its secret stash – relying on its sense of smell rather than memory to locate it. However, many other animals have not achieved even squirrel's limited level of planning. Squirrel represents forgetfulness as much as preparedness.

In spite of the mixed nature of squirrel's gift, its medicine has more benefits than disadvantages. It is a survivor, a guardian. Its chatter can alert one to unseen danger. It can teach foresightedness, if not farsightedness.

Squirrel medicine can be invoked when under attack, to perplex one's attacker. It imparts the instinct of when to run – probably more realistic medicine to call upon in our day and age. Summoned, it is supposed to bestow invisibility.

Of course, attacks can come in many forms. There can be verbal attacks or attacks on one's character or reputation. One should never belittle an animal's gift, least of all squirrel's. Squirrel lends speed and spontaneity. It assists in one's escape from disaster. Squirrel's appearance suggests a time of gathering, or perhaps warns of the need to store something away for later. Even a poor memory has its advantages, for in nature it serves a purpose – allowing others to make use of what was lost before.

The squirrel person is a good planner and organizer, if somewhat lacking in follow-through. This individual will astound, as he or she dodges and darts along several paths simultaneously, jumping from one to another. However, with squirrel, the ground work is usually so well laid that in the event of difficulties, such as a squirrel-like memory loss, contingencies will already be available. This person can be annoying, as squirrel medicine chatters and worries at details. Today's crisis, though, is usually not tomorrow's. Whatever squirrel was into the previous day will quickly be forgotten, as it finds something new about which to scold and fret.

# SWALLOW

*Hirundinidae*

## BIOLOGICAL INFORMATION

There are 80 species of swallow worldwide, eight in the US. In England, *Hirundo rustica* is one of the best-known migrants. It arrives in April and leaves in October. Swallows are about the same size as sparrows. They are characterized by their long pointed wings.

### HABITAT

The most common species in the US is the barn swallow. The tree swallow is found in Nebraska up through northern Manitoba and into Alaska; the ruff-wing swallow covers the entire 48 continental States, while the barn swallow's territory includes the US and lower Canada. The cliff swallow and the smaller New Mexico cave swallow likewise encompass most of the US and Canada, except for the extreme corners of the southeast and northwest. Indeed, they are adapted to most environments. The introduction to the US of the house swallow from Europe was disastrous for the cliff swallow, since they compete for the same environment, with the result that larger house swallow often ousts the smaller cliff swallow from its nest.

### CHARACTERISTICS

Swallows are excellent flyers, capable of great aerial acrobatics. Swift and graceful, adult swallows have been recorded as travelling as far as 960 km (600 miles) a day in search of food. Barn and house swallows, as their names suggest, often nest in buildings. The former migrates as far south as Argentina. All swallows are migratory birds. They raise four to six chicks; however, the parents may lose them all during wet rainy springs.

## LEGENDS AND TRADITIONS

GODDESSES Isis (Egyptian), Venus (Roman)
GODS Osiris

The swallow is primarily a bird of the grasslands. Therefore it was held sacred by the people of the Plains. All birds were honoured as representative of the sky, hence closer to heaven and to the spirits than land-bound mammals and reptiles. Some tribes referred to the swallows as the messengers of the south wind; others found a correspondence between swallows and the thunderbeings. The swallow seemed to precede storms, and its appearance augured rain.

The humble swallow was ascribed with the same attributes as eagle, hawk and dragonfly, a mysterious power which enabled the warrior to remain unharmed by bullets, arrows, lightning and hailstones. Seeing a swallow in a vision imparted its medicine to the warrior. The swallow was agile; the swallow was swift. One called upon swallow medicine to endow one's horse with speed and agility.

For the Lakota, swallow was one of many diverse animals which represented *Heyoka*. If a man saw a swallow in a dream or a vision quest, he became Heyoka. This person taught through satire and ridicule. Once in a contest of medicines, three holy men called upon their spirit animals. The Heyoka chose the tiny bee to the others' bear and eagle. Heyoka defeated the greater powers, for with his constant buzz-buzz-buzz and pricking sting he wore down his opponents, who finally quit. Thus he taught that superior strength did not rely on greater size.

The Cherokee celebrated swallow's return as the bringer of spring. This perspective reflects the European one. It's no great surprise that swallow retained its aerial associations in the Old World.

The Egyptian hieroglyph for swallow was used in the word *wer*, or 'great'. Swallows were associated with the stars; thus, with the souls of the dead. The bird was frequently shown sitting on the prow of the barque of Re (Ra), guiding the god through the underworld each night. The swallow was sacred to both Isis and Venus. It was an allegory of spring. Isis changed herself into a swallow and fanned life back into Osiris, and as such she was the goddess of the winds.

Heraldry called the swallow the harbinger of spring. Its arrival ensured a pleasant season. Swallow is especially favoured in Europe, and misfortune will happen to anyone who interferes with it in any way. In Germany, a swallow's nest built in the eaves of a house ensures it against fire and storm damage. If the swallow was seen flying high, good weather was indicated; if flying low, rain was on its way.

## MEDICINE AND POWER

| | |
|---|---|
| DIRECTION | East (Spring) |
| ELEMENTS | Air, Sunshine |
| TRAITS | Speed, agility, protection |
| ASSOCIATIONS | Resurrection, rebirth, warmth, herald of Spring and storms; thunderbeings |

For Osiris, swallow was bringer of breath and life. As Isis, swallow was feminine nurturing and sustenance. Thus, swallow speaks of love and devotion. Swallow was guide during the god's sojourn in the underworld, keeping him safe and on the right path. So, swallow gives protection in periods of darkness and its energy should be summoned at such times.

As *akicita*, swallow acted as escort to humans as they walked along the 'good red road', the Lakota-Dakota way to wisdom. Swallow imparts discernment and insight. Linked as it was with dragonfly, it also represented Heyoka. As predictor of the weather, swallow was one the many faces of the thunderbeing.

As thunder energy, the swallow lends its wings to give speed and manoeuvrability. It was believed that if a rider wore the appropriate charm, representing this energy, his pony could turn in an instant. Swallow, then, was protection for both rider and horse. Translated into modern needs, swallow's gift is swiftness, precision and security. With its association with good cheer, it seems the perfect medicine to invoke during a traffic jam.

Swallow warned of storms at the same time it welcomed the spring, for on the American Plains spring is a period of thunderstorm activity. Therefore, swallow means acceptance of the good with the bad.

European tradition attributes to swallow domesticity and felicity. Its medicine can be used to protect the home. Its arrival bodes happiness. Therefore, it might presage a time of gain. However, it doesn't necessarily promise a peaceful transition. Its appearance implies turbulence while endowing the individual with all the skills he or she needs to ride out the storm on the wings of bird. Swallow provides a shield against the metaphoric hail, bullets and arrows of life. Therefore, swallow can be called upon when defence is needed. Its medicine can be raised when one is likely to face the stress of competition. It imparts the power to find unusual solutions for familiar problems.

Swallow in the classical definition means guidance. It is connected with spirit and soul. As messenger, swallow brings communication from the spirit world, for this bird has the ability to speak to the ancestors. It gives wise counsel and advice. When swallow is around, spiritual guidance is near, and the recipient should listen.

The direction in which a swallow is seen flying should be noted. This indicates the way to escape, should escape be necessary. Conversely, the direction it is flying from indicates the direction of an approaching storm. As signs, these can be interpreted figuratively or taken quite literally.

The swallow person would be described as a sunny individual. The swallow has grace and speed without being boastful or too mendacious about it. This person will be a wise counsellor. People with swallow medicine seem to be able to soar through difficulties, even better than eagle or hawk. This trait may instill jealousy or envy in others; however, usually the swallow individual is so pleasant that any rancour quickly dissolves.

# SWAN

Whistling Swan: *Olar columbianus*
Mute Swan: *Synus olar*

## BIOLOGICAL INFORMATION

Along with ducks and geese, the swan is a member of the Anatidae family. There are 150 species worldwide. Four breed in the United States. The mute swan (1.4 to 1.5 m/4¾ to 5 ft) is larger than the whistling swan (1.2 to 1.4 cm/4 to 4¾ ft). Both breeds are white. The bill of the mute swan is orange and black, while that of the whistling swan is yellow and black.

### HABITAT

The mute swan was introduced into the Americas from Europe. Therefore, in the US the mute swan is limited to the northeastern seaboard. In England, swan has long been protected under law by the crown. It is found throughout the United Kingdom and northern Europe. It inhabits freshwater ponds, rivers and coastal lakes in both the Old World and the New.

The whistling swan is a creature of the Arctic. It prefers to live in marshy tundra. It ranges from Alaska east into the Northwest Territories of Canada.

### CHARACTERISTICS

The swan mates for life, and if its mate dies it usually spends the rest of its time alone. A beautiful bird, it glides peacefully across waters, but this impression of gentleness is deceptive. The average male swan is able to break a grown man's arm with a single wing beat.

The female lays four to six eggs. Both father and mother care for the cygnets. The parents often carry their young on their back in order to protect them from attack from below, for cygnets are often prey to large fish. The parents extend their wings to provide their young with protection against falling, thus producing one of their most characteristic majestic poses. They will defend their nest against all animals, including man.

The whistling swan holds its head upright, while the mute carries its neck in a graceful curve. The whistling swan migrates from the far north to the Atlantic coast. It stops briefly along the Great Lakes region; it has been saved from the fate of the trumpeter swan (its closest relative), driven nearly to extinction because it breeds in remote locations.

## LEGENDS AND TRADITIONS

GODDESSES Aphrodite (Greek), Venus (Roman), Wolpe (Dakota/Lakota)

Swan has many associations for the indigenous peoples of North America. Archie Fire Lame Deer refers to swan as a symbol of peace and tranquillity. Elsewhere, swan's strength captured the attention of all who saw it. Despite its graceful, gliding beauty, swan is an ill-tempered bird. Therefore swan is as fierce a protector as goose.

The monogamous swan was associated with marital fidelity, constancy and loyalty. Swan also stood for parenthood and family. As faithful partner and good parent, swan was primarily considered women's medicine. In the Medicine dance, the women of a tribe imitated the call of the female swan and mimicked its cumbersome gait.

To date, this author has yet to find a resource that lists swan as a food source in North America, which would seem to suggest that swan was so sacred it could not be killed. It did not receive the same treatment in Europe, however, where it often graced the king's table.

Probably the most important manifestations of white swan for the Lakota and Dakota peoples was Wohpe. She was the daughter of Skan (the mystery of change). Her beauty was legendary. Her name meant 'Falling Star', and she came often to earth in the form of a white swan. She wed Okaga, the giant of the south. Most people who have studied Native American history have heard of her as the White Buffalo Calf Woman, who brought the peace pipe to the tribes. She was also responsible for the seven sacred rites. Thus, she was the most important figure in Lakota religious life, and she seems to have been a historical personage, too – the Winter Count of Standing Bear cites the year when they captured the Wakan Tanka woman; a subsequent entry refers to the introduction of the sacred pipe. Her association with the white swan is lesser known than that with white buffalo, but important nonetheless. If white buffalo was Wohpe's agent on earth, then white swan was her representative in the air.

In Greece swan was sacred to Apollo, god of music, so it was believed that swan would sing sweetly at the time of death. The white swan was emblematic of Venus. The swan of European tradition speaks of the satisfaction of desire. For the Greeks, swan by night replaced the horse which towed the sun god's chariot by day. Therefore, swan suggested protection against the underworld and a connection with the souls and the spirits of the dead, similar to that which was attributed to swallows.

Swan represents Samhuinn in Druidic tradition, and the transition of the soul. The fairy story of the children turned into a swan by a witch (Aoifa) originated with the Celts. In this tale, the purity, love and goodness of the children was revealed despite their transformation into animals, and so this story of the king of Tuatha De Danann Lir's children was later adopted by Christian priests, although the names were changed in order to disguise any link with the pagan faith.

In England generally, swan was the symbol of royalty and strength, along with innocence and purity. It became the royal bird, after a fashion, only answerable to the king or queen. European fairy tales reflect this imagery. Swans were symbols of chastity, artistry and beauty. Hans

Christian Anderson credited swan with spinning the thread of thought and, by association, communication.

It is illegal to kill a swan in Britain; traditionally the implications were more lethal. It was said that anyone who killed a swan would be dead within a year. The Scottish believed that if a flock of swans were seen flying together, national disaster would ensue.

## MEDICINE AND POWER

| | |
|---|---|
| DIRECTION | South |
| ELEMENTS | Water, Air |
| TRAITS | Strength in beauty; elegance and refinement |
| ASSOCIATIONS | Peace, serenity, purity, all things spiritual, royalty |

Swan embodies the virtues of chastity and innocence. It, as much as the dove, is a symbol of divinity. It signifies the peace that can only be found with acceptance. In the book *Medicine Cards*, authors Jamie Sams and David Carson equate the bird with trust in the future and the ability to surrender with grace to the rhythm of the universe.

As one manifestation of the White Buffalo Woman, the white swan is connected to the most sacred mysteries of the Lakota/Dakota faith. Wohpe brought the pipe, which speaks of sacred breath and the air that binds us all together. Smoke carried prayers to the heavens. Wohpe, who often came in the form of a swan, was the bringer of the wisdom which allowed the Native Americans to communicate with the Great Spirit and the sacred ancestors. Swan, therefore, is a messenger of faith.

Swan medicine is a means of achieving the highest spiritual plane. Swan, especially when depicted with the harp (death), represented the mystic journey, the dreamtime. It was the corresponding axis of water and fire, which creates steam or fog. Thus, swan teaches one to find clarity in the face of confusion, to be at one with all planes of consciousness, and to trust in the divine spirit. Swan medicine sometimes calls upon one to make a sacrifice.

Swan energy can be invoked to expand one's consciousness. It imparts self-esteem. Similarly, it allows one to view the good in others. People should call upon swan when needing encouragement to experience life as a precious and sacred gift. It can be used to power one's prayers to the heavens. The bird's wing can knock a human off his feet. The bill can easily sever a child's fingers. Swans are extremely protective of their mate and their children. Therefore, swan reveals might in beauty, potency and power. It can be summoned when an individual needs protection coupled with calm.

The swan person will naturally attract others. This individual, whether male or female, is graceful. Often they appear to be floating through life, which can make others jealous. Everything seems to come easily for them and they rarely get ruffled or lose their composure. Yet people with swan medicine are not as compliant, nor is their life as blessed it may first appear. Swan combines melancholy and passion, comeliness with brawn, and those who forget this will eventually come to regret their error. The swan, once threatened, fights with its wings and beak, and it aims to do harm; but the swan person does this only in defence. This person is a faithful partner and loving parent.

# TOAD

*Bufonidae*

## BIOLOGICAL INFORMATION

Toads are frog-like – so much so that some people cannot differentiate between the two species. Toads have heavy bodies and short, muscular back legs, as frogs do. They can grow up to 32 cm (13 inches) including their legs, although some species grow larger. Unlike the frog, the toad's skin is dull and covered in bumps and warts. The typical toad is brown in colour rather than green, with darker stripes and elongated dots along the back and flanks, and a whitish underbelly. Toads have a prominent parotid gland which exudes poison. Many have poison glands on the thigh.

As with any large biological family of animals, looks and size vary widely among toads. For example there's the great horned toad which resembles a lizard more than a frog.

### HABITAT

The toad is more land-bound than the frog – hence the variation in colour – but, like any amphibian, toads need to maintain a certain skin moisture. Therefore they are found in wet forests, gardens, and near ponds, lakes or rivers and marshland. Some species have adapted to a desert environment, yet they still require some kind of water source nearby.

In the US the toad is more common than the frog. It can be found throughout the US except the most extreme desert conditions. Toads can survive in some of the harshest environments, including the cold northern regions of Canada. Some species have developed a kind of 'antifreeze' that keeps their blood flowing, and they go into suspended animation during the winter months. In the UK, both frogs and toads are protected species. Of the two, the toad is more rare.

### CHARACTERISTICS

Toads are explosive breeders. They congregate in large numbers for mating, in garden ponds, streams and marshes. The females leave a thick nest of egg strings shaped like a ball. Hundreds of babies are born at a time.

Toads go through the polliwog or tadpole stage of development when they are completely aquatic. At this time the tadpole has gills and a predominant tail which later disappears. Within a few weeks of birth they develop legs, losing their tail and gills; at this time they disperse from the nest.

The adult toad dwells underground or in small dens of gathered rocks and stone – any place which remains damp or where water is likely to accumulate. They are carnivores, living mainly on insects.

## LEGENDS AND TRADITIONS

Toad was one of four animals sacred to the Peruvian Incas – along with condor, llama and serpent. The culture reached its climax around 1500 AD, stretching from southern Mexico down to Chile, encompassing an area larger than the Roman empire. The Incas worshipped the Milky Way, and toad was associated with the black cloud formation of the Southern Cross. In this form, toad was considered one of the gateways to the sun.

Toad was the hero in the eastern Huron creation story. In the beginning there was naught but water and sky for the animals to inhabit, and it was decided that something else was needed – a place where the animals could crawl about and dry off for a while. So they got together to figure out how best to build land. Turtle, floating like an island in the sea, pointed out that there was dirt on the bottom of the ocean, and he volunteered his back as a platform. But this meant that he could not dive to get the dirt himself, because each time he did, he'd lose everything he had already collected.

Playful otter tried first to dive down to the depths, but he lost his breath before he reached the bottom. Then dutiful beaver took a turn. Even mighty muskrat tried, but it was only ugly old toad who was successful. Thus, Toskwaye the toad made trip after trip into the deep, bringing up dirt. Thus he fashioned the world upon turtle's back. Toad expelled his dying breath to spit the last mouthful of earth onto turtle's back, sacrificing his life so that others might live and thrive. To this day toad is honoured by the Native Americans, and no man is allowed to harm them.

While toad is more terrestrial than frog, this does not mean that it is not associated with water. The Orinoco did not separate frog from toad. Both were gods of water. Thus these creatures were protected up to a point. Killing one was prohibited. Unfortunately, if a draught ensued the animals were punished. People kept one in a pot, and they would beat it with a stick if the rains did not come.

The Aymara made figures of frogs, toads and other aquatic creatures and placed them on a hill top to bring rain. The tribes of British Columbia would sacrifice a frog or a toad to bring on rain.

The Lakota/Dakota mystery (god) *Gnaska* (*Hnaska*) was ruler of mischief, floods and water, and ablutions. Although Gnaska is used specifically for frog – in other words, it is the common name for frog – some of the descriptions seem to refer to toad, which is called in common Lakota speech *natapeha*. How many frog characteristics are attributed to toad is difficult to ascertain.

In the Old World, if frog meant creation, then lumpy old toad was its antithesis. According to Christian tradition, toad inverted the good of frog to something infernal. It was linked to Satan and often thought to be his messenger.

In England, toad is associated with witchcraft. It was believed that witches used them as familiars, and as such a toad could be hanged or burned right alongside the witch. One presumes that the creation of a noose to handle a toad's physiognomy was an engineering feat of the first magnitude.

Yet toad was not always credited with evil. For example, it was believed that if a toad should cross the path of a wedding party, the marriage would be fertile. The couple would have many children, be prosperous and happy.

Even in the Old World there was a link between toad and water. To kill one caused rain. Sometimes this would be considered a blessing, other times a curse.

## MEDICINE AND POWER

| | |
|---|---|
| DIRECTION | Varies according to tradition |
| ELEMENTS | Earth, Water, Sky and Rain |
| TRAITS | Metamorphosis, water, toxicity |
| ASSOCIATIONS | Witchcraft, magic, transformation, death and birth |

Toad's medicine shares many of the attributes of frog's. Both creatures go through a tadpole stage of development, when they are best suited to a water environment. Both lose their gills. Toad becomes land-based, returning to the water mainly to breed. Frog prefers water. The toad keeps his skin wet, but this is accomplished by remaining in the shade or in a dark, moist environment during daylight hours.

Frog, with its wide mouth and strange posture, appears funny to the human eye, but toad, with its horns, lumps and bumps, presents a devious image. One breed of frog is the most toxic in the world, but all toads possess a gland that exudes poison.

Toad has many of the same regenerative and transformative powers of frog, but utilizes this energy in a different way. Frog energy is more gentle, while toad can be an emotional purgative. If frog is the healer, then toad is a magician, the worker of deep medicine.

If frog is for cleansing, then toad is for reaching inside and confronting the Jungian shadow which each individual contains. If frog has dominion over the subconscious, that which is suppressed, then toad controls the unconscious, that which is never revealed but which continues to have a controlling influence throughout one's life.

Toad medicine should not be underestimated or avoided. Through toad the individual gains access to the rich resources of the instinct. Toad energy is the portal to primal powers, akin to the *materia prima* of the alchemist. It is embryo; it is seed; it is the explosion of growth and regeneration.

One can summon toad's strength during times of transformation or, more appropriately, rough transition. It is first magic and the cleansing burst of rain. Its appearance heralds a beginning which inevitably results from an ending and which may not always be welcome. Toad suggests either a period of solitude or a sudden burst of enforced activity within a crowded pond. But eventually it means growth – volatile development to be sure, but fertility and progress just the same. Few of us enjoy the grey dreary days of rain, but the world would be barren without them.

If emotions become too hard to handle, call upon the emetic qualities of toad. Its medicine can assist in times of crisis, for toad is flexible and knows how to adapt. Toad's energies can be raised when it is time to retreat into solitude to contemplate affairs which are emotional or spiritual in nature. Both frog and toad medicine can be used to help anyone who is forced to confront past emotional issues which surface from time to time.

Those individuals with toad medicine are shy, retiring, even secretive. Often misunderstood or rejected by others who don't understand them or appreciate their power, toad stays alone much of the time. Toad is a hermit. Others will often exhibit an innate revulsion or distrust for toad. This is a mistake, for toad contains deep wisdom, perhaps more profound than frog's. Toad's looks, or external packaging, may repel – in the same way, many people are unwilling to confront the ugliness or shadow in themselves.

# TURKEY

Wild: *Meleagris gallopavo*
Domestic: *Meleagris galliforme*

## BIOLOGICAL INFORMATION

Male turkeys are larger than the females, measuring 1.2 metres (4 ft) to the females' 91 cm (36 inches). The feathers are black and brown with a bronze sheen. Their wings are barred. The head may be either blue or red. More slender than the domestic turkey, the wild turkey has a brown tipped tail. The male has a comb that dangles over its beak most of the time and inflates during courtship or confrontations with other males.

### HABITAT

The wild bird lives in deciduous forests. At one time turkeys were found throughout the woodlands of the US. Then they were hunted almost to extinction. Until in the late 1970s their range was limited to the southern and eastern portions of the States. However, careful management has meant that these birds can now be found in the wild as far north as Wisconsin and as far west as Montana.

The turkey in England is the domesticated descendent of the original bird. Selective breeding may have increased the amount of white meat and changed the feather colour, but it has done little to alter the basic design. Very little separates the domesticated from the wild bird.

### CHARACTERISTICS

Turkeys fly only in short bursts. Otherwise they spend most of their time on the ground. The turkey's neck is longer than that of the grouse or chicken. Thus, turkeys have a peculiar, and endearing, gait where they tuck their head back into their chest and then thrust it out again with each step. They are swift runners, flattening their head and tail to form a straight, aerodynamic line.

Turkeys are gregarious and form flocks. Like the grouse and the peacock, the male fans out his tail and struts to attract a female. The comb stands upright and the feathers on the body also inflate, making the bird look larger. The males will compete for females, often fighting off other males in contests of flapping wings, flashing beaks and posturing. The males strive to maintain a harem. The female produces as many as 15 eggs which she keeps in a hollow depression upon the forest floor.

## LEGENDS AND TRADITIONS

The Mayan included the image of turkey in their codices, along with the horned owl, the screech owl (moan bird) and eagle. In each case, one of the birds is nocturnal (the owl) and the other affiliated with daylight. This coupling seems to suggest solar versus lunar influence, day versus night. The moan bird was specifically associated with death. Eagle represented life, as did turkey. It had a more female and earthy quality than the other birds. The moan bird often appeared with a headdress of maize and seems to have represented years of crop failure. Conversely, turkey symbolized increased fertility. The moan bird (screech owl) in a codice indicated evil – turkey good. Turkeys, together with other birds, were decapitated and given as offerings at rituals where turkey priests officiated to ensure an abundant crop. The turkey was domesticated by the time of the Mayan and plentiful during the time of the Aztecs.

Many tribes considered the turkey a good source of food, although some Native American groups refused to consume its flesh. The Dakota believed the turkey was stupid and cowardly. The warrior would not partake of its meat for fear of acquiring these traits. Some referred to turkey as the 'give-away bird', equating it with the buffalo, who sacrificed its life so that the Native American people might survive. Others thought of it as the 'south eagle', or 'earth eagle' – attributing to the more land-bound turkey medicine and powers comparable to those of the eagle. Turkey represented the earth mother, just as eagle was messenger of the father sky. Therefore, if one prayed to or invoked this bird, turkey carried the message to mother earth.

Turkey's medicine, like that of the buffalo cow, was women's medicine. Many tribes of the woodland and Plains held turkey, prairie chicken or grouse ceremonies in which the women danced, mimicking the mincing steps and head movements of all these birds. These would be the equivalent of the spiral dance of the Druids and Celts.

The appearance of turkey was supposed to presage a period of fertility and growth. It was linked to abundance, and as 'give-away bird' it endows the spirit with generosity.

Americans of European descent have adopted the attitude of the native peoples. Turkey is the main culinary feature of the American holiday of Thanksgiving. Here the bird has come to represent the plenty of the harvest. Benjamin Franklin suggested the turkey rather than the eagle for the American national symbol, since the turkey was the only exclusively American bird.

The turkey was first introduced into England during the reign of Henry VIII. It may have been an American bird, but the English court was eager to accept it as part of the menu. It even merited a mention in books on heraldry, where it was mentioned as one of the most difficult birds to rear.[1]

## MEDICINE AND POWER

| | |
|---|---|
| DIRECTION | South |
| ELEMENTS | Earth, and to a lesser extent Air |
| TRAITS | Mating dance, speed, fertility |

ASSOCIATIONS Women, abundance, self-sacrifice, harvest, altruistic love, generosity

Turkey medicine is giving of oneself. It may entail a loss in the form of a sacrifice, but the medicine itself makes this easier to bear. If tribute is necessary, turkey permits it to be given gladly. Its appearance can herald returns, or the harvest, for those sacrifices previously made. Turkey reminds us that in Native American culture the chief cannot eat until he makes sure the rest of the people have eaten. 'Potlatch', or give-away, is one of the most important Native American traditions. The name comes from the West, but the concept was almost universally practised. In potlatch a family or an individual distributed everything they possessed, because a truly powerful hunter and warrior could always replace property. Turkey medicine embodies the spirit of potlatch. Turkey medicine is not only the medicine of giving, but of receiving, for turkey medicine assures abundance and that an individual's generosity will not go unrewarded.

A person could call upon turkey during periods of financial need. Shamans advise against such invocation if wealth is the intent, which would most assuredly backfire. Yet turkey medicine provides comfort and ensures one's physical needs are met. Its appearance suggests the return of good fortune, being able to harvest the fruit of one's labour. The turkey's mammalian counterpart would be buffalo – though turkey does not share buffalo's unpredictability or dangerousness.

The turkey individual is charitable. However, this is part and parcel of turkey medicine. People with turkey as a power animal give joyously. They can be gullible, like the hunted turkey who, once confused, is as likely to run towards the hunter as away from him. The person with turkey medicine may appear clumsy, but they are quick and capable when needed.

# TURTLE/ TORTOISE

Turtle family: *Chelonidae*
Tortoise family: *Testudinidae*

## BIOLOGICAL INFORMATION

The first turtles evolved 200 million years ago from group of cotylosaurs. A fossil of a turtle some 2 m (approximately 7 ft) in length was found in India, and there remains a type of sea turtle reaching 4 metres (12 ft) in length.

Smaller species exist – usually these are the more landbound – their sizes range from 15 cm (6 inches) to about 60 cm (2 ft). Generally speaking, turtles are better adapted to an aqueous environment and tortoises to land, but like everything in nature this is not a hard and fast rule. For example there is the land-dwelling box turtle, with its rounded back and stubby legs. On the other side of the spectrum there is the sea tortoise which only comes on land to breed. However, as a rule of thumb the differences between the two are noted on the following chart:

| TURTLE | TORTOISE |
|---|---|
| Stream-lined shells (for less resistance in water) | Domed shells |
| Webbed feet | Large, stump-like feet |
| Swims at 16 kph (10 mph) | Walks at 0.27 kph (0.17 mph) |
| Omnivore (insects, carrion, fruit, fish) | Herbivore (land-based tortoises)/ Carnivores (aquatic tortoises) |

Turtles and tortoises live in temperate, semi-tropical and tropical environments; therefore they are found in a band centred around the equator. Within this band they have adapted to woods, ponds, rivers, lakes, marshland, prairies, bays, estuaries, open oceans, even deserts wherever there is a water source nearby.

## CHARACTERISTICS

All turtles and tortoises are eggs-layers; this more than anything keeps them tied to land. The sea turtles and tortoises are among the largest. They can lay hundreds of eggs. The two species are so well adapted to their environment that even sex takes place in the water. Their eggs have leathery shells. The mother buries them on the same beach where she was born. The turtle and tortoise travel thousands of miles between clutches. Each animal is tied to its birthplace, and if something happens to disturb this beach, then they stop clutching.

Once the eggs are laid, the exhausted mother makes her way back to the sea. This is her first and last interaction with her young. When the eggs hatch, the young head unerringly for water, but they must run the gauntlet of predators. Only a small percentage of them survive their first trip back to the water.

The snapping turtle is the only aggressive turtle. It has a sharp beak. When it bites, it does not let go. If a snapping turtle grabs a human hand, it has more than enough power in its jaws to take a few fingers with it.

# LEGENDS AND TRADITIONS

GODDESS Earth mother
GODS Vishnu (Hindu), Kwei (China)

The Mayans gave special honours to turtle. It was part of their mathematical and astronomical systems. They attributed to turtle rather than toad the ability to bring rains. Since turtles often lived through forest fires, the Mayan believed turtles held the secret of eternal life. An altar carved and dedicated to the Great Turtle existed in a temple at the site of Quirigua.

A Huron legend from the American northeast describes how the world was built from soil spread on a turtle's back to create the landmass of the Americas or Turtle Island. The name has become almost universally adopted by the native peoples of North America, as has the concept of turtle as the creator, or at least supporter, of the earth. Therefore turtle was associated with the earth mother.

The Iroquois tell of a time when the world was covered with nothing but water. A woman fell from the sky. Ducks came and spread out their wings to break her fall. The creatures of the deep got together to see what they could do to help her, and decided that the great tortoise should carry her on his back. So he stretched himself and, as he did so, the world got larger. The woman who fell from the sky had children – one was the spirit of good, the second a spirit of evil. The Mohawk, which has joined the Iroquois nation based in New York State, share this mythology.

These legends bear a striking similarity the Chinese myth of the world turtle whose domed back carries the sky and whose flat belly forms the landmasses. Some believe that the early East Asian peoples, who migrated to the Americas across the Bering Strait from Siberia and the Orient, carried this tale with them.

Turtle drums were used by the semi-sedentary Mandan of eastern Nebraska and South Dakota as part of *O-kee-pa*, a renewal ceremony. The drums were considered so sacred that they were guarded by one particular village, the *Nuptadi*. The turtle drums had to be borrowed whenever the *O-kee-pa* was held by another village.

The Zuni worshipped turtle and tortoise in another way, as housing the souls of their ancestors. Once a year the men would leave the village, returning a few days later with captive turtles. How each turtle reacted to its release in a family's home foretold the future. If the turtle ran away and refused to return, then the future was bleak. If, however, it came to the hand to be fed, good would most assuredly follow. The family said prayers over it – special imprecations for their dead relatives. The creature was then allowed to die, and its bones returned to the rivers. The process created a link between turtle and man, the living and the dead. At midsummer a similar ritual was held by the Zuni to honour tortoise. The ceremony ensured the return of the rains. The Moqi tribe of the southwest also held corresponding rites for its clan animals. Thus, members of the Turtle Clan would capture a turtle in order to contact their ancestors.

Turtle's association with mother earth gave it healing properties. The women of the Cherokee wore box-turtle rattles tied to their calves during the Green Corn Festival, a renewal ceremony. Turtle, as a powerful healer, was illustrated in one Cherokee tale where the silly creature angered wolf. Wolf decided to punish him, but turtle tricked wolf into putting him in the river as punishment. So turtle escaped wolf's wrath, but his plan backfired. Wolf was so mad when he realized he had been duped that the next time he ran into turtle, wolf threw the animal onto a rock. Turtle's back shattered into a dozen pieces. Turtle healed his shell with his knowledge of medicine, but wears this 'shattered' pattern to this day.

In ancient myth the turtle was a symbol of stability, strength, benevolence and wisdom. The Lakota held a similar view. Turtles conferred strength, shielding and protection. They were put upon Ghost Dance shirts of the Dakota in the hope of invoking their aid.

The only tribe who did not revere turtle was the Creek. They believed turtle controlled droughts and floods. Thus, any Creek who ran across a turtle killed it on sight.

The Egyptians held the turtle as sacred, but believed it to be the enemy of Ra. The ancient Greeks commemorated the abilities of turtle in Aesop's fable *The Tortoise and the Hare*. In China, Kwei the dragon turtle emerged after the world was destroyed and re-created heaven and earth. He then passed this responsibility to a series of guardian turtles, who helped men pursue wisdom and truth. Thus in the Far East, turtle was seen as a symbol of longevity and immortality.

For the Hindu the turtle represented the god Vishnu. After the great flood that occurs every four billion years, Vishnu transformed himself into a turtle. He carried the god and the demon on his back so they could remix the elements and re-create the planet. Then turtle transported an elephant on his back who, in turn, supported the world.

The turtle is still considered sacred in Asia. Turtles are kept in the Buddhist temple at Wat Po in Bankok. As symbols of immortality they serve as a temporary dwelling place for the human soul on its way to Nirvana.

Interestingly enough, in the east tortoise was considered an animal of ill repute. In 1882, a new temple was erected in Shanghai which resulted in a rebellion when it was discovered that the new building resembled a tortoise. The priests filled in the two wells that were part of the complex, for the animal, once blinded, was considered unable to do mischief.

## MEDICINE AND POWER

| | |
|---|---|
| DIRECTION | South |
| ELEMENTS | Water, Earth |
| TRAITS | Toughness (the hard shell), fecundity, slowness, stability |
| ASSOCIATIONS | Mother earth, women, fertility, plenty, health and healing |

Throughout the section on Legends and Traditions (above) we have referred to turtle, with little of tortoise. This is because few Native Americans, apart from the Zuni, made a distinction between the two creatures. Turtle medicine would depend entirely on the species abundant in the area, which could very well be tortoise. Turtle/tortoise medicine is basically the same. Some living shamans may make a distinction, but the concept of a difference between the species is relatively new even in European society, having first been described in a scientific paper late in the 1700s.

In Native American legend, slow, passive turtle was primarily seen as women's medicine. The curve of its back reflected the fecund female. Therefore, turtle speaks of fertility, literally and metaphorically. Turtle suggests creativity on all levels.

Turtle medicine was women's medicine, but this does not mean that warriors did not call on turtle's protection. Often something of the turtle would adorn their robes, or an image of turtle would be painted upon shields in the hopes that the warrior would develop the thick hide from which arrows rebounded.

The turtle's association with earth and water, women and mother suggests nourishment, sustenance and healing. The native peoples of the regional northwest used turtle as a symbol of health. The turtle is a wise-woman. Her skin is a shield, hence protection.

The Lakota, too, saw turtle as the guardian of life, patron of surgery and preventer of accidents. It was *keya*. The turtle is wise and hears many things, but remains circumspect. Its skin is like a shield so that arrows cannot wound it. The shaman of turtle medicine used the dried and powdered heart, sprinkling the powder over wounds in order to heal them.

Turtle is one of the oldest symbols for earth. With its broad body and wide base, it is the essence of stability. Pagans have adopted turtle as the personification of the goddess. For European and Native American alike, turtle is the eternal mother. Certainly the many species are influenced by elemental earth, for they must return to land to clutch. Tortoises, for their part, are almost completely landbound. Therefore, tortoise more than turtle should be invoked for grounding.

Turtle medicine can also be summoned to provide emotional support and protection. The turtle/tortoise is self-contained, and once breeding is complete the animals go their separate ways, so turtle can teach self-reliance. One of its gifts is the ability to enjoy solitary pursuits. Along with protection, turtle imparts strength – if not speed – for it takes muscle power to lug such a heavy shell around.

Turtle medicine is healing medicine. For the Lakota this referred specifically to wounds, but many other tribes attributed to turtle wisdom other forms of healing. Similarly, the wisewoman of the northwest was also a seer, therefore turtle endows the individual with psychic insight.

Turtle/tortoise medicine should be summoned when someone needs to work from a steady base, or when one has become lost, as this sea creature has the ability to circumnavigate the globe and return to the same breeding spot season after season. The fact that they were seen to survive fires suggested resurrection to native peoples. Meanwhile, turtle's return from semi-hibernation marked the onset of spring, so spoke of seasonal rebirth after winter's sleep. The mastery and triumph of life over death. Thus, turtle medicine can help if making a major life change, or if one is having to re-create one's life in some way.

Turtle provides comfort and feelings of safety when dealing with intense or new situations and environments. Turtle permits one to focus on, and have an appreciation of, the present.

The appearance of turtle can indicate a new and beneficial beginning. Unlike other animals which portend change, turtle's action is gentle, slow and easy. If turtle arrives, it is usually a good time to pause. Close examination will usually reveal that many changes have already taken place, changes of which one has been only subliminally aware.

People with turtle/tortoise medicine are slow and deliberate. They will not be hurried into action or a decision, and will retreat back into their shells if harried. Tortoise/turtle needs roots, a base to which they can return. Their attachment to their home or place of birth is strong no matter how far they travel. Tortoise people enjoy cultivating the earth. Once the immediate responsibilities of parenting are met, the turtle is not a devoted parent – viewing the world with a more global perspective.

# VULTURE (CONDOR)

*Cathartidae*
California Condor: *Gymnogyps californianis*

## BIOLOGICAL INFORMATION

The European vulture descended from eagle. Studies indicate that the American vulture is from an entirely separate biological family whose ancestors have yet to be identified. Of the three primary species found in North America, the California condor is the largest with a wingspan of 3 metres (about 10 ft). The black vulture is smallest, at 56 to 61 cm (22 to 24 inches) with a wingspan of 1.4 metres (54 inches). The turkey vulture measures 63 to 81 cm (24 to 35 inches) with a wingspan of 1.8 metres (6 ft).

### HABITAT

All totalled, there are seven vulture species in the Americas; they inhabit both tropical and temperate climates. Three breed in North America and between them cover the entire continental US. A few range into southern Canada. The black vulture prefers open lands of prairie or plain. The condor dwells in hills or mountainous regions, while the turkey vulture lives in or near deciduous forests.

In Europe the vulture is concentrated in the Mediterranean region and in mountainous, wooded areas throughout the Continent. It is common in Egypt. Some species live in Greece, Sicily, Italy and the Carpathian

Mountains. The bone-breaker is a special breed which lives and breeds only in Spain.

### CHARACTERISTICS

All vultures are scavengers, with stomach juices that are able to digest food and neutralize bacteria that would kill most other animals. Many people consider them dirty creatures. However, some of their more distasteful habits have reason based on their unique biology. For example the vulture defecates on its own legs, but does so to use these digestive juices to eliminate germs picked up when eating. Similarly, the vulture's head is bald specifically to prevent the growth of bacteria in what would be a fertile medium, feathers.

Some vultures have a strong sense of smell and can pick up the scent of carrion over a mile away; others have no sense of smell at all. All possess good vision. The group with no sense of smell work co-operatively: when one vulture has sighted carrion it adopts a certain pose which signals the find to others. Soon the sky will be crowded. Once they have landed, though, it is every bird for itself and fights often erupt.

The bone-breaker is a solitary hunter. It feeds strictly on marrow. It searches the mountains for skeletal remains. Then it will drop the long bones from a great height until they break to get at the meat inside. The vulture exhibits intelligence and highly specialized skills. As a group they serve a vital function: recycling waste.

Generally vultures raise one or two chicks at a time. They might be considered casual parents. They build no nest, laying their eggs on stacks of wood on the ground, in rock piles or in crevices.

## LEGENDS AND TRADITIONS

GODDESSES Mut, Nekhbet, Isis, Hathor (Egyptian)
GODS Ares (Greek), Mars (Roman)

Vulture was featured on the Pampas Colorado illustrations of Peru created by the Nasca culture. The Nasca were remembered by the later inhabitants of the region for many years thereafter and achieved almost semi-divine status. The natives of Peru, including the Incas, often returned to the Pampas Colorado to worship the animal illustrations of the former valley civilization.

The condor, a species of vulture, became one of the most sacred species for the Incas of the Peru. As an eater of carrion, the condor was associated with death and the 'recycling of life' – hence, the afterlife. It was believed that the condor carried the human soul to the hereafter, and an image of condor was sculpted into the earth at each cemetery or major necropolis. In some cases whole hills were reshaped to create a silhouette of the condor in the landscape.

The Mayans pictured both black vulture and turkey vulture in their codices. The black vulture was shown eating a snake (the latter being one of the Mayan's most sacred animals), while turkey vultures were illustrated devouring sacrificial victims. The link with death is obvious.

Other Native American tribes made similar associations, but did not necessarily deify vulture. However, the Native Americans understood that vulture filled a niche in the cycle of life and death; therefore, they tolerated it. The tribes of California refused to eat any carrion bird, from eagle down to crow.

The Lakota seem to have largely ignored the bird in their mythology, although both the black and turkey vultures flew within the Lakota's territory. Some suggest that it was vulture rather than eagle who was portrayed as the thunderbeing, a giant bird with the antlers of a deer. *Wakinyan* (the thunderbeing) was linked with the west since prevailing winds in the region flow from west to east. Therefore, vulture would have been associated with all things *Heyoka*.

In the desert realm of Egypt, vulture was revered. It was associated with any number of female deities, especially Mut, who was the first divinity of Thebes. At one time the word 'mut' meant both goddess and vulture, but later *neret* became the word for the bird, while Mut was reserved for the goddess. *Neret* also means 'mother', so the symbol was adopted by the goddess Nekhbet, the national deity of Upper Egypt.

Eventually she was elevated to the protector god of the king; her outspread vulture's wings were synonymous with safety and preservation; when shown along with the solar disk, the wings represented those of the hawk.

Mut, too, was raised in status when she became the consort of Amun in 2040 BC. The name means 'Invisible or Hidden One', and Amun was god of the air. Therefore the link between Amun and Mut was a natural one to make. Amun symbolized male fertility (ram) while Mut was the original mother goddess. Together they ensured abundance of the kingdom.

As mother goddesses, both Hathor and Isis were often equated with the vulture, and in some *nomes* (or districts) they picked up the vulture symbol. Coupled with the cobra, the vulture was used in the diadem of the two kingdoms.

The Greeks and later the Romans came to worship vulture; however, their perspective of the bird was the opposite of the Egyptian. The later cultures retained the concept of vulture as protector, but they put a greater emphasis on vulture's ties with death and its inevitable presence after battle. So vulture was connected with the gods of war – Ares (Greek) and Mars (Roman).

## MEDICINE AND POWER

| | |
|---|---|
| DIRECTION | South |
| ELEMENTS | Earth, Air, Sky, Fire and Sun |
| TRAITS | Scavenger, ingenuity, versatility, hygiene and cleanliness |
| ASSOCIATIONS | Mother, protection, the cycle of life and death, the souls of the dead, war, recycling |

Poor vulture with its bald head, hunched shoulders and neck, and its peculiar habit of defecating upon itself has got a lot of bad press. The European settlers of America developed an aversion to carrion fowl despite the fact that they fulfil an essential function. It was only the near eradication of the magnificent California condor that led the white population to realize its importance and its virtues. Vulture speaks of life, death and recycling. Vulture medicine imparts the ability to make the best of a bad situation. Vulture has the unique ability to turn death and war into regenerative life. What better protection can there be?

Instead of filth, vulture should be equated with cleanliness; its internal digestion is so antiseptic that it can eat meat that other creatures would not dare to consume. Furthermore, its stools are actually a powerful germicide. Again, vulture reveals itself as taking a disadvantage and transforming it into an asset. Additionally, vulture's bald head developed to ensure that it did not pick up bacteria from its food. Thus, vulture medicine bestows the capacity to adapt and to come up with new and creative solutions to problems which others would prefer to ignore.

No one could deny vulture's link with death. The Inca saw this ability to build new life from waste and believed that vulture was the messenger between the living and the dead. It carried their spirits to the afterlife. Therefore, this bird is connected with mediumship and communication with the dead.

All things considered, vulture medicine could be called upon in times of crisis, especially when the solution requires mental adjustment or acceptance. Roman and Greek tradition suggests that vulture's energies can be summoned during a fight. However, even there the bird's function was to pick up the pieces in the aftermath of battle. By extrapolation, then, vulture can be raised after the struggles are over, to help clean up the mess.

Some believe that vulture can be summoned to communicate with the spirits of the dead, our ancestors or grandfathers. Therefore the person who has vulture medicine might be considered a natural born medium. This individual is a good organizer and is able to salvage what other people would dismiss as of little consequence.

Vulture has acute senses. Those with a highly developed sense of smell may be interested in or benefit from aromatherapy. The vulture individual is serious most of the time, even grave, and they are willing to undertake the work that others refuse to do. This does not mean that they are thanked for it. Other people tend to avoid getting too close to those who have vulture medicine. All told, the distasteful tasks which they undertake, their unusual appearance and others' innate distrust of those things occult or hidden does not make people with vulture medicine very popular. They get along best with others of their own kind and those who understand the value of vulture medicine.

# WHALE

*Cetacea*

## BIOLOGICAL INFORMATION

There is no 'generic' whale. They can range in size from the pygmy sperm whale (4.3 metres/14 ft) to the Blue whale (22.9 to 30.5 metres/76 to 102 ft). Whales, along with dolphins and porpoises, come under the Latin heading *Cetacea*. They are fully aquatic mammals. They are not even tied to the land to breed. Whales are so highly adapted to their environment they are fish-like in appearance, except that the tail is horizontal rather than vertical. Toothed whales (*Odonceti*) include the beaked (*Ziphiidae*) and sperm (*Physeteridae*) whales. The white whale and narwhale (*Monodontidae*) have no dorsal fin and blunt snouts. Baleen whales (*Mysticeti*) have no teeth. The latter group are plankton-feeders which sieve their bounty from the seas. These include the grey whale (*Eschrinichtiidae*) and the fin-backed (*Balaenopteridae*), which are among the largest whales in the world. The blue, the humpback and the white whale also belong to this group.

### HABITAT

Whales inhabit the oceans of the world. Many species seem to prefer the cold water of the Arctic regions, both north and south, the northern coast of the Atlantic and Pacific, and the areas around Cape Horn and the Cape of Good Hope. This does not mean they do not traverse the warm waters, for most whales are migratory, covering thousands of kilometres every year.

## CHARACTERISTICS

Whales are social, communicative creatures which travel in groups or pods. The humpback actually hunt in packs like wolves, and have developed a strategy to breach the defence of fish. One humpback stays in the deep, and when the school of fish dive to escape the rest of the whale pod, who have remained close to the surface, the first whale sounds off. The fish then reverse their course. The other whales continue to drive the school upward. When the fish are within a certain distance of the surface, the pod form a circle around and slightly below their prey. They release a curtain of bubbles which forces the fish into the air, where they are helpless against their predators.

Some whales are more easily studied since they spend part of their year close to land. Others like the blue whale remain at such great depths and live so far out in the ocean that very little is known about them.

One of the most beguiling aspects of whales is their song. Even when travelling singly, whales keep in touch with others of their kind with calls and songs. Each whale has its own particular signature whistle that it uses to identify itself to others. The sound actually travels for many kilometres underwater, and it has been wondered if some of these 'solos' may be a form of echo-location.

Although some whales, such as the humpback, are efficient hunters, all are gentle and protective parents; the cow usually raises a single calf alone which she will keep with her for several years. The babies suckle just like any other mammal, but they are so adapted to their environment that they can accomplish this under water. Thus, unlike the seal, whales are not linked to land even to breed. Calves are usually born in one part of the world and must be prepared to swim thousands of kilometres within a few weeks of birth to their winter feeding grounds.

## LEGENDS AND TRADITIONS

The coastal Nasca, who created their gigantic pictures on the Peruvian plains, honoured whale. Whales were also worshipped by the Native Americans of the Pacific northwest from northern California, Oregon and Washington up to Vancouver and into Alaska. Whale became especially important for the seafaring peoples. It was also an animal of great power for the native peoples of northeastern America far into the 20th century. A large percentage of the Native American population along the New England seaboard were still making their living from whaling until it was banned.

An Inupiaq legend from the Arctic tells how the Great Spirit created the sun, moon and stars, the mountains and the snows. Then Great Spirit made the fish and the birds. He fashioned the Inupiaq as his favourite people. Last of all he made the most perfect of all animals, the bow whale, and the Great Spirit created a path which led his people to the whales and the sea, and so it was that the Inupiaq thrived. Then Great Spirit made mist. Although he did not begrudge the people their food, he did not want to watch the most noble of all his creations die.

As the most perfect, the whale was treated with a great deal of respect. Each hunter had to be initiated into the hunt. After the first kill, the young hunter touched the whale all over – flukes, mouth, and fins. He had to crawl over it from top to bottom, with prayers and reverence. By getting close to the animal the hunter assimilated its spirit and learned not only its medicine, but its pain. Before the rite was completed the novice had to find the join between neck and skull which would ensure a clean, relatively painless kill. Finally the animal was thanked for sacrificing its life to give the Inupiaq sustenance.

The Aleuts of the islands in the Bering Strait between Alaska and Siberia tipped their spears with aconite to ensure the kill. Special training was required in the handling of this poisonous monkshood. Only a few men qualified to hunt whale. They wore special amulets to call the animal to them, along with amulets to appease its spirit – including hematite, feathers of the rosy finch, and the most gruesome of all, the body fluids of mummified hunters. As soon as whale was sighted, a single hunter would depart in his Baidarka (kayak), then he would throw his poison dart. When he returned home he would go into self-imposed exile for three days. By this magic he would share the animal's pain. Three days later the whale would surface where the people could finish it off quickly.

Whaling was the most prestigious way of making a living for the Makah of the Olympia Peninsula in Alaska, and the occupation was passed from father to son. The Haida of British Columbia and the Swinomish warriors also reaped the bounty of the deep, and may have on rare occasions taken the opportunity to hunt whales, although seal and sea lion formed the bulk of their diet.

The Salish Sxwayxwey mask combined the wings of the eagle with the face of a whale, to illustrate that these two creatures shared the same qualities. As late as the 1930s the maritime Koryak of northeast Siberia (another Inuit tribe) held a festival after killing a whale where it was incited to return again next year, for the Koryak consider the whale a member of their family.

The European, too, esteemed whale. It was used as a symbol of the world. It also represented the body and the grave, 'Davy Jones's Locker' at the bottom of the sea. Whale was the ocean that contained and concealed an alien environment which was both vital and fatal to man. More recently, whale has become an allegory for the mystic mandala, the intersection of opposite worlds, heaven and earth.

In the Old World, if a whale was seen swimming it was considered lucky. However, if one became grounded this boded ill. The beached whale portends disaster for an entire community. This superstition is founded on fact, for the animal decaying on a beach brought the stench of death, which at one time was attributed to plague, although history has since proven otherwise. Still, the putrefying corpse becomes a breeding ground for bacteria. Consequently a beached and dying whale could present a real health hazard for a village and cause the spread of disease.

## MEDICINE AND POWER

| | |
|---|---|
| DIRECTION | Varies by tribe |
| ELEMENT | Water |
| TRAITS | Parental devotion, communication, migration |
| ASSOCIATIONS | Power, strength, the gentle giant, intelligence and intuition; the rhythms of the ocean tides and the universe; the bounty of the deep; knowledge; the keeper of history |

The direction attributed to whale differed according to the tribe. For the peoples of the US west coast, the whale was linked to the west, while east coast tribes would have looked to the east to see it. The tribes of Aleutians who depended upon it for food associated whale with the south.

Whale, as the most perfect of all God's creations, was a symbol for the world. Some aboriginal peoples equated it as much with earth as water since it would appear like an island rising in the mists. Even in the Old World, whale was often used to represent the globe. Whale was both life and death. Therefore, whale speaks of the totality of life – without any of the negative implications of spider or snake.

Whale was the primary giver of life and power for the peoples of the Arctic. The derogatory name once given to the Eskimo means 'blubber eater'. Although the modern definition of whale medicine retains some of these elements, the meaning has been greatly enhanced, at least in part by humanity's increased awareness of this mammal. As whales are studied, their songs recorded and their intelligence and communication skills proved, many of these new attributes have been grafted onto the old traditions.

So whale represents communication and song. It is the storyteller who retains both the knowledge of the deep and the secret of time's beginnings. Whale's ability not only to speak, but to hear over great distances has lead some to attribute to it clairaudience, the ability to hear spirit voices.

Recent developments in Native American faith have come to associate whale with the Dog Star. Others believe that the first beings on this planet came from the Pleiades. These believers hold the whale as recorder and keeper of history. Tribal legends state that whale first lived on land, only moving to water after the earth's axis shifted. Biological and zoological studies of their bone structure confirm the fact that whales were once adapted to land. The front fins still retain the digits of a hand under the thick skin.

Therefore, whale has gained a profound understanding of the planet, both land and sea. Whale is linked with movement and change at a most profound level. With whale's global connections, this suggests something that could affect all of humankind.

Whale medicine can be used for connecting with the rhythm of mother earth or with higher planes of consciousness. Whale can be invoked when a person needs to confront the watery realm of the emotions, or for spiritual expansion at the deepest levels. Whale medicine instills calm and clears the mind. Whale's appearance can indicate a time to connect with a higher intelligence, or it can mean something more literal, promising abundance, nourishment, sustenance and growth.

The whale individual is not easily flustered and, once set upon a path or course, is not easily turned aside. These individuals are so unaffected by what goes around them that at times they will appear as if they are on another world. Certainly they view life from a different perspective. Those with whale medicine need both companionship and solitude, for they are social animals with a strong sense of privacy and independence. The whale individual also has acute hearing, with the capacity to hear things beyond the range of normal human faculties.

# WOLF

Grey wolf: *Canis Lupus*
Red wolf: *Canis Niger*

## BIOLOGICAL INFORMATION

The timber or grey wolf stands 66 to 97 cm (26 to 38 inches) at the shoulder. It is 1 to 2 metres (approximately 3 to 7 ft) long with a tail that measures 35 to 50 cm (14 – 20 inches). It weighs 26 to 59 kg (57 – 130 lb). The red wolf is smaller, about half the height and weight of the grey.

'Grey' is something of a misnomer, since wolves in the far north tend to be white, while black wolves are found in other areas. The grey colouring comes from a combination of black, brown and white hairs. All one species, the many different kinds of wolves are all considered 'subspecies' of *Canis*, and any variation in colouring is essentially a variation in the concentration of colours. The Egyptian subspecies is the smallest in the world, at 16 kg (35 lb); the Alaskan wolf is the biggest, weighing in at 80 kg (175 lb).

### HABITAT

Wolves inhabit wooded land. The grey wolf is almost nonexistent in the continental United States, except for small areas of the northern Rockies and in the woodlands around the Great Lakes. In North America, Canada is wolf's primary home. Most wolves stay as far away from humans as they can get. The red wolf is found mainly in the swamps of Louisiana. After being driven close to extinction, it has only recently been reintroduced into the wild.

In Europe, the wolf can still be found in the mountainous forested regions of the Pyrenees, the Alps, the Carpathian Mountains, Poland, Russia and Scandinavia. It was virtually eliminated in Western Europe by the end of the 19th century. Like its American counterpart, it avoids man. Recently there has been a movement to reintroduce the wolf to remote areas of Scotland and England, though this has been much resisted by farmers.

## CHARACTERISTICS

The wolf is a pack animal, with an alpha (breeding) male and female. Packs may number up to 20, although 10 is average. Most if not all wolves in a pack are related. The alpha female rules, and she may oust any member she pleases. The pack has a definite social strata, along with many elaborate rituals, postures and growls required to maintain this structure. In fact it has been suggested that it was not man who socialized wolf to create dog, but wolf who tamed man. Dogs and wolves share enough of the same genes that they can still interbreed. It is said that wolves and dogs are more closely related than frogs in a single pond.

With their thick fur, wolves are more comfortable in cold environments. Even the Ethiopian wolf stays at such high altitudes that the summer days begin with frost.

Wolves hunt in relays, chasing the herds of elk or buffalo for long distances, during which they assess the weakest or eldest animals. There is nothing random about the selection. Once the animal has been chosen, the wolf is so intent upon its prey that the quarry cannot lose itself even by diving deep into the middle of the herd. Thus, wolves perform a service, culling the herd of the weak or the injured – those who would most likely not survive the winter. Wolves rarely kill livestock. Only in extremely cold winters when they are starving would wolves come close enough to man to threaten cattle or sheep, and there has never been a recorded attack on man by a healthy wild wolf in North America.

In the northern hemisphere wolves mate in February or March, although the closer one moves to the Arctic the more this is delayed. The young are born in April or May – some as late as June. Both male and female wolves secrete the hormone prolactin (usually associated with nursing mothers) in summer. Not only the parents, but all pack members release this substance into their bloodstream. This helps with bonding within the pack. The entire group cares for the young. Once the pups are weaned, both male and female siblings of previous years will be called upon to mind them while the parents hunt. Wolves remain playful throughout their lives. They are loving creatures. Wolf fathers are the most devoted and gentle in all the animal kingdom.

Wolves love to howl. They do this for several reasons: to contact other members of the pack outside the range of visual sighting, to announce their presence and boundaries of their territory, and for the sheer joy of doing so. Wolf 'song' has often been equated with whale song, as maintaining the history of the universe.

Thus, wolves are not the savage, ravenous beasts of old fairy stories, but communicative, family-oriented creatures who live, work, hunt and play in a spirit of co-operation rather than competition. There is a great deal we could learn from them.

## LEGENDS AND TRADITIONS

GODDESSES Acca Larentia (Etruscan), Rhea Silvia (Roman), Spako (Persian)
GODS Wepwawet, Khentyamentiu (Egyptian), Apollo (Greek)

The religion of the Great Basin peoples of California placed much emphasis on immortality. After the hunt, the Paiute would position the body of any animal caught in the hunt so the head faced east. Prayers would be said for the animal's spirit. The Shoshone believed that after death the human spirit went to the land of coyote who, along with wolf, created the world. Wolf guarded the path walked by the dead. Wolf would awaken and wash the human soul in the river, thereby making it sacred, and then the newly cleansed spirit gained entry into the promised land.

Elsewhere in northwestern America wolf was linked with raven, especially with those tribes who credited raven with the origin of the universe. So wolf is inextricably bound with the creation story.

In real life wolf and raven quite often work together, the raven flying ahead of a wolf during the hunt. Raven warns wolf of the presence of other predators, and the bird is repaid by sharing the wolves' repast.

For the natives of Nootka Sound, the Wolf Clan was one of the primary clans. The ceremony of initiation consisted of a symbolic death (hunt) of the new initiate who was reborn with the spirit of a wolf. The Niska people of Canada's British Columbia also marked the initiation of a new member into the wolf clan with symbolic death and resurrection. Thus, wolf was linked not only to creation, but to death and rebirth.

The wolf was one of the most important predators. The peoples of California and the Great Plains often associated wolves with mountains, since the shy, retiring creatures retreated into the hills away from the advance of man. This connection with high places – spirit – made wolf one of the most important teacher-animals. As wolf withdrew to more and more remote territories to avoid humanity, it became the pathfinder or trail-blazer. Because they wandered, it was believed that they knew everything.

This is reflected in the languages of the various Native American peoples. The Lakota word for wolf was *sungmanitu* (or *sunkmanitu*). One wonders if there is any coincidence that the Lakota used *manitu* or *manitou*, the name for Great Spirit in a neighbouring tribe. Translated, *sunkmanitu* means 'divine dog'.

The wolf as teacher was so integral an idea to the Native Americans that in sign language – used across the Plains, the Mississippi valley and spreading into the Rockies – the hand position for medicine (power) was nearly identical to that for wolf. For the latter the hand, with index and middle fingers extended, moves forward tracing a diagonal path – indicating something which walks abroad on land. The sign for medicine also has the middle and index fingers extended, the hand spiralling up towards the sky, signifying the heavens, the sacred circle and the spirit.

The Plains tribes invested much in the wisdom of wolf. They studied the animal in order to learn the arts of war. Again, this is reflected in their sign language, where the single sign for wolf embraces such concepts as 'scout', 'spy', 'strategy' or 'ruse'. The wolf sign combined with other signs meant 'patrol'. The Pawnee were one of the most feared tribes upon the Plains, and the sign for Pawnee was also 'wolf'.

Almost all tribes had some kind of Wolf (sacred dog/warrior) Society. Where animals represented lineages, wolf was inevitably among the most important. The Lakota based much of male society on the wolf, just as female society was constructed on the model of the buffalo. They emulated wolf's loyalty to pack, mate and children. Before a war party, the men would smear red on their mouths, cheeks and eyes to emulate the feeding wolf and invoke its power. Immediately prior to setting out, the holy man with wolf medicine would lead the men in a wolf-like howl, for it was thought this would instill them with wolf's fighting spirit.

Wolf was a friend of *Wazi*, the Wizard (old man) of the North; therefore indirectly connect to Iktomi. The relationship between the wizard and wolf was so close that wolf let Wazi ride upon its back. There seems to have been a transformation over time in the attitudes of the Lakota. In monographs written in the 1880s wolf was only spoken of as *Wakan*. At that time, the Kit Fox Society was the primary warrior society. Later documentation (such as that recorded by Joseph Epes Brown) listed the Wolf Society rather than the Kit Fox as the primary warrior society. By that time the Kit Fox Society had more to do with internal policing of the village and the tribe.

The woodland Dakota were not as impressed with wolf as some other Native American peoples. As part of Ohiyesa's teaching in 1862, his grandfather outlined the many predators to be feared and how to deal with them. Wolf was not among them. The grandfather referred to wolf as lazy and cowardly, a creature who never attacked a man, particularly if the wolf was alone. By this time, though, wolves would have been scarce and shy of man. A little more than 50 years later, the wolf had been completely exterminated in the continental United States.

The Lakota Oglala of the Great Plains, however, maintained their respect for wolf. It was believed that if a horse was used to chase a wolf, it would be ruined, for the wolf would curse the horse and it would become lame. And only the Cherokee brave who knew the proper rites of atonement was allowed to kill a wolf.

According to one Ojibwe shaman, wolf is so important it was not considered a power animal. It does not deign to appear to an individual solely to endow him with wolf medicine; rather it comes as a teacher, a temporary energy when there are important lessons of spirit to be learned.

Despite all its wit and wisdom, this did not mean that wolf couldn't be outfoxed. In one legend, wolf is duped by the humble rabbit. The two were neighbours and they took a fancy to two beautiful women who lived nearby. They went to the women's teepee to pay court, but the women ignored rabbit. Finally rabbit pulled one of the women aside and explained that wolf was, in fact, his horse. She laughed and challenged rabbit to ride the wolf. The next day when wolf called to take rabbit with him to visit the women, rabbit complained that he was tired, and refused to go until wolf agreed to let rabbit ride upon his back. The women saw this, and wolf was shamed. Rabbit won their hearts for his courage and was able to keep both lovely women to himself.

As mentioned, wolf was associated with the Dog Star, Sirius, by some tribes. The Egyptians believed that Sirius was home of the gods. The Egyptian god Wepwawet was originally a wolf-god who was supplanted by Khentyamentiu as the foremost god of Abydos after the 1st and 2nd Dynasty. The wolf-god remained as a presence until the end of Egyptian self-rule, for it was the beast god of the city the Greeks called Lycopolis.

Uncertainty has often been associated with Anubis. Jackal seems to be the preferred animal associated with Anubis, but this is often debated. Some claim that the hieroglyph represents dog, fox or even wolf. Indeed, once one has seen the Ethiopian wolf (whose range was undoubtedly larger then than it is now) it is difficult not to see a direct resemblance to the symbol for Anubis.

A legend of Celtic Ireland relays the tale of King Cormac, who was raised by wolves. The pack often accompanied him, and during his inauguration he walked through two rows of wolves, receiving their blessings as he went. Merlin in his time of madness found the companionship of a she-wolf, who remained with him until he was well – thus illustrating the loyalty of wolf.

The Roman view was similar to the Native American one. The wolf was a symbol of valour, often used in insignia. This notion did not carry further north, however. In Norse and German mythology, wolf had a much more negative connotation. It was a symbol of destruction and death. The Vikings commemorated wolf with Fenris (chaos) who, at the end of time would bite through his chains and devour the sun. Thus, the world would end. Gnostics also saw wolf as chaos and destruction.

In England during the time of King Edgar, wolves were so numerous that punishment for a crime would be commuted if the criminal could present a specified number of wolves' tongues. Wolf is first mentioned in the Stowe Bestiary of 1067, where it was proclaimed: 'if a wolf sees a man before the man sees the wolf ... [the man] will be struck dumb.' In France, it was thought that if a child wore a wolf's tooth, he would be protected from evil spirits. In other European countries, mentioning the animal during the month of December invited attack.

Neither wolf nor fox fare well in fairy tales of old, where they are mainly known for trickery. Russian folk tales speak of a wolf who disguises his voice, forces his way into the home of a goat and eats up all the kids. More often than not, wolf is made a fool by wily fox. Thus it would appear that, for Europeans, wolf fulfilled much the same place as coyote, both a trickster and one who is easily taken in.

This opinion hadn't changed much in England by Victorian times, where in Clark's *Introduction to Heraldry*, it states: 'Wolf is a cruel, ravenous, and watchful creature, able to endure hunger longer than any other beast; but, when pressed by it, breaks out and tears the first flock it meets with ...' Still, Clark reflected some of the respect of the Romans: '[Wolf] ... is therefore compared to a resolute commander, who having been long besieged, being at last reduced to famine, makes a desperate sally upon his enemies, and drives all before him; having vanquished his opposers, returned into his garrison laden, with honours, plunder and provisions ...'[1]

Some European superstitions mirror the Lakota belief that a horse could be ruined by wolf. It was said that a horse who stepped into a wolf track would be seized with numbness. In France and Germany, the 'corn spirit' was often conceived of as a wolf or dog. In East Prussia, where wolves were common, it was thought that seeing a wolf running through a field dragging its tail brought blessings; but if the tail was held erect, the villagers would curse the animal and try to kill it. This is not as illogical as it might seem, since the tail down indicates a submissive posture, and a wolf affecting such a pose would mean no threat. The upright tail, on the other hand, signifies dominance and, as such, could constitute a menace.

## MEDICINE AND POWER

| | |
|---|---|
| DIRECTION | North |
| ELEMENTS | Earth (mountains), Sky |
| TRAITS | Loyalty, camaraderie, parental devotion, efficient hunter |
| ASSOCIATIONS | Creation; death, afterlife and rebirth; the chase and war; teacher, pathfinder and trail-blazer; solidarity, co-operation and courage; chaos |

Many correlations can be made between the medicine of wolf and that attributed to snake and spider. Like those creatures, wolf was associated with creation, death, the afterlife, resurrection and rebirth. Unlike snake and spider, wolf doesn't appear to have had quite as many negative connotations – unless one looks to Europe, where wolf was feared rather than respected. In Europe wolf becomes destruction, even linked to the end of the universe. Therefore, wolf embodies the totality of life, especially for the warrior.

More than spider or snake, wolf is teacher. In this context wolf medicine is attainable by all, not just the select few who are able to detoxify the snake's venom. This teaching role remains for wolf to this day. Wolf has now replaced the deer as the symbol of the wild. More importantly, wolf epitomizes everything man has done wrong in reshaping nature to his own preferred image and likeness. Wolf is a lesson of what can happen if the ecological balance is destroyed. For example, the buffalo of the Canadian plains, one of the only places where wolf still exists in the wild, is reputed to be the biggest, the strongest and most healthy of all North American buffalo, for no other reason than that they are regularly hunted and the herd culled of the old, the weak and the infirm. This tends to confirm that wolf as a predator is necessary for the successful completion of the cycle of life and for the natural economy as a whole.

Though often misunderstood, wolf teaches the trust of self. Similarly, the impression of the wolf as savage, hence cruel, is erroneous. Rather, wolf's attributes are speed, wisdom and solidarity. Its medicine should be invoked when these traits are needed, in a time of stress or competition. Wolf medicine imbues the individual with courage and endurance to face problems or obstacles. Wolf medicine allows one to 'ferret' out the truth, to pinpoint and isolate the weakness in any person, plan or scheme.

The wolf pack is the essence of social co-operation. Therefore, one of its lessons is learning one's place in the social hierarchy. The pack works for the benefit of all. It is only when at rest or play that individuality comes to the fore. Thus, wolf gives a knowledge of proper conduct and demeanour in a group setting. It teaches when to sublimate the personality for the good of all. Yet it does not require that anyone gives up his or her sense of identity.

As an instructor, wolf's lessons may be hard. It appears to those who need the skills of the warrior in order to survive. As a pathfinder, wolf reveals itself to those who have lost their way. This author tends to accept the view that wolf medicine is rare, and those who possess it have wolves as life-time partners, and have a particular path to follow. Usually wolf appears as a temporary teacher, in response to a specific need. It should never be invoked lightly, if at all. In this position, wolf is inevitably the alpha male or female, or leader. Thus, they do the choosing – if or when they accept someone into a pack – and their lessons should always be heeded.

Wolf medicine is the divine walking abroad on earth. It represents the fine balance in the cycle of life, nature and spirit, and it imparts this medicine to others when they need it. Wolf's arrival heralds a time for accessing one's ability to know the truth. Wolf medicine helps one define relationships and set boundaries. It encourages kinship and a sense of community. Therefore it grounds.

Wolf has an innate ability for knowing when to retreat and when to attack; therefore, it anticipates right action, and its medicine instills this skill in others. Until the quarry is chosen, the hunting pack appears playful. They may pause to wrestle or chase one another. This serves two purposes. The playful attitude will lull the herd into a false sense of security. As the presence of the pack goads the herd into action, the wolves can assess the animals and choose a victim. Thus, wolf makes fun or takes pleasure in all activity, and so it grants a spirit of joy even in work. Wolf medicine imparts strength of character and integrity. It speaks of honouring lifetime commitments.

People who possess wolf medicine seem to follow one of three paths – that of alpha, or leader, that of pack member, or that of the lone wolf. The first and second are self-explanatory, since human society, business and governments are built on a similar model of leaders and followers. Perhaps the wolf person will play all these roles at different times during the course of their lives. This is certainly true for the animal itself, which starts as a pup (lowest in ranking) and later gets assimilated into the pack as a secondary member. Eventually, if this member is ever to achieve alpha status, it must leave the pack or it will be driven away. The lone wolf is one of the saddest of all creatures. Yet it is a necessary part of the transition to founding one's own pack, or else there would be interbreeding.

All three wolf-types will exhibit 'martial' characteristics when threatened. Yet the wolf personality is shy. This person will usually have a select group of friends with whom he or she associates. All other comers will be spurned, even attacked, if they approach. These people believe in family solidarity; they are good and loyal friends. In competition they are sharp, able to assess a weakness and take advantage of it.

The lone wolf is a weakened wolf. To cover this weakness the lone wolf appears to prefer his or her own company; even though he or she craves the companionship of others. Often this individual has been hurt (driven from his or her family or pack) and will snap rather than let people get close. Such odd behaviour may be a survival tactic, for in the natural world the lone wolf who approaches a strange pack is most often killed on sight. At best, the animal will be subjected to a several-hours-long ordeal before acceptance. If the newcomer does not pass muster, it is summarily killed rather than driven away. The lucky ones are those who have been expelled.

The lone wolf has the same view of the world as the others; it still adheres to the belief in loyalty, fidelity, partnership and family; it simply lacks opportunity. It is at this time when the wolf individual must confront him- or herself; thus, it is a time of honing skills – those who don't, won't survive – and honouring the spirit within. In the life of a wolf, this is the time of the greatest growth. Those who stay with the original pack and never embark on their own, never get to breed.

The senses of the wolf (animal or individual) are keen. It is allied with the moon. The visual cones and rods of the wolf are adapted to see well after dark. This is one reason why it does not see colours, since these are not necessary. A secondary effect is that wolves – and supposedly dog, although there are dog owners who would debate this – cannot assimilate and recognize two-dimensional images. At night, in a world of shade and shadow, depth perception becomes paramount – especially for the hunter, who must be able to single out one animal from a group of 50 to 200 individuals and track it.

Once people with wolf medicine set their sights on something, they won't give up. Only complete exhaustion, utter futility or death will divert the wolf from its prey. So these are not the people to anger or push at any time.

# WOLVERINE

American wolverine: *Gulo luscus*
European wolverine: *Gulo gulo*

## BIOLOGICAL INFORMATION

The largest member of the weasel family, the wolverine is about the size of a large dog. It measures about 1 m (a little more than 3 ft) in length and weighs between 15 and 25 kg (20 and 35 lb). The wolverine has the same long body and short legs of the weasel. Its fur is brown to black. It has a yellowish band across its forehead that runs down the neck and the full length of the body along the flanks. The wolverine has broad padded feet which act as snowshoes. Its eyesight is poor. It relies on scent rather than vision.

### HABITAT

The wolverine prefers high altitudes. It ranges through the wild, coniferous forests of the Cascades (Oregon, Washington and British Columbia) up through Canada and Alaska to mainland Russia. Once found throughout Canada and down into the northern US, wolverines have not been seen in the eastern provinces of Quebec since 1983, nor in Labrador since 1985. In Canada, wolverines have completely disappeared from the plains. The wolverine is listed as endangered even in the Cascades.

The wolverine is not exclusive to the New World. It makes its home in the taigas and wooded tundras of Europe and Asia. In the former, wolverine is found in the northeastern forests and in Scandinavia.

## CHARACTERISTICS

Wolverine means 'glutton', although the name is not deserved. It gained this reputation when it was observed driving bears and cougar from its kill. A wolverine can bring down animals as large as caribou, but the wolverine stores its prize, marking it for later use. Therefore, the wolverine does not waste its food. It is known for ferocity and resourcefulness. Yet it is shy by nature and will not fight unless provoked. Most people living within the 320-km (200-mile) territory of the female wolverine have never seen one. The wolverine has no predators.

The wolverine appears clumsy, but it is surprisingly quick and agile. It can run, climb and swim. It lives on Arctic rodents such as voles and lemmings. It varies its diet with birds, eggs, lizards and frogs. It will also eat berries and fruit. Wolverine has more than a passing resemblance to a bear crossed with a raccoon, in both looks and personality – and, like them, will raid homes to obtain food. It marks its territory – including houses – with urine and scat, a less than endearing characteristic.

The male traverses a range of up to 1,600 km (1,000 miles), which is shared by three or four breeding females. The mating period is July and August in Europe. After a gestation period of eight to nine months, the female gives birth to from one to four young. The lair is usually located in the cleft of boulders or a tumble of rocks. When the young leave the mother, the siblings will stay together to hunt for a couple of years, after which time they separate. The wolverine does not obtain full maturity for three years. In North America the breeding season is longer, lasting from April through September. Implantation occurs in January.

# LEGENDS AND TRADITIONS

The Crow of the Plateau Basin of Wyoming and Montana, like many Native American peoples, honoured the sacred tobacco. They even had a Tobacco Society. Men and women who belonged to the Wolverine group devoted themselves to the planting and harvesting of this sacred herb. Men wore the skins of the wolverine to symbolize their association with this group during rituals. Deer claw moccasins were also worn by members of the Tobacco Society.

Natives of the northeast and the northwest invoked wolverine power before going to war. Once cornered, the wolverine is nearly impossible to beat. The wolverine will take on a mountain lion or a bear if the need presents itself.

One legend relays the origins of wolverine.[1] When God was creating the universe, He had some leftover parts – the claws of a badger, the mask and tail of a raccoon and the temper of a bear. The Great Spirit threw these together, and wolverine was born.

## MEDICINE AND POWER

| | |
|---|---|
| DIRECTION | North |
| ELEMENT | Earth |
| TRAITS | Shyness, but ferocity when cornered, strength and endurance |
| ASSOCIATIONS | Warfare, the sacred tobacco, prudence and persistence |

The wolverine has, sadly, remained unstudied. Hence, little is known about its habits, and now so few remain it is unlikely they will ever be completely understood. They weren't particularly popular in the past, as the one tale of wolverine having been created from the rubbish of the universe illustrates. Their fur was too long, too mottled, too marked to have economic value, and they were savage and dangerous when surprised. They were almost always killed by white fur traders when found in traps, since the animal had a) the audacity to get caught and occupy a trap that could have been used to catch a more profitable furbearing creature, and b) as predators it was believed that they would kill and eat the more important animals. Of course the trapped and wounded animal would not have survived in any case, and it would have been impossible for the hunter to free it without sustaining injury.

Yet wolverine contains some powerful medicine, particularly in the area of defence. This creature won't pick fights, but once confronted it is more than capable of taking care of itself. Furthermore, the animal who attacks or corners a wolverine never makes the same mistake twice. Therefore, this medicine speaks of learning painful lessons and retaining that knowledge. Its medicine can be called upon during times of confrontation.

Wolverine is a symbol of the last vestige of the wilderness. It is master of the forest. Wolverine medicine forms a bridge between the physical and spiritual realms. Wolverine provides protection from attackers and teaches one how to stand one's ground. Some make a connection between the wolverine and revenge. Wolverine medicine is elusive and imparts resourcefulness when under attack, courage when needed, and endurance.

Wolverine is so pacific, though, that it prefers to avoid conflict and will run away or retreat into the nearest available hole and hide. Therefore wolverine, like possum, not only endows one with the ability to fight, but more importantly imparts the discretion to beat a strategic retreat and avoid unnecessary battle. Wolverine medicine knows when to fight and when to withdraw.

Thus, wolverine medicine endows foresight and caution. This animal does not assume that it will have a successful hunt tomorrow, so it does not leave its kill for the carrion. It sprays its food and saves it for the next day.

The wolverine person will reflect many of these qualities. This individual is frugal, storing away food or money for times of want. This person is shy. He or she will stay in the background and rarely put him- or herself forward. However, don't make a mistake. This is not somebody to anger, for wolverine can bring down a moose. Not even wolf can do that. This individual is strong, and once angered not about to back away from a fight.

# WOODPECKER

*Picadae*

## BIOLOGICAL INFORMATION

There are four species of woodpecker native to Great Britain, and 20 common in America – with a total of 210 species worldwide. The Great Black is the largest in Europe, and an occasional visitor to England, and can grow up to 32 cm (13 inches) in length; however, most breeds are smaller, averaging around 15 to 20 cm (6 – 8 inches). The green woodpecker is the most common. As a group, they have sharp beaks designed for digging insects, larvae or grubs from tree trunks, long claws to cling to bark, and a short spiny tail to act as a prop.

### HABITAT

Woodpeckers are found almost everywhere except Australia, New Guinea and Madagascar. As the name suggests, they prefer forested or wooded lands, although woodpeckers can be found in city parks and suburban environments. Between the many species, woodpecker completely covers the United States, the southern strip of Canada from coast to coast, and up the west coast of British Columbia to Alaska.

### CHARACTERISTICS

Woodpeckers lay between three and eight eggs, depending on the species, in the spring (April to May). They build their nests in the holes they create themselves in trees, or use existing holes which they clear out and adapt to their needs. The parents care for the chicks co-operatively, both male and female contributing to their needs.

All woodpeckers hammer to find food, but also as a form of communication. The male will tap out a certain rhythm to attract the attention of the female as part of the courtship ritual. It may also tap to announce its territory. Once mated, the birds will drum to keep track of each other. The woodpecker becomes more active immediately prior to a storm.

## LEGENDS AND TRADITIONS

GODS Silvanus (Roman), Wakinyan (Dakota/Lakota)

The Lakota observed that the woodpecker became agitated just before a storm, especially if the storm was going to be electrical in nature. Like many other animals, woodpecker became associated with thunder, and some believe that it is the woodpecker, and not the eagle, that is portrayed as the thunderbird. The crest depicted on most representations of the thunderbird is reminiscent of woodpecker.

In the Lakota way of being, to see woodpecker in a vision was to become *Heyoka*, the backward actor whose animals were coyote, dragonfly, and swallow. The feathers of woodpeckers adorned the Sun Dance pole used to call upon the thunderbeings. Black Elk spoke to woodpecker in a vision; the bird sat on the offering pole and warned him to be cautious of any bad thing he heard. The guardian of Fools Crow's, one of the most noted holy men of his people in the 20th century, was the red-headed woodpecker.

Woodpecker was particularly valuable in the coastal regions of the western US and Canada. The Yokut shamans of southern California used woodpecker feathers as part of their sacred attire. The scalp of the woodpecker, along with eagle feathers and dentalium shells, were used as a medium of exchange by the Hupa, Yurok and Karol peoples of northern California. One redwood canoe could be exchanged for 10 large woodpecker scalps or 60 small ones.[1]

The Hupa wore buckskin headbands with woodpecker scalps during their primary festivals, the Whiteskin deer dance and the Jumping dance. The Wintu, another of the California hill tribes, wore wool caps adorned with woodpecker scalps for their ceremonies.

The nearby Yurok developed a sophisticated 'monetary' system which included fines. Everything from theft to marriage, even fraud, had its related price. Thus, they were a property-oriented society. To wear a hat or a coat of woodpecker indicated wealth and success. Further north near Bodaga Bay – where the movie *The Birds* was filmed – the Mitok reserved feathered coats or cloaks which included woodpecker and flicker feathers for people of prominence like the wife of the chief or the chief himself. Therefore, woodpecker feathers were used to make a statement about a person's position and status.

The Haida of Alaska and British Columbia placed the image of the thunderbirds on their boats for protection, although from the stylized images used it is difficult to tell if this is supposed to represent a woodpecker, hawk or eagle.

In classical mythology the woodpecker was associated with the Roman god of the woods Silvanus, who was the counterpart to Diana. Besides claiming dominion over things in the forest, Silvanus ruled over cattle. Sir James George Frazier surmised that both were probably involved with the type of generative magic that eventually became watered down – devolving into May Day, Whitsunday and midsummer festivals.

## MEDICINE AND POWER

| | |
|---|---|
| DIRECTION | West (thunderbeings) |
| ELEMENTS | Air, and to a lesser extent Fire and Earth |
| TRAITS | Rhythm, drumming, flight |
| ASSOCIATIONS | Storms, thunder, invisibility, calling of the rains, sacred cycles, mother earth |

The woodpecker gives a particularly shrill call before storms, so it could predict the weather and was associated with thunderstorms. It was also noted that the bird became particularly active before a storm; therefore, by watching woodpecker many could divine the weather. This was no superstition, but fact: scientists have discovered that all animals become agitated before an earthquake, even before the first tremors are felt, and can be good indicators of seismic activity. Some believed that woodpecker's tapping actually called the storms.

Nearly all the Plains tribes link woodpecker with the thunderbeings. Anyone who has ever been through a thunderstorm on the exposed Plains can understand just how powerful they can be and how important the powers were who controlled them. Thus, the medicine of woodpecker can been seen as nearly as forceful as that of eagle, despite woodpecker's diminutive size. Fools Crow kept a skull of a woodpecker to invoke its medicine

The thunderbeings were:

- mighty, as represented by the force of the storms
- imperceptible, for this destructive force, like the wind, remained unseen until it struck
- invulnerable, or invincible, because storms were unstoppable.

These were important beings to placate; useful in warfare and while hunting. Woodpecker became male energy.

Conversely, some associate woodpecker with rhythm. Its tapping against the trunk of a tree is supposed to duplicate the heartbeat of mother earth. This of course suggests more female magic. The concept of rhythm connects woodpecker to cycles – all cycles: day and night, the seasons, etc. To tap like woodpecker is to summon the aid of the earth mother. Likewise, woodpecker is linked with drums, drum 'magic' or the use of the drum for meditation and shamanistic rituals.

As representative of Silvanus, woodpecker is associated with forests, trees and tree magic, regenerative and vegetative magic, and sexual magic (the sacred marriage).

Woodpecker energies invoke the power of wind (air), lightning (fire/electricity), earth/trees, and rain. Thus it is one of the most elemental of all magic. It represents air, fire, water and earth, and as such woodpecker medicine is good 'all-round' medicine to have. It conveys warrior powers in times of trouble. It can be raised for fertility and growth. The Native Americans of the northwest attributed to the feathers a certain intrinsic value; hence woodpecker is a symbol of abundance and plenty. It can even be used for grounding or to assist when one needs to get in touch with life's rhythms and cycles.

One Native American cure for fatigue was to call upon the thunder-beings, who could bestow unlimited energy and renewed vigour when reserves were low. The woodpecker's ability to walk up and down trees suggests the ultimate in balance.

If woodpecker appears, mighty forces are working their way through one's life. The precise type of energies can be discovered by context, to be judged by either the accompanying visual imagery, the circumstances of the sighting, or by the events surrounding the individual. It can mean trouble: a big storm is about to blow through one's life. Perhaps there is to be an uprooting, such as a change of residence. Certainly the period will be busy; but woodpecker also gives not only the energy but the skills to combat any potential problems.

Woodpecker can also bode that the individual is out of synch or out of step. A period of rest may be required, or it might be necessary to get in touch with mother earth. Even when it comes as a warning, woodpecker also protects. If none of these conditions applies, it is said that woodpecker calls one to a shamanistic path. Thus, whenever woodpecker arrives, it is time to listen.

The woodpecker person clings to things. This individual might be something of a nit-picker. These people are always active, hopping from one project to the next, one tree or another. They can walk places where others cannot follow. These people can strike like lightning one minute and sit back and contemplate the breeze the next. Woodpecker medicine can often carry potent lessons with it, so try to have some sympathy for people who possess it.

# REFERENCES


INTRODUCTION

1 Joseph Epes Brown, *Animals of the Soul* (Element Books, 1997): page 52

ANT

1 Jamie Sams and David Carson, *Medicine Cards* (Santa Fe, NM: Bear and Co, 1988): page 165
2 Ron Baxter, *Bestiaries and their Users in the Middle Ages* (Sutton Publishing, 1998): page 78

ANTELOPE

1 No true antelopes of the family *Antelopinae* reside in the area of our study (Europe or North America). European knowledge of the antelope comes from North Africa.

BEAVER

1 Hugh Clark, *A Short Introduction to Heraldry* (John Walker, 1810): page 108
2 Ron Baxter, *Bestiaries and their Users in the Middle Ages* (Sutton Publishing, 1998): page 205
3 'antelope, turtle and rabbit', which is a direct contradiction to other mediaevel sources that attributed imprudence to antelope, and coward and lust to rabbit

BEE

1 Hugh Clark, *A Short Introduction to Heraldry* (John Walker, 1810): page 108

BUTTERFLY

1 Kenneth Meadows, *Earth Medicine* (Element Books, 1989): page 42

COUGAR

1 Ted Andrews, *Animal Speak* (St Paul, MN: Llewellyn Worldwide, 1998): page 259

DEER

1 Not to be confused with Saysun, the goddess

DOG

1 Hugh Clark, *A Short Introduction to Heraldry* (John Walker, 1810): page 151

DRAGONFLY

1 In older text, this 'mystery' or deity is referred to as male; however, in more recent publications *Yum* is depicted as a woman.
2 Jamie Sams and David Carson, *Medicine Cards* (Santa Fe, NM: Bear and Co, 1988): page 145

EAGLE

1 Ron Baxter, *Bestiaries and their Users in the Middle Ages* (Sutton Publishing, 1998): page 68
2 Hugh Clark, *A Short Introduction to Heraldry* (John Walker, 1810): page 158
3 We relay this tale so that his sacrifice will not be forgotten.

FOX

1 Wa Na Ne Chee and Eliana Harvey, *White Eagle Medicine Wheel* (NY: Connection Books, 1988): page 55
2 Ron Baxter, *Bestiaries and their Users in the Middle Ages* (Sutton Publishing, 1998): page 81

HAWK

1 John Cummings, *The Hound and the Hawk, The Art of Medieval Hunting* (Weidenfeld & Nicholson, 1988): page 189

HORSE

1 Colin F Taylor, *The Natives of North America* (NY: Smithmark Books, 1991): page 44
2 Hugh Clark, *A Short Introduction to Heraldry* (John Walker, 1810): page 182

HUMMINGBIRD

1 A Kiva is a specially constructed ceremonial place dug in the earth or hollowed from a cave

LARK

1 The Lakota and Dakota do not speak of gods. Rather they talk of mysteries, as something unknowable and unknown.

LIZARD

1 Ron Baxter, *Bestiaries and their Users in the Middle Ages* (Sutton Publishing, 1998): page 204
2 Hugh Clark, *A Short Introduction to Heraldry* (John Walker, 1810): page 223
3 Clark, *Heraldry*: page 193

LYNX

1 For the Pawnee

MOLE

1 Hugh Clark, *A Short Introduction to Heraldry* (John Walker, 1810): page 199

OTTER

1 Wa Na Ne Chee and Eliana Harvey, *White Eagle Medicine Wheel* (NY: Connection Books, 1988; reprinted 1997): page 30
2 Hugh Clark, *A Short Introduction to Heraldry* (John Walker, 1810): page 208

SKUNK

1 Marie L McLaughlin, *Myths and Legends of the Sioux* (Bismarck, ND: Bison Books, 1842)

2 When going through nurse's training in Kansas, the author shared a house with a family of four skunks. Not voluntarily, mind, but once a mother and her kits have taken up residence in one's kitchen, one doesn't argue too strenuously. No exterminator can trap them, kill them or even tranquillize them without causing them to spray, which can make a house unlivable for months. Yet, this living arrangement lasted quite comfortably for two years. Not once did the skunks spray despite the fact that the cat found the fluffy black-and-white tails fascinating and played with them for hours, pouncing on them or batting them about. The skunks sensed no threat. Their reaction was usually studied boredom and less often they would join in the game, more than living up to their reputation for nonchalance.

SNAKE

1 The desert scorpion embodies the worst traits of snake.

SPIDER

1 Hugh Clark, *A Short Introduction to Heraldry* (John Walker, 1810): page 243

SQUIRREL

1 Northern California

TURKEY

1 Hugh Clark, *A Short Introduction to Heraldry* (John Walker, 1810): page 254

WOLF

1 Hugh Clark, *A Short Introduction to Heraldry* (John Walker, 1810): page 263

WOLVERINE

1 Tribe unknown

WOODPECKER

1 Colin F Taylor, *The Natives of North America* (NY: Smithmark Books, 1991): page 137

## BIBLIOGRAPHY

1 No relation to Charles Eastman; although not uninfluenced by the family. As a missionary, it was Mrs Eastman's husband who converted Ohiyesa's father to Christianity. Hence, the name was adopted when he was released from prison following the 1862 uprising.

# BIBLIOGRAPHY

Andrews, Ted. *Animal Speak* (St Paul, MN: Llewellyn Worldwide, 1998)

Baxter, Ron. *Bestiaries and their Users in the Middle Ages* (Sutton Publishing, 1998)

Beltrami, Constantino. *Sioux Vocabulary 1823 in the Archivio Beltrami of Count G Luchettie* (Filottrano, Italy; reprinted by NJ: Lakota Books, 1995)

Budge, E A Wallis. *An Egyptian Hieroglyphic Dictionary* (vols 1 and 2; NY: Dover Publications, 1978)

Burland, Cottie and Forman, Warner. *The Gods and Fate in Ancient Mexico* (Mexico: Panarama Editorio, 1975)

Carson, David and Sams, Jamie. *Medicine Cards* (Santa Fe, NM: Bear and Co, 1988)

Cirlot, J E. *A Dictionary of Symbols* (NY: Philosophical Library, 1962)

Clark, Hugh. *A Short Introduction to Heraldry* (John Walker, 1810)

Cummings, John. *The Hound and the Hawk, The Art of Medieval Hunting* (Weidenfeld & Nicholson, 1988)

de Rosa, Stanislas Klssowski. *The Secret Art of Alchemy* (Thames and Hudson, 1973)

Eastman, Charles (Ohiyesa). *Indian Boyhood* (Boston: Little, Brown and Company, 1902)

Eastman, Mary Henderson.[11] *Dahcotah, Life and Legends of the Sioux* (NY: John Wiley, 1849)

Epes Brown, Joseph. *Animals of the Soul* (Element Books, 1997)

Fabricius, Johannes. *Alchemy – The Medieval Alchemists and their Art* (Diamond Books, 1976)

Frazer, Sir James George. *The Golden Bough* (London: McMillan Publishing Company, 1922)

Hausman, Gerald. *Meditations with Animals, A Native American Bestiary* (Santa Fe, NM: Bear & Co, 1986)

Jordan, Michael. *Encyclopedia of the Gods* (Kyle Cathie Ltd, 1992)

Lame Deer, Chief Archie Fire & Sarkis, Helen. *The Lakota Sweat Lodge* (Rochester, VT: Destiny Books, 1994)

McLaughlin, Marie L, *Myths and Legends of the Sioux* (Bismarck, ND: Bison Books, 1842)

Marindin, G E. *Smaller Classical Dictionary* (London: John Murray, 1852)

Meadows, Kenneth. *Earth Medicine* (Element Books, 1989)

Meadows, Kenneth. *The Medicine Way* (Element Books, 1990)

Powers, Marla. *Oglala Women* (University of Chicago Press, 1984)

Powers, William K. *Sacred Language, The Nature of Supernatural Discourse in Lakota* (University of Oklahoma Press, 1986)

Spence, Lewis. *The Illustrated Guide to Egyptian Mythology* (London: Studio Books, 1996)

Spinden, Herbert J. *A Study of Mayan Art, Its Subject Matter and Historical Development* (NY: Dover Press, 1975)

Stein, Diane. *Women's Spirituality Book* (St Paul, MN: Llewellyn, 1988)

Stone, Merlin. *When God Was a Woman* (NY: Harvest Books, 1976)

Taylor, Colin F, *The Natives of North America* (NY: Smithmark Books, 1991)

—. *The Plains Indians* (Tiger Books International, 1997)

Tomkins, William. *Indian Sign Language* (NY: Dover Publications, 1929)

Warring, Phillipa. *The Dictionary of Omens and Superstitions* (Secaucus, NJ: Chartwell Books Inc, 1978)

Walker, James R. *Lakota Belief and Ritual* (Lincoln, NB: Bison Books, 1991)

—. *Lakota Society* (Lincoln, NB: Bison Books, 1992)

Wa Na Ne Chee (Dennis Renault) and Eliana Harvey. *White Eagle Medicine Wheel* (NY: Connection Books, 1988; reprinted 1997)

Watterson, Barbara. *Gods of Ancient Egypt* (Sutton Publishing, 1996)

Westwood, Jennifer (ed). *The Atlas of Mysterious Places* (Weidenfeld & Nicholson, 1987)

Wilkinson, Richard H. *Reading Egyptian Art, A Hieroglyphic Guide to Ancient Egyptian Painting and Sculpture* (Thames and Hudson, 1994)

Wissler, Clark. *The Protective Designs of the Dakota* (originally published as an archaeology paper by the American Natural History Museum, New York, 1907; reprinted NJ: Lakota Books, 1998)

Wright, Barton. *Clowns of the Hopi, Tradition Keepers and Delight Makers* (Flagstaff, AZ: Northland Publishing, 1994)

# INDEX